The Great Community

The Great Community
Culture and Nationalism in Ireland

David Dwan

Field Day Files 5

Series Editors: Seamus Deane and Breandán Mac Suibhne

Keough-Naughton Institute for Irish Studies, University of Notre Dame/Field Day
Dublin, 2008

ISBN 978-0-946755-41-7

Published by Field Day in association with the Keough-Naughton Institute for Irish Studies at the University of Notre Dame

Field Day
Newman House
86 St. Stephen's Green
Dublin 2
Ireland

Set in 10.5pt/13.5pt Quadraat
Designed and typeset by Red Dog Design Consultants
Printed on Arctic Gloss and Munken Lynx

for Liam and Anne Dwan

Contents

Acknowledgements

This book was written over a long time and has benefited from the help of many. I began the research at Queen Mary, University of London, and I remain grateful for the support of my supervisor, Morag Shiach, and other staff members — Paul Hamilton, Rachel Potter and Clair Wills. Richard Bourke was particularly helpful and I've gained much from his intellectual generosity and acumen ever since. Joe Lee offered advice and encouragement during my time in New York University, and Denis Donoghue kindly commented on a section of the book. Steven Connor and Roy Foster provided invaluable criticism at an early stage of the project and I've benefited from their advice and support ever since. My greatest debt is to Seamus Deane who accepted the manuscript for publication and brought immense knowledge and rigour to bear on all aspects of its argument. Thanks also to Breandán Mac Suibhne who has been enormously helpful at every stage of its production. I also owe much to the diligence of Ciarán Deane and Hilary Bell.

Many of the arguments in the book were aired at conferences and seminars and gained much from others in these outings; I am particularly indebted to Joe Cleary, Colin Graham, Conor McCarthy, and Emer Nolan for their insightful remarks on a paper delivered in Maynooth. Some parts of the book have appeared previously as articles. I am grateful to a number of editors and publishers for permission to adapt and to republish the following:

'Civic Virtue in the Modern World: The Politics of Young Ireland', *Irish Political Studies*, 22, 1 (2007), 35–60;

'Young Ireland and the Horde of Benthamy', in Roger Swift and Christine Kinealy, eds., *Politics and Power in Victorian Ireland* (Dublin: Four Courts Press, 2006), 109–18;

'Abstract Hatred: Yeats and the Counter-Revolutionary Paradigm', *Literature and History*, 15, 1 (2006), 18–36;

'Culture and Democracy in Ireland', *Irish Review*, 32, 1 (2004), 23–38;

'That Ancient Sect: Yeats, Hegel, and the Possibility of Epic in Ireland', *Irish Studies Review*, 12, 2 (2004), 201–11;

'Abstract Communities: Performativity and the Press in Late Nineteenth- and Early Twentieth-Century Ireland', *Foilsiú*, 2, 1 (2002), 31–42.

My debts to colleagues at Queen's are too extensive to track fully. But I have learned an enormous amount from those in Irish Studies — in particular, Fran Brearton, Eamonn Hughes, Michael McAteer, and the late Siobhán Kilfeather. Others have been kind enough to comment in detail on the book and to provide other forms of counsel: to Debbie Lisle, Andrew Pepper, and Adrian Streete I am eternally grateful. Particular thanks is due to my colleague, Caroline Sumpter, who has listened to me huff and puff about my labours with great patience and humour; her help has been unstinting and is greatly appreciated. I am also grateful to Mark Burnett, Natalie Dalberg-Acton, Theo and Eileen Dombrowski, Steven Donovan, Alessandra Fantini, Caroline Holmqvist, Tom Hunt, Tarik Kochi, Barry McCrea, Maeve McCusker, Shelley Meagher, Madhu Sandrasagra and Ramona Wray for their advice and friendship. Chris Insole has operated both as a source of support and as a standard of academic excellence for a number of years. Aida Edemariam has proved to be one of my most austere editors and kindest friends. The book would not have been possible without the help of my family. It is dedicated to my parents to whom I owe everything.

Abbreviations Used in the Notes

W. B. Yeats

A	*Autobiographies* (London, 1955)
CL 1	*The Collected Letters of W. B. Yeats. Volume 1: 1865–1895*, ed. John Kelly and Erick Domville (Oxford, 1986)
CL 2	*The Collected Letters of W. B. Yeats. Volume 2: 1896–1901*, ed. Warwick Gould, John Kelly and Deirdre Toomey (Oxford, 1996)
CL 3	*The Collected Letters of W. B. Yeats. Volume 3: 1901–1904*, ed. John Kelly and Ronald Schuchard (Oxford, 1994)
CT	*The Celtic Twilight* (London and Stratford-upon-Avon, 1902)
E	*Explorations* (London, 1962)
EI	*Essays and Introductions* (London, 1969)
IR 1 and IR 2	*Interviews and Recollections*, 2 vols., ed. E. H. Mikhail (London and Basingstoke, 1977)
L	*The Letters of W. B. Yeats*, ed. Alan Wade (London, 1954).
LNI	*Letters to the New Island* (Houndmills, Basingstoke, and London, 1989)
M	*Memoirs*, ed. and trans. Denis Donoghue (London, 1972)
PI	*Prefaces and Introductions*, ed. William H. O'Donnell (Houndmills, Basingstoke, and London, 1988)
SS	*The Senate Speeches of W. B. Yeats*, ed. Donald R. Pearce (London, 1960)
UP 1	*Uncollected Prose by W. B. Yeats. Volume 1*, ed. John P. Frayne (London, 1970)
UP 2	*Uncollected Prose by W. B. Yeats. Volume 2*, ed. John P. Frayne and Colton Johnson (London, 1975)
V	*A Vision* (London, 1937)
VP	*The Variorum Edition of the Poems of W. B. Yeats*, ed. Peter Allt and Russell K. Alspach (New York, 1957)

Edmund Burke

W & S   *The Writings and Speeches of Edmund Burke*, 10 vols., ed. Paul Langford, William B. Todd et al. (Oxford, 1981–96)

Works   *The Works of the Right Honourable Edmund Burke*, 16 vols. (London, 1803–27)

Introduction

1 Nationalisms, Cultural and Romantic

W. B. Yeats hoped to create a 'great community'; 'what other game,' he asked, 'is so worth the labour?'[1] He insisted that the greatness of a nation derived from its pursuit of 'fine life'.[2] For much of his career, he remained committed to the idea of an ethical community organized around a shared conception of the beautiful and the good.[3] Before Yeats, the most articulate advocates of this view of political association in Ireland were the Young Irelanders of the 1840s. These patriots subscribed to a set of civic and humanist principles that stretched back to Aristotle and Cicero and which gave their nationalism a distinctive orientation. A nation, for Young Ireland, was not reducible to the possession of a common domicile or collective identity; it was a moral entity or 'spiritual essence'.[4] It supplied ethical horizons to its citizens and invested them with a sense of shared purpose. The expression of this common purpose was the object of all genuine culture. Neither Yeats nor Young Ireland deployed the word 'culture' frequently or systematically, but it is a term that may be used to designate a set of values and practices that they regarded as central to the well-being of the nation. The aim of this book is to examine this vision of culture and to study the model of nationalism to which it gave rise.

---

1 W. B. Yeats, *Explorations* (London, 1962), 28. Hereafter cited as E.
2 W. B. Yeats, *Memoirs*, ed. and trans. Denis Donoghue (London, 1972), 180. Hereafter cited as M.
3 For influential accounts of nations as ethical communities in recent times, see David Miller, *On Nationality* (Oxford, 1995), 24–25, and Margaret Moore, *The Ethics of Nationalism* (Oxford, 2001), 25–51.
4 Thomas Davis asserted that the nation was a 'spiritual essence', but he attributed the term to Edmund Burke. *Nation*, 17 December 1842. 'Nation is a moral essence,' Burke had argued, 'not a geographical arrangement'. *The Writings and Speeches of Edmund Burke. Volume 9. I: The Revolutionary War, 1794–1797, II: Ireland*, ed. Paul Langford, R. B. McDowell, and William B. Todd (Oxford, 1991), 253. Hereafter cited as W & S 9.

The term 'culture' has, of course, a complex history and is extremely difficult to define, but there are at least four interrelated ways in which the notion operates. First, the word 'culture' functions, as it did for Matthew Arnold, as another term for what the ancients might have called 'the good life'.[5] A genuine community, for Young Ireland and for Yeats, necessarily pursued this supreme end. Young Ireland also believed, however, that this pursuit needed to be rooted in a particular tradition or historical community. This accounts for the group's emphasis on culture in a second or sociological sense. But if culture implied a set of goods that were internal to historical forms of life, there were also privileged settings for its acquisition. This links with a third interpretation of culture in which specific activities and institutions such as 'the arts' played a dominant role. Young Ireland and the early Yeats often assumed that there was a natural unity between these three versions of culture, but the relations between each were often extremely dissonant. Moreover, while Young Ireland assumed that culture was a public good, Yeats soon discovered that such a notion was severely tested by another (or fourth) view of culture as a private value. What J. S. Mill called 'self-culture' did not necessarily harmonize with certain collective ends.[6]

These different and often rival conceptions of culture play a key role here. I begin by outlining Young Ireland's efforts to promote a vision of an ethical community through the forum of the Nation newspaper and then move on to consider Yeats's initial enthusiasm for and subsequent rejection of these ideals. He was deeply attracted to the Young Irelanders' communitarian vision: they 'were not separated men; they spoke or tried to speak out of a people to a people; behind them stretched the generations'.[7] But he ultimately concluded that their ideals were at odds with the basic facts of modern social organization; they also violated core values that moderns had fought for and cherished. The 'superficial ideality' of Young Ireland was not simply mistaken, it was also oppressive.[8] I examine the grounds for this conviction and explore Yeats's alternative — and highly problematic — account of the good life, which he opposed to the 'wreckage of Young Irelandism'.[9]

---

5 According to Matthew Arnold 'true culture teaches us to fetch sweetness and light' or beauty and truth. The Greeks were 'the great exponents of humanity's bent for sweetness and light united'. See Matthew Arnold, *Culture and Anarchy and Other Writings*, ed. Stefan Collini (Cambridge, 1993), 106, 141. For Plato, both truth and beauty derived from 'the form or character of the good'. See Plato, *The Republic*, ed. G. R. F. Ferrari, trans. Tom Griffit (Cambridge, 2000), 215.

6 J. S. Mill, *The Collected Works of John Stuart Mill. Volume 10: Essays on Ethics, Religion and Society*, ed. J. M. Robson and D. P. Dryer (London and Toronto, 1969), 'Bentham', 75–116, 98: 'There is no need to expatiate on the deficiencies of a system of ethics which does not pretend to aid individuals in the formation of their own character; which recognises no such wish as that of self-culture.' Mill did not invoke the term 'self-culture' in 'On Liberty' but he provided his most famous defence of the principle in its third chapter. See *The Collected Works of John Stuart Mill. Volume 18: Essays on Politics and Society*, ed. J. M. Robson (London and Toronto, 1977), 213–10; 260–75.

7 W. B. Yeats, *Essays and Introductions* (London, 1969), 510. Hereafter cited as EI.

8 E, 447.

9 M, 154.

These ideological battles are worth exploring in some detail, because they reveal much about the nature of what scholars have called 'cultural' or 'romantic' nationalism in Ireland.[10] This terminology has its uses, but it has also produced conceptual muddle and historical error. Isaiah Berlin regarded nationalism in general as a form of 'political romanticism'; from this perspective, the phrase 'romantic nationalism' is tautological.[11] Berlin, on the other hand, made a strong distinction between 'political' and 'cultural' forms of nationalism, but the sense and historical validity of this distinction is open to question.[12] All nationalism, Ernest Gellner argued, aims to render politics and culture co-extensive; in this context, 'cultural nationalism' has also a circular aspect.[13] If it is difficult to isolate 'cultural' or 'romantic' sub-species of nationalism, this reflects the indeterminate character of the species itself.[14] Nationalism is a vague ideology, not least because it draws upon a broad range of different and even rival political vocabularies.[15]

'Romantic' or 'cultural' nationalisms are not entirely discrete political doctrines. In the most reductive accounts, nationalism becomes a free-floating identity politics isolated from broader questions of sovereignty, citizenship and the nature of freedom and justice; analyses of its 'cultural' or 'romantic' strains yield second-order simplifications that often appear to be removed from all recognizable forms of politics. For some scholars, the defining feature of cultural nationalism in Ireland is its non-political character.[16] But

10 D. George Boyce, *Nineteenth-Century Ireland: The Search for Stability* (Dublin, 1990), 78, maintains that the Young Irelanders were 'cultural nationalists'; Alvin Jackson, *Ireland 1798–1998* (Oxford, 1998), 53, declares that 'the Young Irelanders were primarily cultural nationalists'. But Oliver MacDonagh, *States of Mind: A Study of Anglo-Irish Conflict, 1780–1980* (London, 1983), 76, insists that the *Nation* was the mouthpiece of 'romantic nationalism of the German and more specifically the Prussian type'. S. J. Connolly, *The Oxford Companion to Irish History*, 2nd edn. (Oxford, 2002), 633, has also described Young Ireland as a 'romantic nationalist group'. Richard English, *Irish Freedom: The History of Nationalism in Ireland* (London, 2006), 142, presents them as 'romantic, cultural nationalists'.

11 Isaiah Berlin, 'Nationalism, Past Neglect and Present Power', in *Against the Current: Essays in the History of Ideas*, ed. Henry Hardy (London, 1979), 333–55, 349. Berlin provided other and somewhat different assessments of nationalism in 'The Apotheosis of the Romantic Will: The Revolt against the Myth of an Ideal World' and 'The Bent Twig: On the Rise of Nationalism', in Isaiah Berlin, *The Crooked Timber of Humanity*, ed. Henry Hardy (London, 2003), 207–37; 238–61.

12 He distinguished between 'political' and 'cultural' forms of nationalism particularly in the case of Herder. See Isaiah Berlin, *Vico and Herder: Two Studies in the History of Ideas* (London, 1976), 181–82. For this distinction in an Irish context, see John Hutchinson, *The Dynamics of Cultural Nationalism* (London, 1987).

13 See Ernest Gellner, *Nations and Nationalism* (Oxford, 1983), 13: 'that fusion of culture and polity which is the essence of nationalism'. J. S. Mill was convinced that democracy can only flourish where 'the boundaries of government ... coincide in the main with those of nationalities'. This reflected his conviction that a functioning democracy required a shared civic culture. See J. S. Mill, *The Collected Works of John Stuart Mill. Volume 19: Essays on Politics and Society*, ed. J. M. Robson (Toronto and London, 1977), 548.

14 Henry Sumner Maine, *Popular Government* (London, 1885), 27: 'Nobody can say exactly what Nationalism is.' Indeed, the dangerousness of the theory, for Maine, 'arises from its vagueness'.

15 The parasitical nature of nationalism leads one commentator to conclude that it 'has no necessary substantive content'. See Andrew Vincent, *Nationalism and Particularity* (Cambridge, 2002), 6.

16 Hutchinson, *The Dynamics of Cultural Nationalism*, 15, distinguishes 'cultural nationalism' from 'political nationalism' in Ireland. He puzzlingly claims, however, that the cultural nationalist 'has a politics, but it is very different from that of the political nationalist in its goals and modes of organization'.

this is an unhelpful simplification that reflects a historically impoverished conception of politics. Yeats liked to suggest that culture supplanted politics after the death of Charles Stewart Parnell, but this was an inaccurate description of the historical reality; it was also a misconstruction of his own practice.[17] The ethical community of Yeats and of Young Ireland was not a 'romantic' distortion or aesthetic sublimation of politics, but had a distinctive political logic which this study sets out to describe. This logic cannot be understood, however, outside of the democratic context in which it was articulated.

2 Culture and Democracy

In 1843 the *Nation* declared that 'the principle of rational democracy is advancing in every land'.[18] Its advance seemed to be particularly fast in Ireland. Daniel O'Connell's extraordinary mobilization of the masses — in his respective campaigns for Catholic Emancipation and the Repeal of the Act of Union — was interpreted by many as the dawn of democracy in Ireland.[19] In 1837, J. S Mill proclaimed that in Ireland 'the spirit of Democracy has got too much head ... too prematurely'.[20] Gustave de Beaumont, on the other hand, provided a more upbeat assessment of democratic developments in Ireland; he spoke of O'Connell's Catholic Association in rapturous terms, noting 'the deep democratic character in this government of a people by one central power emanating from the universal will, expressed or understood; collecting within itself all the national elements; omnipotent by popular assent; absolute in every one of its actions, though constantly subjected to the control of all'.[21] Here a fanasty of popular sovereignty supplanted the concrete realities of O'Connellite politics, but other, more sceptical commentators regarded O'Connell as the harbinger of democracy. The Young Irelanders were initially supporters of O'Connell and endorsed his campaign

---

17 E, 45: 'The fall of Parnell had freed imagination from practical politics, from agrarian grievance and political enmity, and turned it to imaginative nationalism, to Gaelic, to the ancient stories, and at last to lyrical poetry and drama'. See also *Autobiographies* (London, 1955), 559. Hereafter cited as A.

18 *Nation*, 5 August 1843.

19 Catholic Emancipation, according to one commentator, 'inaugurated the liberal democratic era'. Fergus O'Ferrall, *Catholic Emancipation and the Birth of Irish Democracy* (Dublin, 1985), 273. For a more sceptical assessment of O'Connell's commitment to democracy, see Paul Bew, *Ireland: The Politics of Enmity 1789–2006* (Oxford, 2007), 172–74.

20 At this point Mill sponsored 'a good stout Despotism' for Ireland. See *The Collected Works of John Stuart Mill. Volume 12: Earlier Letters, 1812–1848*, ed. F. Mineka (Toronto and London, 1963), 397. For a comprehensive account of Mill's views of Ireland, see Bruce Kinzer, *England's Disgrace?: J. S. Mill and the Irish Question* (Toronto, 2001). See also E. D. Steele, 'J. S. Mill and the Irish Question: Reform, and the Integrity of the Empire, 1865–1870', *Historical Journal*, 13 (1969), 419–50.

21 Gustave de Beaumont, *Ireland: Political, Social and Religious*, 2 vols., ed. W. C. Taylor (London, 1839), 2. 67–68.

for manhood suffrage, shorter parliaments and ballot reform. 'Democracy', the Nation boldly proclaimed, 'is the destiny of the world'.[22]

For Yeats, writing in the wake of the crucial Reform Acts of 1867 and 1884, this destiny seemed to have come to fruition. He was initially sanguine about the development of democracy in Ireland. In his youth, he claimed that ancient Ireland was 'above all democratic and communistic' and he made no obvious objection to the revival of these traditions.[23] But he gradually came to feel that the democracy that had evolved in Ireland lacked all sense of excellence. In his eyes, an event such as the *Playboy* riots of 1907 confirmed that the Irish were repeating 'the same mistakes of the newly enfranchised everywhere'.[24] His misgivings hardened over time into a thoroughgoing rejection of democratic principles. In later life, his 'anti-democratic philosophy' took on a strong fascist dimension.[25] He averred that he would probably despise a fascist government in Ireland, though not as much as he professed to 'hate Irish democracy'.[26] The Young Irelanders had celebrated the birth of democracy in Ireland; an embittered Yeats prayed for its demise.

It was against such a background of mass democratization that debates about culture in Ireland developed their ideological substance and specific passion.[27] The worry that democratic rule would undermine cultural excellence was standard fare in the nineteenth century and remained a staple part of twentieth-century debates. 'The difficulty for democracy,' Matthew Arnold declared, 'is how to find and keep high ideals'.[28] How would democratic societies sustain those cultural and political activities that had traditionally depended upon the existence of a wealthy and leisured aristocracy? W. E. H. Lecky declared that 'modern democracy is not favourable to the higher forms of intellectual life'.[29] The issue did not simply reflect concerns about the absence of a leisured class

22 *Nation*, 29 April 1848.
23 W. B. Yeats, *Uncollected Prose by W. B. Yeats. Volume 1*, ed. John P. Frayne (London, 1970), 165. Hereafter cited as UP 1.
24 W. B. Yeats, *Uncollected Prose by W. B. Yeats. Volume 2*, ed. John P. Frayne and Colton Johnson (London, 1975), 351. Hereafter cited as UP 2.
25 W. B. Yeats, *The Letters of W. B. Yeats*, ed. Alan Wade (London, 1954), 812. Hereafter cited as L. For a discussion of Yeats's fascist views, see Conor Cruise O'Brien, 'Passion and Cunning: An Essay on the Politics of W. B. Yeats', in A. Norman Jeffares and K. G. W. Cross, eds., *Excited Reverie: A Centenary Tribute to William Butler Yeats 1865–1939* (London, 1965), 207–78; Elizabeth Cullingford, *Yeats, Ireland and Fascism* (London, 1981); Paul Scott Stanfield, *Yeats and Politics in the 1930s* (London, 1988); R.F. Foster, *W. B. Yeats: A Life. II: The Arch-Poet, 1915–1939* (Oxford, 2003), particularly, 466–83; W. J. McCormack, *Blood Kindred. W. B. Yeats: The Life, the Death, the Politics* (London, 2005).
26 L, 813.
27 For a seminal account of Irish cultural debate which adopts modernity more generally as its interpretative framework, see Seamus Deane, *Strange Country: Modernity and Nationhood in Irish Writing since 1790* (Oxford, 1997).
28 Arnold, 'Democracy', in *Culture and Anarchy and Other Writings*, 14.
29 W. E. H. Lecky, *Democracy and Liberty*, 2 vols. (Indianapolis, 1981), I. 112. This was a late and disillusioned text that reflected Lecky's disgust for recent forms of Irish nationalism. In his youth, Lecky had believed himself to be a patriot in the tradition of Henry Grattan and of Young Ireland. According to Donal

in a democratic setting; Lecky believed that the very ethos of democracy was in itself antithetical to the idea of cultural excellence. He claimed that the principle of equality contradicted the standard procedures of intellectual practice and eliminated the basic norms of better and worse upon which any meaningful form of normative inquiry relied. Democracy was incapable of producing or even recognizing intellectual authority. He would not accept that democracy allowed for an authority based on merit; for Lecky, this merely begged the question, because the very principle of merit was itself subject to democratic adjudication.[30] An authority putatively based on merit would merely reflect the 'omnipotence of numbers'.[31] And when it came to numbers, Lecky was convinced that his sums were correct: 'In every field of human enterprise, in all the competitions of life, by the inexorable law of Nature, superiority lies with the few, and not with the many, and success can only be attained by placing the guiding and controlling power mainly in their hands.'[32] Culture and democracy, in Lecky's eyes, were implacably opposed.

Yeats ultimately came to share similar views. The logic of his critique of 'democracy in artistic matters' applied to life in general.[33] He stressed the necessity, therefore, of dominant élites in politics as well as in the realm of culture. Enthusiasts on the left or right of the political spectrum, he suggested, implicitly conceded this point in their commitment to the administrative structures and the skilled oligarchies of the modern state: whatever one's ideological orientation, the practical reality of governance demanded that it was the few who ruled.[34] But if democratic ideology did have substance, Yeats remained implacably opposed to its principles. 'What's equality?' he asked. His answer: 'Muck in the yard'.[35] Equality overlooked qualitative differences between human beings; but it was also, he believed, despotic. He was adamant that 'intellectual freedom and social equality are incompatible'.[36] Since, in his eyes, there was no such thing as natural equality in everyday social relations, equality as a principle had to be artificially enforced through the erasure of the real differences and the distinguishing merits of individuals. The prospects here for individual liberty — let alone for cultural achievement — were not

McCartney, W. E. H. Lecky: Historian and Politician, 1838–1903 (Dublin, 1994), 9, he especially admired Thomas Davis and Gavan Duffy and their newspaper, the Nation, John Kells Ingram, and William Smith O'Brien, 'the man in Ireland he most wished to know'.

30   The Young Irelander, John Dillon, believed that a meritocracy was compatible with democratic government: 'Distinctions of rank are no more inconsistent with democracy than aristocracy — the only difference is, that under the former, these distinctions are bestowed according to merit, under the latter they are allotted by chance.' Nation, 3 December 1842.

31   Lecky, Democracy and Liberty, I. 23.

32   Lecky, Democracy and Liberty, I. 22.

33   W. B. Yeats, The Collected Letters of W. B. Yeats. Volume 3: 1901–1904, ed. John Kelly and Ronald Schuchard (Oxford, 1994), 258. Hereafter cited as CL 3.

34   E, 357.

35   W. B. Yeats, The Variorum Edition of the Poems of W. B. Yeats, ed. Peter Allt and Russell K. Alspach (New York, 1957), 547. Hereafter cited as VP.

36   A, 348.

good.[37] Yeats deplored the way democracies both manufactured and enforced equality through bureaucratic management or 'mechanism'.[38] These administrative systems may have set out to produce equal treatment of all, but even democrats conceded that they frequently eroded the freedoms they ostensibly secured.

Yeats's anti-democratic disposition duly converged with a nostalgic commitment to an aristocratic order. 'Ireland has suffered more than England from democracy,' he maintained, because the erosion of its aristocratic influence began so much earlier.[39] The loss of Ireland's native aristocracy after the Jacobite Wars of the seventeenth century had had, he believed, damaging consequences for the nation's cultural well-being. And the decline of the Anglo-Irish aristocracy under the agrarian revolution had contributed further to the rise of democratic vulgarity. In 'Upon a House Shaken by the Land Agitation', Yeats lamented the loss of those noble virtues 'Wrought of high laughter, loveliness and ease' — the beautiful issue of 'the best knit to the best'.[40] A democratic culture organized around the moral cant of equality afforded no space to such superlatives. Cultural excellence, Yeats maintained, could only thrive among 'a leisured class' and in his unwavering commitment to this belief, he gladly declared himself 'a crusted Tory'.[41]

Young Ireland was by no means oblivious to the dangers of democracy, and its cultural policies were in many respects based upon a sense of democracy's shortcomings. Indeed, Thomas Francis Meagher explicitly rejected a comprehensive form of democracy and promoted instead the benefits of a mixed constitution.[42] However, the leaders of the movement believed — like their contemporary Tocqueville whom they read and esteemed — that the march of democracy was irreversible. Young Ireland feared, however, that democracy would lead to the primacy of equality over basic

37 Contemporaries like Max Weber also noted that the enforcement of egalitarian principles under democracy came at a certain price. 'Bureaucracy inevitably accompanies modern mass democracy', because the principle of democratic equality demands the institution of administrative procedures that treat all individuals in equal and uniform ways. See Max Weber, Economy and Society, 2 vols., ed. Guenther Roth and Claus Wittich (Berkeley, 1978), 2. 983. The irony, for Weber, was that bureaucracy developed its own internal logic which stood at odds with the democratic principles — such as the accessibility, accountability and general transparency of political authority to its constituents — it was supposed to guarantee.

38 For instance, in A Vision (London, 1937), 52 (hereafter cited as V), he grouped democracy with among other things 'mechanism', 'science' and 'abstraction' and contrasted this with a set of values that included 'kindred', 'art', 'aristocracy' and 'particularity'.

39 E, 257.

40 VP, 264. According to Louis MacNeice, The Poetry of W. B. Yeats (London, 1967), 97, Yeats chose 'to ignore the fact that in most cases these houses maintained no culture worth speaking of, nothing but an obsolete bravado, an insidious bonhomie and a way with horses'.

41 W. B. Yeats, The Senate Speeches of W. B. Yeats, ed. Donald R. Pearce (London, 1960), 38–39. Hereafter cited as SS.

42 Thomas Francis Meagher, Meagher of the Sword: Speeches of Thomas Francis Meagher in Ireland 1846–1848, ed. Arthur Griffith (Dublin, 1916), 89: 'I am one of the people, but I am no democrat. I am for an equality of civil rights — but I am no republican. I am for vesting the responsibilities and the duties of government in three estates.'

political freedoms such as the security of property and of persons. It was precisely for this reason that Lecky believed democracy and liberty to be largely incompatible.[43] He considered it politically imprudent — if not immoral — to base property rights in its final instance on the political will of the country's less wealthy majority. Even to more sympathetic commentators, democratic rule could all too easily present itself as a ruthless confiscatory force. The history of Jacobin France provided ample evidence of the real prospect and brutal nature of this kind of outcome. Young Irelanders such as Davis and Dillon were more committed to the equitable distribution of wealth than Duffy — who worried about any tampering with the fundamental rights of property — and were strongly critical of aristocratic institutions. Nevertheless, the Nation was careful to insist that 'the democratic principle will progress, not to the detriment of the aristocracy'.[44] In addition to class divisions, Ireland was riven by major religious rivalries which democracy threatened to aggravate. If democracy was organized on majoritarian lines, then it was easy to see how majorities could override the basic rights of minorities. Davis was acutely worried that tolerance would not be extended to religious minorities within an Irish democratic setting. The fact that this anxiety presented itself to O'Connell, in the sectarian circumstances of the time, as the exemplification of 'Protestant monomania', did little to assuage such concerns.[45]

It was to allay anxieties about the damaging effects of class conflict and religious sectarianism in a democratic setting that Young Ireland promoted a redemptive ideal of culture. Cultural institutions, in their eyes, allowed for the collective articulation of shared values that transcended differences of class and creed.[46] This was also an ideology of culture which Yeats at first enthusiastically entertained, then dismissed as a vague dream.[47] But Young Ireland's promotion of culture was not simply a response to class strife and religious sectarianism in Ireland. It was also a reaction to a more subtle and pervasive danger which Tocqueville had recently detected at the heart of democracy. Tocqueville's concern was not solely that democratic equality would erode political liberty, but that a reductive view of liberty itself would supplant an earlier and more capacious interpretation of freedom and citizenship. He feared that freedom would be construed as the untrammelled pursuit of private advantage and pleasure. This danger seemed to threaten modern democracies in particular. Aristocracies, for instance, were not rooted

---

43 As Lecky put it in 'Democracy and Liberty, I. 217: 'a tendency to democracy does not mean a tendency to parliamentary government, or even a tendency towards greater liberty. On the contrary, strong arguments may be adduced, both from history and from the nature of things, to show that democracy may often prove the direct opposite of liberty ...'

44 Nation, 11 February 1843 [Nation's emphasis].

45 Mary Buckley, 'Thomas Davis: A Study in Nationalist Philosophy', Ph.D. thesis, University College Cork, 1980, 31. See also Boyce, Nineteenth-Century Ireland, 78–80.

46 The group's desire was 'to conciliate every Irish party, to separate nationality from creed, to raise our reputation in art and literature'. Nation, 8 June 1844.

47 F. S. L. Lyons largely agreed with Yeats's assessment and argued that culture did as much to foment as to assuage conflict in Ireland. See F. S. L. Lyons, Culture and Anarchy in Ireland, 1890–1939 (Oxford, 1979).

exclusively in a sense of paternal responsibility or *noblesse oblige*; aristocrats enjoyed the actual and necessary independence that allowed for a patriotic dedication to public interests.[48] Democracies, on the other hand, delegated power to those who lacked this independence and the political virtues it fostered. The sovereign people in a democracy were potentially so consumed by the satisfaction of private needs that *de facto* sovereignty would be in the hands of administrative élites presiding over an increasingly centralized state. Both Tocqueville and his contemporary J. S. Mill entertained a dystopian vision, whereby a centralized administration enjoyed unchallenged rule over large aggregates of isolated individuals.

Young Ireland also worried that democratic individualism would culminate in either a bureaucratic tyranny or simple anarchy. In the face of this awful possibility, Davis explicitly drew on Tocqueville's advice: 'if you would qualify Democracy for power, you must "purify their morals and warm their faith, if that be possible"'.[49] Religious sentiment in America, according to Tocqueville, laid the basis for a shared moral framework upon which civic unity relied, while religious associations provided Americans with a form of collective experience that curbed the latent individualism of their democratic values. But in Ireland religion was a source of civic strife, not a solution to a divided society. It was in this context that culture — understood both as a vision of the human good and as a practical forum for civic association — acquired its true significance. According to this extremely hopeful vision, culture would provide individuals with a more expansive sense of themselves and a more developed awareness of the common good; it would generate the institutional contexts and discursive resources for the articulation of core values that transcended individual interests. Democracies, as Arnold suggested, may have difficulties generating high ideals, but this made the active promotion of such ideals the more imperative. Young Ireland hoped, therefore, that the pursuit of culture — sustained by a system of public education — would curb the individualism that menaced Ireland's democratic future.

48 E, 351. As Yeats put it in a discussion of Swift, 'the Few are those who through the possession of hereditary wealth, or great personal gifts, have come to identify their lives with the life of the State, whereas the lives and ambitions of the Many are private'.

49 Thomas Davis, *Essays Literary and Historical*, ed. D. J. O'Donoghue (Dundalk, 1914), 45. Davis seemed to be quoting from Tocqueville's introduction to *Democracy in America*: 'The first of the duties that are at this time imposed upon those who direct our affairs is to educate democracy, to reawaken, if possible, its religious beliefs, to purify its morals; to mould its actions; to substitute a knowledge of statecraft for its inexperience, and an awareness of its true interest for its blind instincts, to adapt its government to time and place and to modify it according to men and to conditions. A new science of politics is needed for a new world.' Alexis de Tocqueville, *Democracy in America*, ed. Alan Ryan (London, 1994), 7.

3 Politics and the Good Life

Young Ireland's emphasis on the civic significance of culture was a response to democratic developments in Ireland, but it also reflects the group's commitment to a particular — and to our eyes, perhaps, bizarre — conception of political life. Basic to Young Ireland's outlook on politics was its neo-classical conviction that the purpose of a political community was not simply to furnish material well-being or basic securities for its citizens, but to promote a collective vision of the good life. It was on the basis of this view of public affairs that Socrates, for instance, could declare himself in *Gorgias* the only true politician of Athens.[50] For his life, he maintained, was dedicated to improving the souls of Athenians and not to the more material concerns of adding new buildings or new riches to the city. In their celebrated attempts to 'bring a soul to Ireland', Young Ireland possessed a similar understanding of the moral substance of politics.[51] Modern political thought had generally conducted itself in a more sceptical vein. Peaceful co-existence, for instance, was presented as a more modest and more tangible objective of government than the purification of the soul.[52] This condition was often better secured by an appeal to the individual's rational self-interest than by a demand for self-sacrificing virtue.[53] When moderns argued that the public well-being did not *directly* depend on personal virtue, they repudiated an entire tradition of classical thought which insisted on the identity between the moral integrity of communities and their individual constitutents.[54] Young Ireland believed in the direct relationship between the good citizen and the good country — a fact that helps to explain the moralizing zeal and high-minded rhetoric of the movement. Here the active pursuit of the good was the ultimate goal of political endeavour.

50 Plato, *Gorgias*, trans. Robin Waterfield (Oxford, 1994), 127.

51 John Mitchel explicitly contrasted ancient virtue with modern corruption: 'They did actually imagine those ancient wise men that it is true wisdom to raise our thoughts and aspirations above what the mass of mankind calls good to regard truth, fortitude, honesty, purity, as the great objects of human effort, and *not* the supply of vulgar wants.' See *Jail Journal; or, Five Years in British Prisons* (Glasgow, 1876), 42 [Mitchel's emphasis].

52 In Thomas Hobbes's *Leviathan* (1651), the fundamental law of nature was 'to seek peace'. See *Leviathan*, ed. Richard Tuck (Cambridge, 1996), 92. The same law, however, presupposed virtues that were the means to peace, 'modesty, fairness, good faith and mercy'. See Thomas Hobbes, *On the Citizen*, ed. Richard Tuck and Michael Silverthorne (Cambridge, 1998), 55.

53 See Albert O. Hirschman, *The Passions and the Interests: Political Arguments for Capitalism before Its Triumph* (Princeton, 1977).

54 Few assented fully to Bernard Mandeville's account of the benefits derived from private vices in *The Fable of the Bees; or, Private Vices, Publick Benefits*, 2 vols., ed. F. B. Kaye ([1723–28] Indianapolis, 1988). Adam Smith, in his *Theory of Moral Sentiments*, ed. Knud Haakonssen ([1784] Cambridge, 2002), 363, said Mandeville's views were 'in almost every respect erroneous'. But he did acknowledge that the link between public and private well-being was indirect; indeed, he who pursues his own interest 'frequently promotes that of society more effectually than when he really intends to promote it'. See Adam Smith, *An Inquiry into the Nature and Causes of the Wealth of Nations*, 2 vols., ed. R. H. Campbell, A. S. Kinner and W. B. Todd (Oxford, 1976), I. 456.

Many modern commentators on politics would resist such an ascription of a moral *telos* to public affairs, because it seems at odds with the value-pluralism which liberal democracies aim to foster and to defend.[55] The state's legitimate function, according to some liberal thinkers, is not to endorse a univocal concept of the good, but to remain neutral in the face of competing interpretations of the proper ends of human life. A particular, market-based expression of this position promotes the economy as the most neutral arbiter of values and the best insurance that the good will be interpreted in a plurality of ways and pursued through the widest variety of means.[56] Young Ireland's nationalism, I shall argue, arose in opposition to a nineteenth-century version of this outlook on politics. The group invariably associated this doctrine — admittedly, with scant respect for its nuances — with Benthamite utilitarianism and the relatively new science of political economy. Young Ireland acknowledged the importance of economic science and sponsored a specifically Irish version of it as an explicit challenge to English practitioners of the discipline. But the group also condemned the hegemony of political economy in modern political life: it diminished the moral scope of politics and exacerbated the individualism that pervaded modern societies. When politics were reduced to a set of techniques managed by a body of experts, individuals were discouraged from participation in public life and fell back on the exclusive pursuit of their own private interests. At the heart of Young Ireland's nationalist vision was a commitment to active citizenship grounded upon a positive conception of freedom.

Yeats's complicated response to Young Ireland reflects the great appeal as well as the extremely problematic nature of its political ideology.[57] Young Ireland had offered an inclusive model of culture that proved attractive to a young Protestant poet brought up on the margins of Irish life and searching for greater integration within it.[58] Yeats's own hopes for a 'unity of culture' was partly an extension of Young Ireland's attempts to provide a non-sectarian basis for civic interaction. Moreover, Yeats was disturbed by the atomistic nature and alienated character of modern life and was prepared to promote the remedial properties of culture in the face of such fragmentation. He was deeply inspired by Young Ireland's ideal of a community unified in its pursuit of the good. However, it was precisely because states were judged to have this ethical vocation, that political commentators, since the days of Plato, had dismissed democracy as an intrinsically corrupt form of government. Yeats ultimately subscribed to this outlook and it lent a strong authoritarian dimension to his thought. He rejected the populism of

---

55 See John Rawls, *Political Liberalism* (New York, 1993), 201.

56 For a classic statement of this position, see F. A. Hayek, *The Road to Serfdom* (London, 1944).

57 For an account of Yeats's criticism of Young Ireland's artistic practice, see Phillip L. Marcus, *Yeats and the Beginning of the Irish Renaissance* (Ithaca and London, 1970), 3–34; 79–103.

58 Yeats only slightly exaggerated Young Ireland's commitment to inclusiveness when he declared, 'Unionist or Nationalist, Conservative or Liberal, it was nearly all one to them, if they thought you loved Ireland and were ready to seek her prosperity by setting the moral law above all the counsels of expediency'. See UP 1. 258.

Young Ireland, but he did so because he seemed to share the group's conviction that the purpose of a state is to pursue supreme values.

But there was also a less authoritarian Yeats who questioned the tenability of these ultimate ends. Some modern thinkers had dismissed the idea of a *summum bonum* as an elusive, fictitious and even incoherent notion, but much of Yeats's career was based around an ideal of moral harmony that presupposed a unified good.[59] He was nervous, however, about its implications. In 1903 he declared that 'there is only one perfection and only one search for perfection', but he immediately qualified this absolutism by adding that there were many ways of pursuing the same search.[60] He was even more tentative elsewhere: there was, he suggested, a supreme good, but it was not directly accessible to human understanding. Indeed, 'to those who believe in the final victory of Good there is greater heroism in our uncertainty'.[61] And there were good grounds for uncertainty. Modern life, after all, was an incorrigibly plural affair involving large aggregates of individuals engaged in very different activities. To insist upon a common moral purpose in such circumstances was often either unrealistic or authoritarian. Of course, Yeats did not balk at authoritarian solutions to modern problems; when his admiration for Benito Mussolini was at its highest, he pointed to the highly complex nature of modernity as evidence of the need for authoritarian rule: in such a complicated world, decisions could not be entrusted to the unskilled many.[62] But in other situations, he invoked this social complexity to contest the ascription of a unitary end to communal life: access to this final cause, he suggested, eluded human beings; in a more radical revaluation of his former values, he queried the very existence of a *summum bonum*.

It was on this basis that he further attacked the principles of Young Ireland. He believed that its attempt to organize a community around a shared conception of ethical life culminated in either 'simplification' or 'tyranny'.[63] If this common good was to accommodate large numbers of people, it would be vacuous; it would say everything in general and nothing very specific. If a more substantial interpretation of the good was offered, it would be exclusionary and coercive. Either way, Young Ireland's ideal of the ethical community dangerously exaggerated the social and moral coherence of human affairs. Young Ireland's poetry was itself evidence of this blindness: here a claim to moral

---

59 In *Leviathan*, 70, Hobbes famously asserted that there 'is no such *Finis ultimus* (utmost ayme) nor *Summum Bonum* (greatest Good) as is spoken of in the Books of the old Morall Philosophers'. For liberals such as Isaiah Berlin, the idea of a unitary good was incoherent; a moral decision necessarily implied a preference in the face of different and incompatible goods. See Berlin, *The Crooked Timber of Humanity*, 13.

60 EI, 207.

61 E, 309.

62 UP 2. 433: 'Authoritative government is certainly coming, if for no other reason than that the modern State is so complex that it must find some kind of expert government, a government firm enough, tyrannical enough, if you will, to spend years in carrying out its plans'. Cf. Benito Mussolini, *The Doctrine of Fascism*, trans. E. Cope (Florence, 1938), 55–56: 'We were the first to state that, as civilization assumes aspects which grow more and more complicated, individual freedom becomes more and more restricted.'

63 M, 251.

unanimity was often built around an extremely vague notion of the good, culminating in a form of advocacy without content; alternatively, a poetry of shrill conviction precluded from the start any possibility of dissent. Yeats shrank from this coercive fellow-feeling. Instead of looking for the world's lost harmony he began to subscribe — under the influence of Friedrich Nietzsche — to a different philosophy, one wherein life expressed itself as an 'always individualising' force.[64] Here the world did not manifest itself as a unified whole but as a perpetual conflict. On the basis of this account of cosmic struggle, Yeats ratified his own pugnacity in Irish public life. His often ferocious campaigns for a more tolerant Ireland were in many ways self-refuting, but they were aimed in particular at the legacy of Young Ireland.

'Young Ireland,' Yeats maintained, 'sought a nation unified by political doctrine alone, a subservient art and letters aiding and abetting.'[65] He believed, however, that literature should be enjoyed 'for her own sake and not as the scullery maid of politics'.[66] Art, in other words, must pursue a logic immanent to itself. Young Ireland's fusion of art and politics, on the other hand, often presented itself to Yeats as a disastrous conflation of two discrete spheres of value. The sorry child of this marriage, he suggested, was not art but propaganda. Yeats's criticisms of propaganda did not simply amount to a high-minded defence of the purity of art; they were often highly partisan attacks on certain political opinions with which he disagreed. But the serviceable nature of Yeats's efforts to distinguish art from politics — as well as the difficulty of this particular task — should not obscure the broader conceptual point: human life appears to involve a diversity of goods, none of which shares a common principle or an ultimate end. As Max Weber put it, 'the various value spheres of the world stand in irreconcilable conflict with each other'.[67] This conflict of values, according to Weber, was always a feature of the world, but it was exacerbated in a modern context. The division of labour and specification of social function had led to an extraordinary multiplication of ends and means, none of which were reducible to some ultimate end.

Yeats, however, was often appalled by this moral and social dissonance. This is why he would always remain fascinated and tormented by the ideals of Young Ireland. In the midst of a fragmented world, he repeatedly returned to their vision of a moral community unified in its pursuit of the good, an end that was not reducible to peace, material well-being or private satisfaction. For all his misgivings, he found it impossible to relinquish an ideal of politics grounded on a substantive interpretation of the good life.

---

64 E, 120.
65 A, 204.
66 UP 1. 373.
67 Max Weber, *From Max Weber: Essays in Sociology*, ed. H. H. Gerth and C. Wright Mills, new edn. (London, 1991), 129–56, 147.

4 Structure and Method

The first section of this study examines Young Ireland's conception of an ethical community; the second part focuses on Yeats's ambivalent response to this vision of social life. His ambivalence, I argue, resulted in part from the difficulties surrounding the instantiation of an ethical community in modern societies of enormous size. The third section further explores this problem and takes the role of mass communications in Ireland as its main focus. I begin with Young Ireland because it is often regarded as the point of origin for a specific form of 'cultural nationalism' in Ireland.[68] If this means that the group combined explicitly political objectives with an emphasis on cultural pursuits such as poetry and song, then as recent commentators have shown, the United Irishmen had already attempted a similar kind of marriage in the 1790s.[69] But there are also significant ideological differences between the United Irishmen and Young Ireland — one of the most notable is the self-conscious 'historicism' of the latter movement. A sense of history, I argue in chapter 1, was central to Young Ireland's understanding of political discourse, method and right. The United Irishmen were inspired by the French Revolution and were enthusiasts of the 'Rights of Man'.[70] Young Ireland endorsed the Revolution, but it was also critical of the abstract nature of its legitimizing discourses. This reflects the influence of Edmund Burke, for whom Young Ireland had profound admiration. The Young Irelanders shared Burke's criticisms of 'geometrical' reasoning in politics, but they also extended these criticisms to condemn the abstract method of Jeremy Bentham.

The group's opposition to Benthamism also arose from its classical conception of politics, which I explore in detail in chapter 2. Young Ireland's very real affiliation to a classical tradition of civic republicanism emphasises the fraught nature of recent attempts to distinguish the language of republicanism — or patriotism — from the discourses of nineteenth-century nationalism. It is a historical and moral imperative, Maurizio Viroli maintains, to distinguish a patriotic endorsement of free institutions from the nationalist pursuit of the homogeneous community grounded often on illiberal and atavistic ideas.[71] Few would deny the importance of distinguishing between these political ends, but nationalism is a more complex phenomenon than Viroli's polarized account of matters suggests.[72] The Young Irelanders were self-confessed nationalists,

---

68 In this context, Thomas Davis is often regarded as Young Ireland's most influential ideologue. According to one commentator, he was 'about the most important single figure in the history of Irish cultural nationalism'. See Malcolm Brown, *The Politics of Irish Literature: From Thomas Davis to W. B. Yeats* (London, 1972), viii.

69 See Mary Helen Thuente, *The Harp Re-Strung: The United Irishmen and the Rise of Irish Literary Nationalism* (Syracuse, 1994).

70 See Marianne Elliott, *Partners in Revolution: The United Irishmen and France* (New Haven and London, 1982).

71 Maurizio Viroli, *For Love of Country: An Essay on Patriotism and Nationalism* (Oxford, 1995).

72 The difficulty of efforts to distinguish between patriotism and nationalism is testified by the fact that other figures have attempted to draw similar distinctions within nationalism itself. Hans Kohn, for instance,

but they also invoked the language and ideals of a republican or patriot tradition. There were clear problems with this republican advocacy, particularly in a mid-nineteenth-century context, but these difficulties were intrinsic to patriotism as a whole and were not the result — at best, they may be regarded as the cause — of some malign nationalist distortion. Joep Leerssen has argued, nevertheless, that an eighteenth-century patriot tradition was gradually supplanted by 'ethnic nationalism' under Young Ireland.[73] It is hard to say what weight the term 'ethnic' should be given when applied to any nationalism. If it is intended to suggest that Young Ireland based its understanding of a political community upon a racial essence or common blood-line, then the description is inaccurate. Davis criticized even his beloved Augustin Thierry for his excessive emphasis on race and insisted that 'when we come to deal with politics, we must sink the distinctions of blood as well as sect'.[74]

The Young Irelanders certainly had difficulties in adjusting their republican ideals to the realities of modern political life, but there are dangers in judging the case in advance through the sometimes latent but more usually heavily loaded values of terms such as 'romantic nationalism'. Stress on the 'romantic' character of Young Ireland's politics has produced questionable genealogies of influence in which German romanticism plays a disproportionately large role in Irish letters.[75] The German sponsorship of a historical Kultur against the universalizing ambition of French civilisation has clear analogies with Irish attempts to resist English cultural encroachments in the name of a native tradition. But analogies are not causes and too much has been made of Davis's visit to Germany in 1839–40, where he supposedly underwent 'an evangelical-like conversion'

---

famously distinguished between 'Eastern' and 'Western' forms of nationalism. The former was grounded upon atavistic notions of a shared, organic identity, while the latter was a function of rational assent to the laws and institutions of the sovereign nation. See Hans Kohn, *The Idea of Nationalism, Its Meaning and History* (New York, 1964). More recently, Liah Greenfeld, *Nationalism: Five Roads to Modernity* (Cambridge, 1992), 11, adopted a different nomenclature to make a similar distinction: 'nationalism may be distinguished according to criteria of membership in the national collectivity, which may be either "civic", that is, identical with citizenship, or "ethnic"'. See also Anthony D. Smith, *Nationalism: Theory, Ideology, History* (Cambridge, 2001), 39–42. For a critique of the idea of 'civic nationalism', see Bernard Yack, 'The Myth of the Civic Nation', in Ronald Beiner, ed., *Theorizing Nationalism* (Albany, 1999), 103–18.

73 Joep Leerssen, *Remembrance and Imagination: Patterns in the Historical and Literary Representation of Ireland in the Nineteenth Century* (Cork, 1996), 22. The problem with distinguishing an *ethnie* from a nation is that both seem to lack objective or natural foundations and are constituted by belief. Nor is the criterion for distinguishing between these forms of collective belief always clear. For an account of the apparently ethnic character of nationalism see Anthony D. Smith, *The Ethnic Origins of Nationalism* (Oxford, 1991). For a critique of Smith, see T. K. Oommen, *Citizenship, Nationality and Ethnicity* (Cambridge, 1997), 35–40.

74 *Nation*, 26 November 1842.

75 Oliver MacDonagh, in *Ireland: The Union and Its Aftermath* (London, 1977), 152, makes much of the suggestion that Davis visited Germany in 1839–40. But John N. Molony, *A Soul Came into Ireland: Thomas Davis 1814–45. A Biography* (Dublin, 1996), 25, concludes there is no evidence to support this mythic visit. Another recent biography of Davis also makes no reference to the visit. See Helen Mulvey, *Thomas Davis and Ireland: A Biographical Study* (Washington, 2003).

to German romanticism.[76] There is no evidence for these journeys to Prussia or to Damascus. The Young Irelanders certainly owed more to Young England — which they repeatedly extolled in the pages of the *Nation* — than to Young Germany (the German group was, in any event, explicitly hostile to romanticism). This is not to argue that there was no intellectual commerce between Germany and Ireland but the accounts of it have produced some questionable conclusions.[77]

If Young Ireland's politics have been read through a German lens, this may reflect a belief — popularized by figures like Isaiah Berlin and others — that the 'paradigm of modern nationalism' is to be found in Germany.[78] Berlin also presented this nationalism as an understandable but misguided reaction to Enlightenment values. This sharp and overdrawn contrast between 'Enlightenment' principles and 'romantic' ideals has generated a dubious set of dichotomies in Irish scholarship. According to one historian, the 'romantic' character of Young Ireland's nationalism led it to place 'the emphasis on the race rather than the person, the group rather than the individual, instinct and emotion, rather than reason, cultural rather than constitutional liberation, and a subjective and creative rather than a formal or negative concept of independence'.[79] This view is entirely mistaken; although it was produced some time ago, its distortions survive. Certainly, Young Ireland believed that affect was an irreducible feature of politics, but this reflected a specific understanding of political rationality rather than a repudiation of reason as such. Rather than promoting 'cultural' over 'constitutional' objectives, the

76 For an interesting account of the influence of German romanticism on Young Ireland, see Eva Stöter, '"Grimmige Zeiten": The Influence of Lessing, Herder and the Grimm Brothers on the Nationalism of the Young Irelanders', in Glenn Hooper and Leon Litvack, eds., *Ireland in the Nineteenth Century: Regional Identity* (Dublin, 2000), 173–80. The Young Irelanders — as Roy Foster and others suggest — were influenced both in style and content by Thomas Carlyle, who had written a biography of Friedrich Schiller and introduced a British readership to German idealism. See R. F. Foster, *Modern Ireland, 1600–1972* (London, 1989), 311. See also Roger Swift, 'Thomas Carlyle and Ireland', in D. George Boyce and Roger Swift, eds., *Problems and Perspectives in Irish History since 1800* (Dublin, 2004), 117–46. Duffy himself pointed to an affinity between Irish ballads and the achievements of Bürger, Schiller and Goethe, while Davis quoted on occasion from Lessing. Charles Gavan Duffy, *Ballad Poetry of Ireland*, 40th edn. (Dublin, 1869), 32; Davis, *Essays Literary and Historical*, 2. German literature had a profound influence on James Clarence Mangan's work. His *Anthologia Germanica*, a series of essays and accompanying translations of German poets, was published in the *Dublin University Magazine* from 1835 to 1846. He also produced a similar series, *Stray Leaflets from the German Oak*, during the same period. But Mangan's intellectual interests were not necessarily representative of the Young Irelanders as a whole. For a discussion of Mangan, see David Lloyd, *Nationalism and Minor Literature: James Clarence Mangan and the Emergence of Irish Cultural Nationalism* (Berkeley, 1987). For a more general account of the intellectual commerce between Germany and Ireland, see Patrick O'Neill, *Ireland and Germany: A Study in Literary Relations* (New York, 1985).

77 According to Leerssen, *Remembrance and Imagination*, 22, the 'Herderian-cum-Hegelian pattern of ethnic nationalism is firmly entrenched in Irish politics from *The Nation* and the mid-century onwards'. This is questionable on empirical grounds, but it is also conceptually fraught. The coupling of Herder and Hegel in particular overlooks substantial incongruities. Hegel, after all, revered the ethical state as the instantiation of reason in the world, while Herder's intense distrust of state institutions made his thinking appear, to some interpreters, deeply anti-political. See Berlin, *Vico and Herder*, 181–82.

78 Berlin, *Against the Current*, 346.

79 Oliver MacDonagh, *O'Connell: The Life of Daniel O'Connell, 1775–1847* (London, 1991), 310.

group insisted that the separation of these ends led to the moral impoverishment of politics. Young Ireland, moreover, did not prioritize collective over individual liberties, but generally maintained that both spheres of freedom were co-dependent. These patriots were undeniably critical of a purely 'formal or negative' concept of liberty, but their preferred alternative was not some 'subjective or creative' idiosyncrasy. The group drew its positive conception of freedom from a neo-Aristotelian tradition in which the practice of politics was a necessary condition of self-realization. This position may have been impractical in a modern context, but it was not capricious.

A wealth of scholarship has been produced on Yeats's politics, but I intend to shed further light on his complex attitude to Irish nationalism and to Young Ireland in particular.[80] Yeats's criticisms of Young Ireland have sometimes been presented as a critique of nationalist propaganda in the name of art. F. S. L. Lyons maintained, for instance, that 'Yeats approached the Irish past not primarily as a patriot ... but as an artist concerned above all to create. Those whom he sought to convince, however, were too long habituated to regard art as propaganda to be able to think of it as anything other than subservient to nationalism'.[81] This was to take the terms of Yeats's own polemic at face value in ways that divested his quarrel with Young Ireland of its political content. Yeats was certainly distressed by the poverty of Young Ireland's art, but he also objected to the group's politics and, in particular, to the moral and social coherence it seemed to presuppose. Of course, the plural and complex nature of modern societies militated against Yeats's plans for a 'unity of culture' in Ireland. Chapter 3 focuses on his initial attempts to restore a unity to a world dismembered by the division of labour and the specification of function. The failure of these hopes, I shall argue, is bound up with his disillusionment with Young Ireland. Chapter 4 outlines the way his criticisms of Young Ireland and Irish nationalism, more generally, were informed by a counter-revolutionary political tradition. The nationalism of Young Ireland had a distinctly Burkean character, but in response to this, Yeats drew on an Anglo-Irish tradition of Burke interpretation to criticize the group and its paler imitations. His repudiation of nationalism, I shall argue, was also informed by a more general rejection of mass democracy in Ireland.

Yeats's dispute with Young Ireland ultimately centred on competing interpretations of the viability of cultural excellence in a mass political and social setting. The third section of the book develops this claim and examines the fate of culture in an age of mass communications. It is difficult to overestimate the practical and symbolic significance of mass media such as the press for the Young Irelanders: the newspaper made democracy

---

80 The various discussions of Yeats's politics are too extensive to cover here, but, among the works already cited, I have found the following material particularly helpful. Marjorie Howes, *Yeats's Nations: Gender, Class, and Irishness* (Cambridge, 1996), and Michael North, *The Political Aesthetic of Yeats, Eliot, and Pound* (Cambridge, 1990), 21–73. The most exhaustive treatment of Yeats's complex politics is provided by R. F. Foster in *W. B. Yeats: A Life. I: The Apprentice Mage, 1865–1914* (Oxford, 1997), and *W. B. Yeats: A Life. II: The Arch-Poet*.

81 F. S. L. Lyons, *Ireland since the Famine*, rev. edn. (London, 1973), 237.

a viable hope in modern states by removing spatial barriers to collective deliberation over public affairs. If democracies required, as J. S. Mill suggested, a shared civic ethos or national feeling, then newspapers helped to foster these sentiments.[82] It was hardly surprising, therefore, that many influential Irish nationalists were also successful journalists. Cultural nationalists such as Thomas Davis or Eoin MacNeill, Fenians such as John Devoy or John O'Leary, constitutional nationalists such as A. M. Sullivan or William O'Brien, republicans such as Arthur Griffith, and revolutionaries such as Padraig Pearse were all influential ideologues with diverging political views, and all were journalists. Chapter 5 explores the co-dependent relationship between newspapers and nationalism in Ireland.[83] Irish nationalism may have owed much to newspapers, but the relationship between both was often fraught. Patriots repeatedly condemned the newspaper industry for its want of political principle in the search of profit. Yeats, along with many of his literary contemporaries, used nationalist idioms to condemn the corrupting influence of the press on national life. Over time, however, he regarded nationalism as part of the problem rather than the solution. Irish politics and the Irish press, he suggested, were systematic in their promotion of prejudice: 'We are quick to hate and slow to love and we have never lacked a Press to excite the most evil passions.'[84]

Yeats objected to the illiberal qualities of the press in Ireland, but he displayed throughout much of his career a more generalized hatred of newspapers.[85] According to George Moore, he was 'a sort of monk of literature, an Inquisitor of Journalism'.[86] Yeats's reflections on the Young Ireland leader, Charles Gavan Duffy, reflected his considerable contempt for the grubby world of journalism. The objective correlative of Duffy's 'manhood of practical politics' was, for Yeats, 'the dirty piece of orange-peel in the corner of the stairs as one climbs up to some newspaper office'.[87] In a 1907 essay, he noted a kind of poetic justice in Duffy's death: 'I have just read in a newspaper that Sir Charles Gavan Duffy recited upon his death-bed his favourite poem, one of the worst of

---

82 'Among a people without fellow-feeling, especially if they read and speak different languages,' Mill maintained, 'the united public opinion necessary to the workings of government, cannot exist.' *Collected Works*, 19. 547.

83 For a general survey of the development of the press in Ireland, see Brian Inglis, *The Freedom of the Press in Ireland, 1784–1841* (London, 1954); Hugh Oram, *The Newspaper Book: A History of Newspapers in Ireland, 1649–1983* (Dublin, 1983); Brian Farrell, ed., *Communications and Community in Ireland* (Dublin and Cork, 1984). The most comprehensive discussion of the Irish provincial press is provided by Marie-Louise Legg, *Newspapers and Nationalism: The Irish Provincial Press 1850–1892* (Dublin, 1999). See also Virginia Glandon in *Arthur Griffith and the Advanced Nationalist Press, Ireland: 1900–1922* (New York, 1985). For the relationship between the Irish press and the British Empire, see Simon J. Potter, ed., *Newspapers and Empire in Ireland and Britain* (Dublin, 2004), and Michael Foley, 'Colonialism and Journalism in Ireland', *Journalism Studies*, 5, 3 (2004), 373–85.

84 UP 2. 465.

85 Louis MacNeice shared W. H. Auden's view that 'the normal poet includes the journalist', but noted that Yeats dissented from this. 'A wider view of poetry', in MacNeice's eyes, 'might have made him less severe upon journalism'. See MacNeice, *The Poetry of W. B. Yeats*, 30; 41.

86 George Moore, *Hail and Farewell: Ave, Vale, Salve*, ed. Richard Cave (Gerrards Cross, 1985), 210.

87 A, 225.

the patriotic poems of Young Ireland.'[88] His dealings with Duffy were characterized by a specific rancour — issuing from Duffy's apparent hijacking of the New Irish Library project in 1894 — but this only gave an extra charge to his long-standing hatred of journalists. They were the crude mouthpiece of 'tittering jeering emptiness'.[89] These fulminations tend to repress the fact that journalism served as a major source of Yeats's income for much of his writing life. Yug Chaudhry has produced a careful study of Yeats's early journalism, emphasizing the fluid nature of his politics and the supple quality of his prose as he moved between journals of radically diverging outlooks.[90] But the broader political and social ramifications of the poet's anti-newspaper polemic remain to be addressed. I consider these in the last section of the book.

Yeats hoped to create a great community through the forum of art, but in the modern world, at least, this necessarily implied some form of mass culture. He ultimately recoiled from the task, insisting that 'ideas and images which have to be understood and loved by large numbers of people must appeal to no rich personal experience, no patience of study, no delicacy of sense'.[91] A mass culture was, it seemed, a contradiction in terms. This undermined his own hopes for a popular art, but it also confirmed the broader difficulties of Young Ireland's political vision. The group had sponsored a redemptive ideal of culture in the face of a democratic future, but this had turned out to be a destructive illusion in the poet's eyes. Against the degraded forms of public culture that was Young Ireland's bequest to the nation, Yeats increasingly glorified the private virtues of 'self-culture'. Here he produced a complex model of personal authenticity — the tensions and contradictions of which shall be explored in some detail in the final chapter of the book. If a genuine ethical community was impossible in the modern age, a confused ethics of the self was not a credible alternative.

88 EI, 257.
89 W. B. Yeats, The Collected Letters of W. B. Yeats. Volume 1: 1865–1895, ed. John Kelly and Erick Domville (Oxford, 1986), 91. Hereafter cited as CL 1.
90 Yug Chaudhry, Yeats, the Irish Literary Revival and the Politics of Print (Cork, 2001).
91 EI, 313.

Part I
The Political Thought of Young Ireland

1   History and National Character

1 The Political Significance of Historicism

Yeats emerged from the first decade of the twentieth century convinced that Young Ireland had 'wrecked the historical instinct'.[1] This was ironic because the nationalism of Young Ireland was predicated not simply on historical claims — about the nature of English conquest or the origins of Irish independence — but on claims about the importance of historical inquiry as such; a sense of history, in other words, was central to Young Ireland's understanding of political discourse, practice and right. The group repeatedly exalted the benefits of historical knowledge, and entertained wild hopes for a new history of Ireland: 'its first political effect would be enormous; it would be read by every class and side; ... it would clear up the grounds of our quarrels, and prepare reconciliation; it would *unconsciously* make us recognise the causes of our weakness; it would give us great examples of men and of events, and materially influence our destiny'.[2] Ireland's claim to independence lay within its own history.

Thomas Davis attempted to ground his bid for an independent legislature, not on abstract reason, but on historical precedent, tracing the 'pedigree of our freedom' in rights embodied in the Patriot Parliament of James II and the Protestant Parliament of 1782.[3] He was by no means the first or last Irish patriot to base his claims on historical grounds. Although William Molyneux's *Case of Ireland* (1698) drew substantially on a

---

1   EI, 316–17. Young Ireland's historical emphasis, he claimed, had helped to produce a national consciousness which was as narcissistic as it was deluded: 'The man who doubted, let us say, our fabulous ancient kings running up to Adam, or found but mythology in some old tale, was as hated as if he had doubted the authority of Scripture'.
2   *Nation*, 5 April 1845 [*Nation*'s emphasis].
3   *Nation*, 1 April 1843.

Lockean conception of the social contract and rights 'founded on such immutable laws of Nature and Reason', his defence of Irish constitutional liberties was substantially built around a genealogy of rights which had their origins in the medieval past.[4] The eighteenth-century patriot, Charles Lucas, drew on Molyneux and made further appeals to historical precedent as a legal basis for Irish claims, while Henry Grattan — much revered by the Young Ireland movement — again laid claim to legislative rights which Ireland had supposedly enjoyed since the reign of Henry II.[5] What distinguishes Young Ireland's approach, therefore, is less the uniqueness of the group's historical method — which often amounted to no more than an amplification of earlier views — than its extreme self-consciousness.

The political grounds for this kind of historical fetishism lay in reactions to the French Revolution.[6] The nature and legacy of the French Revolution would become for Young Ireland something of an obsession, and it dictated the terms of their own nationalism. Indeed, many commentators regard the French Revolution as the origin of nationalism as such.[7] Genetic inquiries of this kind are inescapably circular and they often collude in the Revolution's own sense of itself as a new beginning or absolute origin. Still, the impact of the Revolution on modern political discourse in general — and on the idioms of nationalism in particular — is undeniable. In his study of nationalism, Friedrich Meinecke noted how the principle of self-determination was transferred from individuals to states during the Revolution, producing 'the lofty insight that the state is an ideal supra-individual personality'.[8] The 'Rights of Man' now seemed to guarantee the 'Rights of Nations'. This advocacy was not necessarily straightforward or coherent, for the universalism of natural law often strained against the particularist ethos of nationalism.[9] In some cases, a commitment to the sovereign nation came at the expense of the individual rights it was meant to guarantee. There was, however, another way of imagining the nation and it began by repudiating the doctrines of the *Droits des Hommes*. This was the method adopted by Burke and it culminated in a concept of 'national character' which was, he argued, a product of history and not of abstract reasoning.[10]

It was Burke, Yeats maintained, who 'restored to political thought its sense of history' and a host of other figures from Lord Acton to Hubert Butterfield have shared a similar

---

4 William Molyneux, *The Case of Ireland Stated by William Molyneux*, repr. from the 1st edn. of 1698 (Dublin, 1977), 93.

5 See S. J. Connolly, 'Precedent and Principle: The Patriots and Their Critics', in S. J. Connolly, ed., *Political Ideas in Eighteenth-Century Ireland* (Dublin, 2000), 130–58.

6 Leo Strauss, *Natural Right and History* (Chicago, 1953), 3.

7 See, for instance, Elie Kedourie, *Nationalism*, 4th edn. (Oxford and Cambridge, 1993) and E. J. Hobsbawm, *Nations and Nationalism since 1780*, rev. edn. (Cambridge, 1990); Otto Dann and John Dinwiddy, eds., *Nationalism in the Age of the French Revolution* (London, 1988).

8 Friedrich Meinecke, *Cosmopolitanism and the National State*, trans. Robert B. Kimber (Princeton, 1970), 15.

9 John Dunn, *Western Political Theory in the Face of the Future* (Cambridge, 1993), 59.

10 Seamus Deane, *Strange Country*, 1–48, has argued convincingly that Burke's *Reflections on the Revolution in France* is a 'foundational' text for intellectual debate in Ireland.

conviction.[11] I want to explore the nature of Burke's historicism in some detail, because it will allow us to recuperate the political significance of Young Ireland's focus on history — a preoccupation that can all too easily be dismissed as a form of atavism or nostalgia or, at best, a simplistic rationalization of irredentist desire. This is not to suggest that the group's interpretation of Burke was either profound or systematic. Young Ireland may have praised Burke as a 'philosopher, and a statesman of the first class', but the group's accounts of his talents were often extremely superficial. One review, for instance, dedicated itself more to 'Burke on the Philosophy of Ploughing' than to anything substantive he had to say about politics.[12] The Young Irelanders' irredentist ambitions — however vaguely set out — meant that Burke would always remain for them a figure of considerable ambivalence. The Nation applauded Burke's commitment to 'the political cause of the Catholics' and was keen to assert the 'hereditary Irishry' of his feelings, but Burke's outlook on Irish constitutional affairs — from his initial defence of Poynings's Law to his general protection of Ireland's status within the empire — was deeply at odds with Young Ireland's political programme.[13] But the historical approach of the Young Irelanders, although influenced by contemporaries such as François Guizot and Thierry, is best interpreted in the light of Burke, because his historicism was so explicitly articlated as a response to a foundational event in modern political culture — the French Revolution.

The central premise of Burke's historicism, I want to argue, is the contextual nature of moral and political judgements. This did not amount to a form of ethical relativism; in his thoughts on Indian affairs, Burke condemned the advocates of a 'Geographical morality' and asserted that 'the laws of morality are the same everywhere'.[14] There was, in principle, no contradiction between Burke's defence of general norms and his strong emphasis on the context-relative nature of moral judgement.[15] He believed that there were formal constraints on what could operate as a moral norm, as well as common features of human nature that needed to be accommodated in any account

11   UP 2. 459. 'History,' Acton maintained, 'hails from Burke, as Education from Helvétius or Emancipation from the Quakers.' See Herbert Butterfield, *Man on His Past: The Study of the History of Historical Scholarship* (Cambridge, 1955), 70. See also Friedrich Meinecke, *Historism: The Rise of a New Historical Outlook*, trans. J. E. Anderson (London, 1972), 227.

12   *Nation*, 12 April 1845.

13   *Nation*, 3 May 1845; *Nation*, 12 April 1845. Poynings's Law (1494) made a royal licence a legal requirement for the meeting of the Irish parliament; all parliamentary activity needed the approval of the King and his Council in England as well as his Deputy and his Council in Ireland. For Burke's reasoning on Irish constitutional matters, see Eamon O'Flaherty, 'Burke and the Irish Constitution', in Seán Patrick Donlan, ed., *Edmund Burke's Irish Identities* (Dublin, 2007), 102–16. See also James Conniff, 'Edmund Burke's Reflections on the Coming Revolution in Ireland', *Journal of the History of Ideas*, 47, 1 (1986), 37–59.

14   Edmund Burke, *The Writings and Speeches of Edmund Burke. Volume 6: India: The Launching of the Hastings Impeachment, 1786–1788*, ed. Paul Langford, P. J. Marshall, William B. Todd (Oxford, 1991), 346. Hereafter cited as *W & S 6*.

15   For a subtle treatment of this issue, see Christopher Insole, *The Politics of Human Frailty: A Theological Defence of Political Liberalism* (London, 2004), 15–40.

of the good.[16] He drew frequently on a classical tradition of natural law in delineating these general principles.[17] But this tradition had always acknowledged the significance of social context in the application and interpretation of these laws. 'Circumstances,' as he put it in the *Reflections*, 'give in reality to every political principle its distinguishing colour, and discriminating effect. The circumstances are what render every political scheme beneficial or noxious to mankind.'[18] It was through an appeal to circumstance that Burke attacked, first, a 'geometrical' or *a priori* approach to politics, second, an atomistic method — an inquiry that began with an account of the individual removed from his social and historical contexts — and third, a reductive positivism, one which derived its concept of proof and evidence from the natural sciences.[19] In Burke's eyes, the French revolutionaries erred on each of these issues in ways that betrayed the essentially anti-historical nature of their political outlook.

Burke was skilled in the rhetorics, both ancient and modern, of natural law, but his historicism also presented itself as an attack on certain conceptions of natural right.[20] In assigning rights to pre-social individuals, the French overlooked the fact that political inquiry is only meaningful within a social and historical context.[21] 'I cannot stand forward,' Burke insisted, 'and give praise or blame to anything which relates to human actions, and human concerns, on a simple view of the object, as it stands stripped of every relation, in all the nakedness and solitude of metaphysical abstraction'.[22] Moral understanding could not be separated from our socially mediated interests in the world. Theories, in other words, derived from the values and practices internal to historical

16 These constraints were imposed by 'the will of Him who gave us our nature, and in giving impressed an invariable Law upon it'. See *W & S* 9. 455.

17 Meinecke, *Historism*, 223, overstated the case when he claimed that, for Burke, 'the innermost enemy who must be slain in order to understand human life and history on a deeper level was the spirit of Natural Law, further exaggerated by the Enlightenment'. See also, Alfred Cobban, *Edmund Burke and the Revolt against the Eighteenth Century: A Study of the Political and Social Thinking of Burke, Wordsworth, Coleridge and Southey*, 2nd edn. (London, 1960).

18 *The Writings and Speeches of Edmund Burke. Volume 8: The French Revolution 1790–1794*, ed. Paul Langford, L. G. Mitchell, William B. Todd (Oxford, 1989), 58. Hereafter cited as *W & S* 8.

19 Burke maintained that his opposition to political geometry was broadly Aristotelian. *The Writings and Speeches of Edmund Burke. Volume 3: Party, Parliament, and the American War 1774–1780*, ed. Paul Langford, Warren M. Elofson, John A. Woods, William B. Todd (Oxford, 1996), 157. Hereafter cited as *W&S* 3.

20 Peter Stanlis followed the lead of Leo Strauss in distinguishing between a classical tradition of natural law and a modern and distinctly inferior paradigm of natural right that derives from Hobbes and Locke. He presented Burke as a defender of the classical doctrine. Peter J. Stanlis, *Edmund Burke and the Natural Law* (Ann Arbor, 1965). For other accounts of Burke's debts to a classical notion of natural law, see Francis P. Canavan, *The Political Reason of Edmund Burke* (Durham, 1960); Burleigh Wilkins, *The Problem of Burke's Political Philosophy* (Oxford, 1967); Joseph Pappin, *The Metaphysics of Edmund Burke* (New York, 1993). For Burke's debts to a more Hobbesian version of natural law, see Iain Hampsher-Monk, *A History of Modern Political Thought: Major Political Thinkers from Hobbes to Marx* (Oxford, 1992), 270–72. See also Richard Bourke, 'Sovereignty, Opinion and Revolution in Edmund Burke', *History of European Ideas*, 25 (1999), 99–120.

21 See Introduction to Edmund Burke, *Reflections on the Revolution of France*, ed. J. G. A. Pocock (Indianapolis, 1987), vii–lvi, vii.

22 *W & S* 8. 58.

forms of life. But the French, he believed, had reversed this relationship and had given a false priority to abstract theory.[23] He criticized the tendency of the *philosophe* to regard his country 'as nothing but *carte blanche* upon which he may scribble whatever he pleases'.[24] This faith in an absolute origin or new beginning was as irrational as it was narcissistic.[25] 'Personal self-sufficiency and arrogance' were the defining traits of those who would purport to transcend their own historical environments and seek to invent things anew. In this operation, time-bound institutions and solidarities were reduced to 'the dust and powder of individuality, and at length dispersed to all the winds of heaven'.[26]

Against the dangerous French propensity for metaphysical abstraction, Burke promoted a more modest and circumstantial form of reasoning, which was, he believed, deeply embedded in English national character. The English had come to see that reason in politics was context-dependent. The criteria for human action, they believed, derived from, just as they are adjustments to, the contingency of life itself. This precluded a simple *a priori* approach to politics, but the contextual nature of political reason also overruled an atomistic method that began with an account of the individual abstracted from his social environments. 'Men', according to Burke, 'are never in a state of *total* independence of each other'.[27] The criteria for right action were internal to the social contexts in which human beings found themselves. 'The *situations* in which men relatively stand produce the rules and principles of that responsibility, and afford directions to prudence in exacting it.'[28] Social contexts necessarily presupposed shared norms which provided individuals with some orientation in moral space. Moreover, there was no neutral position within these environments.

This was the basis for Burke's estimation of prejudice in politics. Prejudice was not something that must be removed for a proper understanding of human situations; it was foundational to such knowledge.[29] However, the French revolutionaries, he

---

23 Burke did not repudiate theory outright. As he put it in his 'Speech on the Reform of the Representation in the House of Commons' in 1782: 'whenever I speak against theory, I mean always a weak, erroneous, fallacious, unfounded, or imperfect theory; and one of the ways of discovering, that it is a false theory, is by comparing it with practice. This is the true touchstone of all theories, which regard man and the affairs of men — does it suit his nature in general; — does it suit his nature as modified by his habits?' *The Works of the Right Honourable Edmund Burke*, 16 vols. (London, 1815–27), 10. 99–100.

24 *W & S* 8. 206.

25 *W & S* 8. 83.

26 *W & S* 8. 146. For a very similar line of argument in a twentieth-century setting, see Michael Oakeshott, 'Rationalism in Politics', in *Rationalism in Politics and Other Essays*, new edn. (Indianapolis, 1991), 5–42.

27 *W & S* 9. 249 [Burke's emphasis]. In 1770 he reported to the Commons 'an old scholastic aphorism, which says, "that the man who lives wholly detached from others, must be either an angel or a devil"'. He had not, he assured the House, come across any angels. See Edmund Burke, *The Writings and Speeches of Edmund Burke. Volume II: Party, Parliament and the American Crisis, 1776–1774*, ed. Paul Langford and William B. Todd (Oxford, 1981), 320.

28 *W & S* 9. 249 [Burke's emphasis].

29 Burke, *Works*, 6. 256. For a philosophical defence of prejudice in the twentieth-century, see Hans-Georg Gadamer, *Truth and Method*, 2nd and rev. edn., trans. Joel Weinsheimer and Donald G. Marshall (London, 1989), 269–77.

believed, sought an objective ground for their values and were consequently at war with prejudice.[30] Burke denied the possibility of such a neutral vantage-point. A political system was not a physical entity, nor a set of facts that could be subjected to scientific scrutiny; rather, it was a moral setting that based its entire constitution on values.[31] For this reason, scientific certainty was not available in moral life, but one could still lay claim to a kind of ethical confidence.[32] Prejudice was the source of this confidence, for Burke, and formed the basis of an everyday, moral know-how. From this perspective, prejudices were not irrational but possessed a cognitive dimension.[33] Burke defended, as he put it, 'not a prejudice destitute of reason, but involving in it profound and extensive wisdom'.[34] Prejudice was not a sufficient justification of a moral attitude, but it was a necessary basis for having such attitudes at all. When the French turned against prejudice in their search for objective certainties, they struck at the foundations of moral life. It was in effect a methodical attempt 'to vitiate our primary morals'.[35]

These primary morals, for Burke, were shaped by historical circumstances and were available on one level in the form of a national character.[36] English national character, he suggested, was inherently self-reflexive; it was not simply shaped by history, but it was also a lived acknowledgement of this shaping. For it was the habit of Englishmen to refer to the past and to the wisdom of their predecessors. The rights that they enjoyed were not established on an abstract basis, but were 'a patrimony derived from their forefathers'.[37] Burke encouraged the critical interrogation of this inheritance, but it could not be abandoned in toto or at will. The legacies of the past checked the voluntarist presumption of the present. A nation was not a product of will or rational deliberation, but was the work of anonymous hands:

> Because a nation is not an idea only of local extent, and individual momentary aggregation, but it is an idea of continuity, which extends in time as well as in numbers, and in space. And this is a choice not of one day, or one set of people, not a tumultuary and giddy choice; it is a deliberate election of ages and of generations; it is a Constitution made by what is ten thousand times better than choice, it is

---

30 Burke, W & S 9. 661.
31 As he put it, 'commonwealths are not physical but moral essences'. W & S 9. 188.
32 For a philosophical discussion of the idea of 'ethical confidence', see Bernard Williams, Ethics and the Limits of Philosophy, 3rd edn. (London, 1993), 170–71.
33 Elsewhere, however, he maintained that it was necessary to 'separate prejudice from reason'. W & S 3. 519.
34 W & S 8. 142.
35 W & S 8. 138.
36 David Hume had argued that 'the English, of any people in the universe, have the least of national character; unless this very singularity may pass for such', and he attributed the richly plural quality of English life to the mixed nature of its constitution. David Hume, 'Of National Characters,' in Political Essays, ed. Knud Haakonssen (Cambridge, 1994), 78–92, 86. Burke also sang the virtues of this constitution, but he strove to consolidate a more definite sense of English traits as a bulwark against French ideas.
37 W & S 8. 82.

made by the peculiar circumstances, occasions, tempers, dispositions, and moral, civil, and social habitudes of the people, which disclose themselves only in a long space of time.[38]

English customs had stood the test of time and did not depend on the impossible rigours of a political metaphysics for their validity. The English constitution, he believed, would always invite criticism and require reform, but its existence and longevity were testimony to its utility and created a presumption in its favour.[39]

'What a sad thing it is,' Burke declared late in life, 'that the grand Instructor, Time, has not yet been able to teach the grand lesson of his own value; and that, in every question of moral and political prudence, it is the choice of the moment, which renders the measure serviceable or useless, noxious or salutary.'[40] These comments may have been formulated with his old antagonists, the Jacobins, in mind, but it is worth noting — as a final point — that they were directed to Irish political affairs.[41] For Burke believed that the oligarchs of Ireland were guilty of their own kind of fanaticism; they were also dedicated to rules of 'vicious perfection', which denied the contingent and circumstantial nature of political life.[42] These rules — Burke had in mind the Penal Laws — were ostensibly historical in character, but they had long outlasted their conditions of use. Their maintenance only protracted a 'theological hatred' which ultimately served the selfish interests of a small minority.[43] To defend these repressive measures on the basis of an appeal to historical precedent was to travesty the form of historicism that Burke recommended. Such an approach denied the spirit of the law in the defence of its letter and converted a contingent measure into a political principle.[44]

---

38 *Works*, 10. 97.
39 See J. G. A. Pocock, 'Burke and the Ancient Constitution: A Problem in the History of Ideas', in *Politics, Language and Time: Essays on Political Thought and History* (New York, 1973), 202–32. However, Burke's enthusiasm for the ancient constitution can be exaggerated. He was arguably more committed to the constitutional settlement of the Glorious Revolution than the compacts of the Saxon past. According to Seán Patrick Donlan, his focus was 'on modern, not ancient liberties'. See Seán Patrick Donlan, 'The "Genuine Voice of its Records and Monuments"?', in Donlan, ed., *Edmund Burke's Irish Identities*, 69–101, 72.
40 *W & S* 9. 666.
41 Burke's view of Ireland has received much attention. See in particular William O'Brien, *Edmund Burke as an Irishman* (Dublin, 1926); Thomas Mahoney, *Edmund Burke and Ireland* (Cambridge, 1960); Conor Cruise O'Brien, *The Great Melody: A Thematic Biography of Edmund Burke* (London, 1992); Michel Fuchs, *Edmund Burke, Ireland, and the Fashioning of Self* (Oxford, 1996); W. J. McCormack, *From Burke to Beckett* (Cork, 1994), 49–93; Luke Gibbons, *Edmund Burke and Ireland* (Cambridge, 2003); Seamus Deane, *Strange Country*, 1–48; Deane, *Foreign Affections: Essays on Edmund Burke* (Cork, 2005); Donlan, ed., *Edmund Burke's Irish Identities*.
42 *W & S* 9. 637.
43 *W & S* 9. 634.
44 Burke also believed that the Penal Laws were anti-historical because they eroded the principle of a moral patrimony derived from one's predecessors. See 'Tracts relating to Popery Laws', in *W & S* 9. 446: '... you punish them for acting upon a principle, which, of all others, is perhaps the most necessary for preserving society, an implicit admiration and adherence to the Establishments of their forefathers'.

Burke's historicism was not a rigid posture adopted in the face of change but was a stance that acknowledged the contingent nature of political judgement. Catholics, Burke believed, no longer posed a threat to the safety of the realm. To continue repressive measures against them was, in fact, to jeopardize, that security. An oppressed people who continued to be excluded from the benefits of the constitution would ultimately, he predicted, find succour in Jacobinism. Even though he had lauded the Glorious Revolution in his *Reflections*, he appreciated that in England, it had secured the liberties of the majority from the tyrannical designs of a faction, while the reverse was true in Ireland. Here the revolution had consolidated the privileges of the few over the basic liberties of the many. 'It was,' as Burke put it, 'not a revolution, but a conquest, which is not to say a great deal in its favour'.[45] As he had argued in the *Reflections*, principles may seem to remain everywhere the same, but it was circumstances that rendered them benign or malignant.

Burke's concerns about the rise of Jacobinism in Ireland were not without substance. A year after his death, the United Irishmen, advocates, it seemed, of distinctly 'French' principles, rebelled.[46] Burke was sympathetic to many of the grievances that spurred Irish Catholics, in particular, to revolt, but the entire corpus of his anti-revolutionary writings was opposed to the importation of the political principles of France for the service of whatever cause. Burke had worked hard to secure Ireland's rights within the empire, and had hoped that the removal of abuses against Catholics would ultimately strengthen the bond between Ireland and Great Britain. He 'never liked, as it is well known, that total independence of Ireland which, without ... adding any security to its Liberty, took it out of the common constitutional protection of the Empire'.[47] But Wolfe Tone, among others, sought this independence. The Young Irelanders shared Tone's republican principles, although they allowed themselves considerable interpretative latitude in deciphering the constitutional implications of autonomy.[48]

Yet the writers of the *Nation* regarded the United Irishmen with considerable ambivalence. They had doubts about the practical benefits of physical-force methods. But the group's scepticism had a deeper ideological character that owed something

---

45 W & S 9. 614. This contradicted his earlier praise for the impact of the English constitution on Ireland. In his 'Speech on Conciliation with America', W & S 3. 140, he declared that it was not 'English arms, but the English constitution that conquered Ireland. From that time, Ireland has ever had a general Parliament, as she had before a partial Parliament. You changed the people; you altered the religion; but you never touched the form or the vital substance of free government in that kingdom. ... This has made Ireland the great and flourishing kingdom that it is; and from a disgrace and burthen intolerable to this nation, has rendered her a principal part of our strength and ornament'. For an account of Burke's attitude to conquest, see Richard Bourke, 'Edmund Burke and the Politics of Conquest', *Modern Intellectual History*, 4, 3 (2007), 403–32.

46 For the influence of the French Revolution on the United Irishmen, see Elliott, *Partners in Revolution*.

47 *The Correspondence of Edmund Burke. Volume 9: 1796–97*, ed. R. B. McDowell and John A. Woods (Chicago, 1970), 122.

48 Davis insisted that independence did not mean total separation: 'they and I do not seek separation, because we think it unnecessary'. See the *Nation*, 23 December 1843.

to Burke.[49] Young Ireland was particularly distrustful of a French language of natural rights which the United Irishmen had enthusiastically deployed.[50] The men of '98 made occasional reference to Ireland's historical rights, but they sometimes dismissed history as a ground for political or moral claims.[51] As one circular put it in 1791: 'we have thought little about our ancestors — much of our posterity. Are we forever to walk like beasts of prey over fields which these ancestors have stained with blood? In looking back, we see nothing on one part but savage force succeeded by savage policy'.[52] They hoped to escape the bondage of the past, and based their claims on abstract reason and universal justice.[53] Young Ireland, however, remained profoundly sceptical of the universal scope and seemingly trans-historical character of the United Irishmen's legitimizing discourses. Here, at least, they remained enthusiastic pupils of Burke's 'grand Instructor, Time'.

2 Young Ireland and the Lessons of History

The deliberate and studied nature of Young Ireland's historicism is set out most clearly in an exchange between Duffy and Dillon after the collapse of the movement in 1848. By that point, Dillon was no longer convinced of the viability of a historically based nationalism in Ireland, but he also retained a very clear sense of what it had initially set out to achieve. As he put it in a letter to his wife:

> The history of Ireland can hardly in truth be called the history of a nation. The glory that could be won in two or three battles is too small a thing for a nation to subsist upon. There is not one link that can bind the past of Ireland to its future. The old forms of society, the old laws, and the old language have perished irrecoverably. For these reasons I would, if I were Duffy, abandon this ground of Celtic Nationality, and take my stand henceforth upon the rights of man. A Federal

---

49 'Who fears to speak of '98?' the *Nation* boldly asked in 1843. Ironically, Young Ireland was often the guilty and timorous party in this regard. For an account of Young Ireland's circumspect attitude to '98 on the issue of violence, see Sean Ryder, 'Young Ireland and the 1798 Rebellion', in L. M. Geary, ed., *Rebellion and Remembrance in Modern Ireland* (Dublin, 2001), 135–47.

50 J. C. Beckett, *The Making of Modern Ireland, 1603–1923* (London, 1966), 355, maintained that although Young Ireland 'helped to revive and continue the revolutionary spirit of the United Irishmen, its appeal was to the history of Ireland rather than to the Rights of Man'.

51 Ian McBride claims, in 'Nationalism and Republicanism in the 1790s', in Connolly, ed., *Political Ideas in Eighteenth-Century Ireland*, 159–69, 167, that in the United Irishmen journal, the *Northern Star*, 'the suasive force of precedent was generally relegated in favour of universal rights'.

52 'Address from the Society of United Irishmen in Dublin to the Delegates for Promoting a Reform in Scotland'. Cited by Nancy Curtin, *The United Irishmen: Popular Politics in Ulster and Dublin, 1791–1798* (Oxford, 1994), 21.

53 See Kevin Whelan, 'The United Irishmen, the Enlightenment and Popular Culture', in David Dickson, Dáire Keogh and Kevin Whelan, eds., *The United Irishmen: Republicanism, Radicalism and Rebellion* (Dublin, 1993), 269–96.

Republic is what Great Britain and Ireland want, and if that object were judiciously pursued it might, perhaps, be realised within twenty years.[54]

Here Dillon identified a basic opposition between a historically grounded nationalism and a more general or universal language of legitimization — a distinction which shaped Young Ireland's entire vision of politics. Unsurprisingly, Duffy rejected his friend's proposal to found a new *Nation* in London defending the universal rights of man and ignored Dillon's deeper challenge to a nationalist movement based on an appeal to history alone. Duffy's interests lay not with 'Radicalism or Republicanism', but with the task of putting 'a sceptre into the hand of Ireland'.[55] It was a picturesque vision, as dreamily evocative as it was soothingly vague, but it reflected Duffy's profound distrust of the abstract nature of universal theories of political right — a scepticism that he shared with many of the key figures in the Young Ireland movement.

The Young Irelanders' ambivalent assessment of the French Revolution reveals much about their political values. In the first edition of the *Nation*, Mangan took pains to point out that 'we take not for motto, *Nul n'a de l'esprit,* | (As they once did in Paris) *hors nos bons amis*'.[56] But the newspaper was soon derided as the work of a 'French party', which led, in turn, to noisy rebuttals of such calumny: 'The National party of Ireland were called a French party by factious Helots. ... We are Irish, and Irish alone, and our purely national objects are now known and cherished in every parish in Ireland.'[57] Nevertheless, France and its revolutionary history continued to exercise the mind of Young Ireland in ways which made them easy targets for those with a sensitive nose for Jacobinism. Reflecting the views of liberal historians such as Thierry and Guizot, Davis saw France as 'the first of the large states to sweep away the feudal despotism'. He declared France 'the apostle of liberty', while England remained 'the turnkey of the world'.[58] Of course, he took pains to dissociate himself from the apparent godlessness of certain French apostles: 'our struggle differs from the French Revolution, in the one great fact that our leaders and our people are Christians, and that their leaders were Infidels'.[59] As for the Revolution itself, Davis criticized its excesses, but he was also prepared to acknowledge its positive effects.

Great as were the horrors of the French Revolution, terrible as was the execution it did upon many things noble, venerable, and beloved, still it compensated for much of its crime by having destroyed the practice and principle of primogeniture.

---

54 Quoted in Charles Gavan Duffy, *My Life in Two Hemispheres*, 2 vols. (London, 1903), 2. 3.

55 Duffy, *My Life in Two Hemispheres*, 2. 6. As far as the Irish people were concerned, Duffy maintained, the 'sordid radicalism of Cobbett never found favour among them, and the desolating doctrines of Jacobinism are utterly unknown'. *Nation*, 29 April 1848.

56 *Nation*, 15 October 1842.

57 *Nation*, 4 February 1843.

58 *Nation*, 22 April 1843.

59 He condemned the writings of Voltaire and Rousseau, in particular, as 'evil, depraved, Atheistic'. *Nation*, 8 February 1845.

It led the way, which all nations will go, to a more just and natural distribution of property. France possesses a nation of proprietors; it is no longer the agitated scene whereon a large serf class is vainly struggling against the immunities and privileges of their oppressors.[60]

Davis called for a similar redistribution of property in Ireland. In his promotion of land reform, Dillon went even further and quoted Mirabeau: 'Society is composed of three classes — those who work, those who beg and those who rob.'[61] The aristocracy in Ireland, he believed, was entirely corrupt and history provided salutary lessons of the disaster awaiting those that failed to reform.[62] However, Young Ireland usually invoked the violence of the French Revolution as a dreadful warning to those who resisted reform rather than as a model for emulation.

Young Ireland's endorsement of the Revolution — however qualified — was at odds with Burke's uncompromisingly negative account of its ideals and consequences. Indeed, in a rare moment of criticism, Davis argued that Burke's 'grand but angry genius could only see the crimes of revolution — he was blind to the vast benefits which were to spring from that bold recurrence to first principles'.[63] By the 1840s, of course, it was difficult to hold a wholly Burkean assessment of the French Revolution, whatever one's political orientation. After the fall of Napoleon, Europe seemed to have returned to a period of relative political calm — one soon to be disturbed by the revolutionary events of 1848. Before this outbreak, however, the rhetoric of apocalypse and cataclysm common to anti-revolutionary writing was difficult to sustain. Since the July Revolution of 1830, many middle-class reformers felt that political transformation need not culminate in anarchy and widespread violence.[64] Young Ireland, for instance, spoke of France's 'second (spotless) Revolution'.[65] Here the achievements of 1789 had been consolidated, it appeared, without major disorder. In retrospect, it also seemed possible to separate the revolutionary ideals of 1789 from the Jacobin terror of 1793. Duffy, like many of his liberal contemporaries, regarded the Girondin party as the Revolution's true representatives. In a two-part review of Lamartine's *Histoire des Girondins* (1847), he noted how the group constituted 'all the glory and interest of the Revolution'. When it came to the Jacobins,

---

60 *Nation*, 16 August 1845.

61 *Nation*, 15 October 1842.

62 Irish aristocrats, according to Dillon, represented 'the very same compound of frivolity, luxury, and rapacity, which in 1789 drove France to madness at first, and then to freedom'. *Nation*, 22 October 1842. One can detect here the influence of Carlyle, whose history of the French Revolution suggested that corrupt aristocracies ultimately meet the fate they deserve. On this point see Brendan O'Cathaoir, *John Blake Dillon, Young Irelander* (Dublin, 1990), 19.

63 *Nation*, 16 August 1845.

64 J. R. Dinwiddy, *Radicalism and Reform in Britain, 1780–1850* (London, 1992), 212.

65 *Nation*, 11 April 1846.

however, Duffy gave full license to an established anti-revolutionary rhetoric, criticizing their 'system of murder and levelling fanaticism'.[66]

Duffy's Manichaean vision of Jacobins and Girondins was a rationalization of his ambivalence for the French Revolution as a whole.[67] His anti-Jacobinism reflected his extreme distrust of social revolution. Rousseau had argued with some force that political equality was meaningless in a polity characterized by vast inequalities of wealth, and Young Ireland would quote from this section of the *Social Contract* in its 'Philosophy for the Nation'.[68] But Duffy was adamant that social equality should not be bought at the expense of political liberty. The Jacobins, he believed, had turned government into a ruthless confiscatory force that pitched one class against another. He was particularly concerned about the 'Jacobin' sympathies of nationalists such as John Mitchel — whom he ultimately deemed to be Robespierre reborn. By 1848, Mitchel had come to accept the argument — propounded by Fintan Lalor — that aristocracy derived from conquest and that national liberation presupposed a redistribution of wealth. 'I believe the time for conciliation of the landlord class is past,' Mitchel declared in May 1848; 'I believe rights of property as they are termed must be invaded.'[69] Duffy recoiled from this language; he would not 'combat tyranny with new tyranny, but with justice'.[70]

Burke had been in essential agreement with many of his antagonists on one important point: the Revolution marked a rupture in European history, a 'total departure ... from every one of the ideas and usages, religious, legal, moral, or social, of this civilized world'.[71] But during the Restoration, French liberal historians such as Guizot and Thierry argued that far from being the exception to the rule of European society, the Revolution was the culminating moment of a long period of historical development. History, in this respect, played an integral role in Restoration liberalism.[72] Indeed, Thierry explicitly counselled against a historical method which was itself 'inspired by abstract right and reason ... a process which may be very well with the view of operating a revolution in men's mind and in the state, but by no means proper in the composition of history'.[73] Davis was an ardent advocate of Thierry's historical method and the political values it sponsored: 'it appeals to history ... for its justification against the aristocrat, the free-trader, and the

---

66 *Nation*, 12 February 1848. In the same article, he condemned 'the hideous, disgusting Marat' and declared Robespierre 'the offspring of vanity'. Saint-Just embodied 'the cold impassibility of a logic which makes the heart dry as a system and cruel as an abstraction'.

67 The Young Irelanders, according to A. V. Dicey, were the 'true Girondins of Ireland'. See A. V. Dicey, *A Fool's Paradise* (London, 1913), 4.

68 *Nation*, 4 February 1843.

69 *United Irishman*, 6 May 1848.

70 *Nation*, 29 April 1848.

71 *W & S* 9. 249.

72 See François Furet, *Revolutionary France, 1770–1880*, trans. Antonia Nevill (Oxford, 1992), 306. 'The Restoration reveals the tyranny of history over French politics which is so characteristic of the French nineteenth century.' See also Ceri Crossley, *French Historians and Romanticism* (London, 1993).

73 Augustin Thierry, *History of the Conquest of England by the Normans*, 2 vols. (London, 1847), 1. xxi.

demagogue'.[74] Rights depended on history as their justification, not pure reason. After the death of Davis, the *Nation* continued to insist that all 'lasting revolutions have been little more than revivals of dormant rights, or the perfection of existing liberties'.[75]

Young Ireland's reluctance to use the 'Rights of Man' as the basis of Irish liberties indicates the group's considerable distrust of particular kinds of universalism in politics.[76] This scepticism was implicit in the very motto of the *Nation* — 'To create and foster public opinion in Ireland, and to make it racy of the soil' — which celebrated concrete rights over abstract principles. Young Ireland derived the phrase from Stephen Woulfe, the first Catholic to be appointed solicitor-general, attorney-general and chief-baron of the exchequer in Ireland. But the *Nation* also claimed that its masthead harmonized with the sentiments of Burke.[77] In 1840 Davis discussed 'the utter hopelessness of any attempt at universalism', in what was a strong echo of Burke's views on politics.[78] 'Nothing universal', Burke had declared, 'can be rationally affirmed on any moral, or any political subject'.[79] He did not deny that there were universal foundations to ethical life — these were inscribed in our very nature — but he remained convinced that this nature was always expressed within social contexts that varied across space and time. Politics needed to accommodate itself to this contingency and had to be guided, therefore, by the circumstantial counsels of prudence rather than the categorical precepts of pure reason. Young Ireland possessed a similar outlook; it accepted that there were basic features of humanity that had to be accommodated under any account of the good, but it criticized attempts to invest *substantive* moral or political doctrines with a universal character.[80]

74 *Nation*, 26 November 1842.
75 *Nation*, 26 February 1848.
76 The Young Irelanders were not always consistent on this point. For instance, the *Nation*, on one occasion, contradicted the assertion that it embraced French doctrines of right by declaring its support for 'Universal principles'. On the whole however, they remained sceptical of *a priori* principles in politics. See *Nation*, 5 November 1842.
77 *Nation*, 3 May 1845: 'The value of that pregnant observation of the late Chief Baron Woulfe (the motto of *The Nation*) could not be enforced with more strength than in Burke's comments upon a free and high-spirited public.' According to Davis, *Nation*, 17 December 1842, 'all that our climate and soil suggest to us, we should do, and so doing, should grow to be different from men of other climes and soils'.
78 Davis, *Essays Literary and Historical*, 35. Davis's audience would have possessed an ear for such resonances. The speech, after all, was delivered to the Dublin Historical Society, of which Burke had been a member, and Davis made explicit reference to his famous predecessor elsewhere in the speech.
79 *Works*, 6. 97.
80 Later currents of nationalism celebrated this feature of Young Ireland's thought, but tended to coarsen its scepticism of political universals into a rejection of all universalism as such. Arthur Griffith, for instance, commemorated Davis as 'one of the first men in nineteenth-century Europe to resuscitate the doctrine of Nationality, and challenge the Universalism and Utilitarianism which both Democracy under the French Revolution and Aristocracy under the Holy Alliance had proclaimed as Truth'. See Arthur Griffith, 'Preface', in Thomas Davis, *Thomas Davis: the Thinker & Teacher: The Essence of His Writings in Prose and Poetry*, ed. Arthur Griffith (Dublin, 1914), v–xiv, vi. Griffith was convinced that Mitchel 'a sane Nietzsche' was implacably opposed to 'theories of humanitarianism and universalism'. He was prepared to defend Mitchel's advocacy of American slavery, insisting that Ireland's claim to political independence is 'dependable in nowise for its existence of justification on the "Rights of Man," it is independent of

It was on this basis that Young Ireland queried both the viability and justice of global benevolence or cosmopolitan concern. 'Patriotism,' the *Nation* declared, 'is a more practical, genuine, and common thing than philanthropy.'[81] Through statements of this kind, the paper attempted to explain its tentativeness on the issue of American slavery — Ireland did not have 'a Quixotic mission to redress all the wrongs of humanity'.[82] Burke had always remained a stalwart opponent of slavery, and insisted that moral duties did not terminate at one's nation's borders. But he also believed that benevolence began at home and was extended outwards.[83] Human beings derived their bearings from the 'little platoon' that was the origin and proper object of their concern.[84] A global benevolence merely served to undermine these attachments, while failing to put anything of moral substance and affective force in their place.[85] Young Ireland made this point again and again. As the *Nation* put it: 'We like not the cosmopolitans who, in embracing universal mankind, forget their closer affinity with their own country'.[86] Not all Young Irelanders were equally convinced about the wisdom of this policy. 'We must be cosmopolitan,' Thomas MacNevin advised, 'and deviate occasionally from our native bogs. We shall have a better chance of success by being less Irish'.[87] Davis, however, was adamant that the cosmopolitan attitude was 'base' and 'unnatural'.[88] According to Dillon, the 'patriot revels in a thousand pure delights which the cold cosmopolite can never taste'.[89]

Cosmopolitanism presented itself as impartial, but this simply lent a universal sanction to values that were themselves contingent. Philanthropists, for this reason, were potentially tyrannical. 'They are,' the *Nation* suggested, 'as intolerable as the Saints who would cram Bibles down the throats of Africans and Hindoos, and make the world religious by the annihilation of charity, enjoyment, and good-fellowship, and the

theories of government and doctrines of philanthropy and Universalism'. Arthur Griffith, 'Preface', in John Mitchel, *Jail Journal* (New York, Paris, Dublin, 1913), ix–xvi, xiv. Griffith seemed to ignore the problematic fact that the terms 'Liberty, Equality, and Fraternity' appeared on every title page of the *United Irishman*, while Mitchel had considered himself for some time to be a Jacobin. However, it is certainly the case that Mitchel and Young Ireland, in general, distrusted theories of general philanthropy and cosmopolitan concern.

81 *Nation*, 12 October 1844. 'Patriotism,' Davis asserted in 1840, 'is human philanthropy'. Davis, *Essays Literary and Historical*, 46 [Davis's emphasis]. Here Davis appears to suggest that patriotic and philanthropic concerns were compatible and co-extensive, but he was, in fact, saying something quite the reverse. By collapsing one term into another, Davis attempted to deny the possibility of philanthropic attachments that remained purely extrinsic to the concerns of the patria.

82 *Nation*, 31 May 1845.

83 *W & S* 9. 461.

84 *W & S* 8. 97.

85 For a discussion of this theme, see Deane, 'Swift and Burke', in *Foreign Affections*, 11–27.

86 *Nation*, 2 September 1843.

87 Quoted in Charles Gavan Duffy, *Young Ireland: A Fragment of Irish History, 1840–1850*, 2 parts (London, 1880), 1. 565.

88 Davis, *Essays Literary and Historical*, 46.

89 Quoted in O'Cathaoir, *John Blake Dillon*, 9.

substitution of Prayer Meetings, fanaticism, and long-visaged hypocrisy.'[90] These attacks on cosmopolitan philanthropy resurrected a language that Burke had deployed against French fanaticism: the revolutionaries, he suggested, were the political equivalent of religious enthusiasts in their fixity of purpose and evangelical zeal.[91] Both forms of enthusiasm, Burke suggested, were predicated on a blind faith in the universal validity of particular statements about a complex world.

In Burke's eyes, the anti-historical disposition of the French also expressed itself through its centralized administration — an inflexible form of rule that was repeatedly condemned by Young Ireland. According to Burke, a purely abstract understanding of political geography had led to the destruction of local institutions and to the redivision of France. People were discouraged, he suggested, from being Gascons, Picards, Bretons, Normans, but were deemed to be Frenchmen enjoying a sovereignty that was one and indivisible. For Burke, however, the destruction of local loyalties in the name of some remote conception of nationhood was self-undermining. Local attachments, he suggested, provided the enabling background for a more expansive patriotism. By destroying historical institutions and loyalties, the revolutionaries had undermined the foundations of public solidarity which they pretended to promote. The French, as a consequence, relied more and more on the 'power and preeminence of Paris' for their conditions of unity.[92] Such unity, Burke was convinced, would not last, but in the meantime it expressed itself as a coercive force.

French liberals like Guizot also worried about the tyrannical nature of a centralized administration in France, but maintained that this concentration of power began long before the Revolution. The destruction of local autonomy was the unintended consequence of the destruction of aristocratic power, first by the monarchy and then by the Revolution. The Young Irelanders took a similar view to Guizot and condemned 'Centralizers of all sorts — Bourbons and Orleans Kings, Directors, Terrorists and Emperors'.[93] This hostility to centralization exposed tensions in the group's own doctrine: while it may have celebrated the emergence of peasant proprietors under the Revolution, it also believed that the destruction of the aristocracy had disastrous political results in France: 'Without a landed aristocracy she has no security against an official despotism, save in its separation.'[94] In the same editorial, the Nation called for the restoration of a natural aristocracy and the resurrection of local parliaments. On the whole, the Young Irelanders tried to ensure that their criticism of centralization did not amount to an absolute rejection of the Revolution. Occasionally, however, their condemnation of centralized power in France developed a fury in which it was difficult to discern anything but contempt for the Revolution as a whole:

90 Nation, 2 September 1843.
91 W & S 8. 341.
92 W & S 8. 244.
93 Nation, 23 December 1843.
94 Nation, 18 February 1843.

The French Republicans, disciples of a negative philosophy, and irritated by emigrants and tyrants, sacrificed their local liberties to central power; Lyons and La Vendee, Bretagne and Marseilles, were levelled by an impartial despotism; Paris became France, and Jacobin Clubs, and Directories, and 'the Emperor,' became Paris, and their gushing energies went revenging and triumphing over the extent of Europe.[95]

Negativity and revenge, foreign intrigue and dangerous enthusiasm, all the staple motifs of Burke's anti-revolutionary rhetoric find a home here, indicating just how volatile Young Ireland's assessment of the Revolution remained.

Young Ireland condemned French centralization, but the group extended this critique to incorporate the government of Westminster. The British Empire, according to Young Ireland, was oblivious to the local character and historical texture of political and social bonds. If these criticisms owed something to Burke, they also reflected the influence of Burke's own mentor, Montesquieu.[96] According to Montesquieu, 'laws should be so appropriate to the people for whom they are made that it is very unlikely that the laws of one nation can suit another'.[97] On this basis he distinguished two kinds of tyranny: 'a real one which consists in the violence of the government, and one of opinion, which is felt when those who govern establish things that run counter to a nation's way of thinking'.[98] Young Ireland applied a similar kind of logic to Ireland. English rule, Davis maintained, had established itself through violent conquest — a view strengthened by his reading of Thierry — and now presided, it seemed, over a tyranny of opinion. However benign its execution, this was a system of government that would always be experienced as oppressive. Dillon insisted 'that a country, like a man, had a character of its own, to which its government and its laws ought to be adapted, and that this character can be thoroughly comprehended by itself alone'.[99] On this basis, Young Ireland demanded Repeal of the Union. Ireland's claim to independence, however, was to be retrieved from its own history; it did not depend on a more abstract justice.

Young Ireland may have promoted the historical claims of Ireland, but it was often unclear to what extent it believed that a defence of these justified violent revolution. The group's interpretation of 1789 and its effects was ambiguous, but its endorsement of

---

95 Nation, 22 June 1844.

96 According to Davis's obituary, Davis owed his interest in 'the popular manifestation of national characters' to the great political philosopher. Davis drew explicitly on Montesquieu in essays such as 'We Need a History', Nation, 14 October 1843. When the Nation declared that 'national literature should be stamped with the popular idiom, inspired by patriotism, breathing of the climate and scenery, and informed of the history and manners of the people' it applied to literature what Montesquieu said about a nation's laws. Young Ireland's poetry collection, The Spirit of the Nation, echoed the title of Montesquieu's The Spirit of the Laws. For Burke's praise of Montesquieu's genius, see Works, 6. 263–64. See also J. P. Courtney, Montesquieu and Burke (Oxford, 1963); Deane, 'Montesquieu and Burke', in Foreign Affections, 28–46.

97 Montesquieu, The Spirit of the Laws, ed. and trans. Anne M. Cohler, Basia Carolyn Miller and Harold Samuel Stone (Cambridge, 1989), 8.

98 Montesquieu, The Spirit of the Laws, 309.

99 Nation, 5 August 1843.

the Revolution of 1848 was emphatic. 'France,' the *Nation* declared, 'seems once more determined to lead the van in the work of European reform.'[100] For Guizot, the event was a personal, political disaster, while, in Thierry's eyes, it amounted to a national tragedy. Young Ireland, however, celebrated the downfall of the July monarchy — which it had always regarded with ambivalence — and cheered the new republic.[101] Moreover, the group now hoped to kindle the spirit of revolution in Ireland. Duffy, of course, remained cautious. 'It is the curse of liberty,' he opined, 'that it is everywhere followed like a shadow by this fiend of anarchy, preaching fatal and revolting excesses. It ruined freedom in 1793, and it bids fair to wound it fatally in 1848.'[102] Duffy was a most reluctant revolutionary and had been an advocate for some time of 'moral' over physical force. But the failure of O'Connellite Repeal and, more particularly, the devastation wrought by the Famine in Ireland had encouraged Duffy and his colleagues to consider more radical methods. In articles such as 'Necessity Knows No Law' the *Nation* outlined why revolution provided the only solution to Irish woes.[103]

The revolt of the Young Irelanders in June 1848 was neither spontaneous nor popular. The rumpus in Ballingarry did little to secure Irish liberties. More generally, the rebellion of 1848 demonstrated the degree to which events in France could still dictate the terms of politics in Ireland. Duffy lauded the French in 1848, but he was also at pains to insist that the *Nation* remained 'an Irish, not a Jacobin journal'.[104] Irishness remained a bulwark, not only to Jacobin terror, but to cosmopolitan theories in general. If a neo-Burkean conception of Irish history and national character allowed Young Ireland to resist the universal scope of French revolutionary doctrine, it also afforded other forms of refuge. In particular, it was a discourse that provided a measure of defence from English attempts to impose a foreign government and character on Ireland. The Jacobin French may have been dangerous evangelists and innovators, but Young Ireland believed that England exported its own form of political enthusiasm to Ireland. Britain's most dangerous ideological export, for Young Ireland, was the creed of Benthamism.

100 *Nation*, 4 March 1848.
101 The *Nation* criticized 'the usurper Louis Philippe'. *Nation*, 24 February 1844. However, Davis later spoke
    ambivalently of the 'wise tyranny of Louis Philippe'. *Nation*, 16 August 1845.
102 *Nation*, 26 February 1848.
103 *Nation*, 1 April 1848. But if the revolution had any chance of success, it demanded, according to Duffy,
    organized leadership. With Mitchel in his sights, Duffy duly criticized the view, which he attributed to
    Thomas Carlyle and Jules Michelet, that popular revolutions were a spontaneous matter. *Nation*, 24 June
    1848.
104 *Nation*, 29 April 1848.

3 Young Ireland and Benthamism

O'Connell often declared himself a committed Benthamite, but his contemporaries in the Young Ireland movement were fierce critics of Bentham's influence.[105] According to the *Nation*, Bentham had 'contaminated to a considerable extent the public mind of his country', and the Young Irelanders were determined not to let such contamination spread to Ireland.[106] Many of these patriots, however, had started out as admirers of Bentham and utilitarianism. They generally shared Bentham's later commitment to democracy and his lifelong frustration with aristocratic institutions. Moreover, the economic views of some Young Irelanders remained for a considerable length of time broadly Benthamite. Nevertheless, the group repeatedly attacked Benthamism as a profoundly destructive force in political and moral life. Terms such as 'Benthamism' and 'Benthamy' had, of course, an extraordinarily wide semantic remit for Young Ireland; indeed, they often operated as simple shorthand for political vice in general. Their criticisms of Bentham, however crude, generally tended to focus on the abstract nature of his political method. His apparent disregard for national feeling and national character was symptomatic in Young Ireland's eyes of a profoundly anti-historical disposition. This was not an uncommon view: even sympathetic commentators like J. S. Mill, believed that Bentham failed to understand the significance of 'national character' in political life.

Young Ireland drew on Mill's criticisms, but its attacks on Bentham also owed much to the Young England movement. After all, one of the first uses of the term 'Young Ireland' appeared in the *Belfast Vindicator* in an initially ironic comparison between the writers of the *Nation* and the Young England movement — a Tory cadre led by men such as Benjamin Disraeli, Lord John Manners, Richard Monckton Milnes and George Smythe. The comparison was intended as a form of criticism and queried the authenticity and political ethos of a nationalist party that so closely resembled a British Tory clique. There were, nevertheless, important, ideological affinities between both groups, which even the writers of the *Nation* were prepared to acknowledge. When MacNevin responded to the *Belfast Vindicator*'s attack in November 1844, he tended to embrace rather than to repudiate comparisons between Young England and Young Ireland. This was because there was 'truth and not hollowness, reality and not sham in these men'.[107] Months

---

105 After his election to Westminster in 1829, O'Connell wrote to Bentham: 'I avowed myself on the hustings this day to be a "Benthamite", and explained the leading principles of your disciples — the "greatest happiness principle" — our sect will prosper'. Quoted in MacDonagh, *Life of Daniel O'Connell*, 280. See also Joseph Lee, 'The Social and Economic Ideas of O'Connell', in Kevin B. Nowlan and Maurice R. O'Connell, eds., *Daniel O'Connell: Portrait of a Radical* (Belfast, 1984), 70–86.

106 *Nation*, 13 April 1844.

107 *Nation*, 2 November 1844. For a glowing review of Young England pamphlets, see the *Nation*, 29 June 1844. For a positive review of the 'highly interesting' speeches given in Manchester by Disraeli and Smythe and Manners, see the *Nation*, 19 October 1844. Despite this collective praise, the *Nation* maintained a singular dislike for Disraeli, whom it presented as a selfish opportunist who 'has coquetted with every faction in

before this spat, the *Nation* had already declared its 'highest respect' for the principles of Young England:

> We sympathise with the intense nationality of their piety; their veneration for their *national* church, and their aspirations for its restoration to pristine zeal and purity; their exertions for the revival of good old customs, and for the increased use of those still remaining; above all, their endeavours to re-vivify society with the spirit of belief, and to rescue it from the state of sulky degradation into which Puritanism, Evangelicism, Socialism, and Utilitarianism, have plunged it; to bring back the days of the archery buts, Mayings, Harvest-homes, Christmas festivities, and village holidays; to make England 'Merrie England,' and not England the abode of pallid cotton-spinners, the living grave of filthy miners, the land of arson, stabbing, cant, infidelity, immorality, and ignorance.[108]

The leaders of the Young England movement were horrified by the social consequences of a burgeoning industrial capitalism. Fatted on Carlylean rage, they denounced England's 'fever-fit of mammon-worship', 'wealth-adoration' and 'harsh utilitarianism' and called for the reinstitution of the social bond that they believed to have characterized feudalism.[109] Chartism, the Welsh riots and disturbances in the eastern counties, according to one fairly typical Young England diagnosis, were the inevitable result of 'the presence of unspeakable poverty in the houses of the mechanic and the peasant; the impotence of the national church, and the virulence of sectarianism; the decadence of a proper sympathy between the great classes of our community, between the employees and the employed, the peer and the peasant, the master and the man'.[110] Bentham's political economy, according to Young England, simply rationalized these injustices rather than offering them suitable redress. Young England, Marx concluded, were practitioners of 'feudal socialism' — a politics that was 'half lamentation, half lampoon, half echo of the past, half menace of the future, striking the bourgeoisie at its very core through bitter, witty, biting judgements that were always comic because of a total incapacity to grasp the course of modern history'.[111] Paeans to the past, according to Marx, did not solve modern problems.

The same might be said about Young Ireland. The Irish patriots grew increasingly distrustful of the practicality and coherence of Young England's project of moral reform, but they shared many of its criticisms of social atomism and exploitation and offered a similar idealization of the collective bond of a pre-industrial past.[112] Both groups cultivated myths of

---

every party'. *Nation*, 8 March 1845. See the *Nation*, 22 June 1844 for a highly derogatory review of Disraeli's novel *Coningsby*.

108 *Nation*, 2 September 1843.

109 John Morrow, ed., *Young England, The New Generation: A Selection of Primary Texts* (London, 1999), 70, 33, 41.

110 Morrow, ed., *Young England*, 42.

111 Karl Marx, *Later Political Writings*, ed. and trans. Terrell Carver (Cambridge, 1996), 21.

112 In the *Nation*, 26 October 1844, Duffy argued that purity of moral intention or the force of eloquence was not enough to secure concrete legislative reform. 'Legislation must be the fruit of their labours,' he

primeval unity. Young England, for instance, glorified the social cohesion of feudal society; figures like Davis, however, dismissed the 'rank feudality of the dark ages' as well as its more benign variants, and promoted an earlier system of land tenure known as udalism.[113] These differences reflected a more substantial disagreement about the merits of aristocratic rule. Young England celebrated feudalism partly because it revered aristocracy, but Young Ireland repeatedly condemned the injustices of aristocratic government. The Irish patriots wanted to revive, not *noblesse oblige*, but the muscular independence of the yeoman farmer. Despite these significant differences, both groups were committed to restoring public solidarity through the celebration of a historically grounded national character. According to the *Nation*'s assessment, Young England was comprised of men 'infinitely superior to the Radical Philosophers who would benefit the world by breaking down everything worthy of reverence, and building up instead a system of undigested crudities, with Jeremy Bentham as the Allah and Roebuck the Mahommed of their veneration'.[114]

Young Ireland's criticisms of Bentham were frequently offered as a general indictment of any political theory for which the fundamental egotism of human beings appeared to be axiomatic. Bentham believed that sympathy for others was a key feature of human experience, but he also suggested that the 'self-regarding' motives were the most powerful.[115] The *Nation* duly attacked 'vile and brutal Benthamism' and dismissed it as a 'selfish creed'.[116] These assaults were not sophisticated, nor were they particularly novel. Earlier critics of utilitarianism, such as Thomas Babington Macaulay, had criticized the vagueness of self-interest as a motivational theory.[117] If self-interest implied a narrow egotism, this was, he suggested, the result of a wholly arbitrary delimitation of human nature; if it implied something broader, it traced an empty circle. The principle of self-interest ultimately means that 'whatever is, is' or 'that a man had rather do what he had rather do'.[118] Macaulay also suggested that utilitarianism's hedonistic motivational theory was at odds with its altruistic accommodation of the greatest happiness of the greatest number.[119] The latter could only be defended on pragmatic terms and,

maintained, 'otherwise their sentiments and their sympathies are words only.' Writing at the high point of the Irish Famine, Duffy maintained that English indifference to the plight of the Irish peasant proved that Young England's project of moral reform had failed. As he put it, 'all the high-flown writings about revival of the ages of faith, symbolic architecture, and Saxon simplicity have never yet reached its long-eared middle classes.' *Nation*, 5 February 1848.

113 Davis, *Essays Literary and Historical*, 61.

114 *Nation*, 2 September 1843.

115 Jeremy Bentham, *Principles of Morals and Legislation* ([1789] Amherst, 1988), 122.

116 *Nation*, 1 June 1844.

117 According to the *Nation*'s assessment of Macaulay, 'Burke had scarcely a grander imagination, a clearer intellect, or a riper knowledge'. See *Nation*, 3 July 1846.

118 James Lively and John Rees, eds., *Utilitarian Logic and Politics: James Mill's 'Essay on Government', Macaulay's Critique and the Ensuing Debate* (London, 1990), 125.

119 According to Bentham, 'the dictates of utility are neither more nor less than the dictates of the most extensive and enlightened (that is *well-advised*) benevolence'. Bentham, *Principles of Morals and Legislation*, 121 [Bentham's emphasis].

as Disraeli argued, could apply to a whole range of political regimes and practices, including the use of torture and mass delusion.[120] The *Nation*, for its part, insisted that the true Benthamite would defend something as vicious as duelling on the grounds of its utility.[121] The failure of utilitarianism to accommodate qualitative distinctions of this kind stemmed, according to its critics, from its basic inability to understand human values as such. This, at least, was the point made by Young Ireland when it condemned Bentham's attempts 'to mechanise the human soul after the fashion of some ingenious ethical engineer'.[122] Values for Bentham were ultimately reducible to pleasure, and the sole evaluative criterion was the maximization of its satisfaction.[123] Only through a radical distillation of this kind could a diversity of human goods be reduced to a common level and provide something akin to a harmony of interests or an optimum happiness.[124]

Bentham ultimately rejected the idea that there was a natural harmony of interests, but he tacitly relied on political economy to generate public good through the prudent pursuit of private ends. The Smithian notion of an 'invisible hand' — in which self-interested activity within an economic system yields untintended public benefits — defused the apparent tension between his psychological egotism and his greatest happiness principle.[125] Political economy, moreover, was a fitting supplement to the Benthamite project because both attempted to place the study of human affairs on a properly scientific footing. As the *Nation* put it, Bentham felt 'he could render philosophical speculation useless — that he could supersede metaphysics, and remove any doubt of the ethical enquirer'.[126] Over time, Benthamism and the harsher aspects of political economy were, in Young Ireland's eyes, virtually indistinguishable. The parsimonious New Poor Law, — 'that monstrous experiment on human wants and passion', according to the *Nation* — which Benthamite Radicals had helped to introduce in 1834, had helped to make

---

120 Benjamin Disraeli, *Vindication of the English Constitution in a Letter to a Noble and Learned Lord* (London, 1835), 8. According to Frederick Rosen, however, Bentham's utilitarianism provides no basis for the sacrifice of individuals. This is overruled in advance by secondary principles such as 'equality'. See Frederick Rosen, *Classical Utilitarianism from Hume to Mill* (London and New York, 2003), 220–31.

121 *Nation*, 5 November 1842. Here Young Ireland may have associated Bentham with Bernard Mandeville, who defended the public utility of duelling in the *Fable of the Bees* (1723–28). Duels, he suggested, were a necessary part of an honour-system that fostered good manners in society as a whole. 'It is strange that a Nation should grudge to see perhaps half a dozen Men sacrific'd in a Twelvemonth to obtain so valuable a Blessing, as the Politeness of Manners, the Pleasure of Conversation, and the Happiness of Company in general.' *Fable of the Bees*, I. 220.

122 *Nation*, 13 April 1843.

123 'Now, pleasure is in *itself* a good: nay, even setting aside immunity from pain, the only good: pain is in itself an evil; and, indeed, without exception, the only evil; or else the words good and evil have no meaning.' Bentham, *Principles of Morals and Legislation*, 102 [Bentham's emphasis].

124 For a modern critique of this reductivism, see Charles Taylor, 'The Diversity of Goods', in *Philosophy and the Human Sciences. Philosophical Papers 2* (Cambridge, 1985), 230–47.

125 In Smith, *Wealth of Nations*, I. 456, the individual 'intends only his own gain, and he is in this, as in many other cases, led by an invisible hand to promote an end which was no part of his intention'.

126 *Nation*, 13 April 1844.

this a common, albeit unfair, assumption throughout Britain.[127] Like O'Connell, Young Ireland was initially strongly opposed to the introduction of an Irish Poor Law. Such opposition did not amount to a repudiation of classical political economy; indeed it was a reassertion of some of its basic *doxa*.[128] The 'father' of political economy, Adam Smith, had distinguished between commutative and distributive justice and insisted that the latter should remain within the sphere of private charity. O'Connell and Young Ireland initially took a similar stand in resisting an Irish Poor Law. 'It is a blundering system of legislation,' the *Nation* declared, 'which converts the whole population of the country into paupers, by taking away the produce of their labour and giving it to idlers, and then sets up a costly machinery for the purpose of relieving their distress.'[129] Arguably, this was a more extreme defence of minimal government and laissez-faire principles than even the Benthamites were prepared to mount.

 Young Ireland gradually accepted the necessity and justice of a Poor Law in Ireland. They also attacked Benthamism for its apparent commitment to laissez-faire notions. These criticisms were again rather undiscriminating, not least because Bentham had always allowed for governmental intervention in the economy.[130] He sponsored state provision, however limited, for the poor, while Young Ireland, as we have seen, opposed policies of this kind in 1842. However, the Famine forced Young Irelanders to reconsider their economic policies.[131] They began to query the universal scope of the 'dismal science' and to condemn its disregard for local circumstances. The Repeal of the Corn Laws in 1846 was a testament in Young Ireland's eyes to the inadequacy of classical political economy when applied to Irish affairs. Repeal, the group argued, might benefit England as a consumer of corn, but it was harmful to Ireland as a producer.[132] Free trade might seem justified as a theory, but the inconsistency of its historical application, according to Young Ireland, meant that its absolute advocacy in current circumstances was both arbitrary and unjust. Political economists encouraged governors to 'leave trade to its "natural laws"', but arguments of this kind had not stopped England from imposing protective tariffs at the expense of Ireland in the eighteenth century.[133] Now, it was morally incumbent upon England to protect Irish agriculture until the asymmetries

127 *Nation*, 26 October 1844.
128 'In principle, we are disposed to agree with the economist, that a legal system of relief for the able-bodied labourer cannot exist without prejudice to the productive industry of the country.' *Nation*, 17 December 1842. Even here, however, Young Ireland conceded that the Poor Law had pragmatic benefits in Ireland, where land was unfairly distributed; it was 'the only check to the rapacity of those who owned the land'.
129 *Nation*, 26 November 1842.
130 For a discussion of the complexity of Bentham's thought in this regard, see J. L. Hume, *Bentham and Bureaucracy* (Cambridge, 1981), 93–109.
131 The Famine, according to the *Nation*, emphasized the absence of self-government in Ireland: its evils 'might be mitigated or turned aside, or haply, transformed into the occasion of great public virtues, if this country were governed by its own people'. The paper also rejected British forms of charitable relief, convinced that it undermined Irish autonomy. See *Nation*, 8 November 1845.
132 *Nation*, 31 January 1846.
133 *Nation*, 17 October 1846.

between both economies were redressed.[134] Whatever the particular merits of these arguments, the catastrophe of the Famine strengthened Young Ireland's belief that the laws of political economy did not enjoy universal validity.

Young Ireland duly called for a form of political economy that was more attuned to Ireland's particular social circumstances. The group began to champion an Irish version of economic science, the origins of which were apparently to be found in George Berkeley and Jonathan Swift. 'Irish Political Economy,' the *Nation* declared, 'is essentially different from that of all other countries, as our circumstances are unlike theirs.'[135] Figures such as Isaac Butt had argued for some time that there was a distressing gap between 'English theories' and 'Irish facts' and had called for policies more accommodating to the latter.[136] Young Ireland lavished praise on Butt's economic writings and reiterated the view that policies should not be made 'upon any universal principles laid down by political economists, but with reference to the circumstances of that country'.[137] With these arguments in mind, Young Ireland questioned the viability of English land tenures and agricultural practices in Ireland, and called for fixity of tenure and peasant proprietorship. These proposals were also a challenge to Benthamism. However committed Bentham may have been to political and economic reform, his staunch commitment to the security of property precluded a more flexible conception of property relations.[138] Even supporters of Bentham, such as J. S. Mill, were forced to relinquish their faith in the inviolable character of property rights in the light of the Famine.

Benthamism in Young Ireland's eyes was a profoundly anti-historical outlook. English Radicals, according to the *Nation*, proposed 'to blot the past out of human memory, and to scribble Benthamism in its place'.[139] A neo-Burkean conception of history and national character, which had seen service against the Jacobins, was also enlisted, therefore, in the battle against Benthamism.[140] The *Nation* defended the integrity of Irish character and condemned 'the meanest doctrines of the Benthamite and Malthusian creeds, the bloodless Utilitarians to whom the high aspirations and hopes of a National Party

---

134 For an analysis of these arguments, see R. D. Collison Black, *Economic Thought and the Irish Question, 1817–1870* (Cambridge, 1960), 140–44.

135 *Nation*, 27 March 1847.

136 For a discussion of Butt's economic views and their relationship to nationalism, see Alan O'Day, 'Nationalism and Political Economy in Ireland: Isaac Butt's Analysis', in Roger Swift and Christine Kinealy, eds., *Politics and Power in Victorian Ireland* (Dublin, 2006), 109–18.

137 *Nation*, 28 February 1846.

138 Bentham may have promoted 'equality' as an end of government, but it was ultimately subordinate to 'security'. See Frederick Rosen, *Jeremy Bentham and Representative Democracy: A Study of the Constitutional Code* (Oxford, 1983), 216–20.

139 *Nation*, 5 November 1842.

140 There was an irony here because Burke's own *Thoughts on Scarcity* was used to bolster 'Benthamite' policies of laissez-faire and free trade during the Famine. This put considerable strain on Young Ireland's advocacy of Burke. For negative references to Burke during this period, see *Nation*, 1 May 1847 and 21 August 1847. For the use of Burke's economic thought during the Famine, see Gibbons, *Edmund Burke and Ireland*, 121.

are either unintelligible or odious'.[141] In Bentham's scheme there were no theoretical limits to the maximization of utility across space; general benevolence trumped a more restricted or local concern for one's neighbours. In Young Ireland's eyes, therefore, the Benthamite was a dangerous 'Cosmopolite': 'to reform the world is his main object'.[142] Dillon condemned the way English reformers showed scant regard for Irish national character. He insisted in a style deeply reminiscent of Burke that

> this character has not been produced in a day, or in a year, or in a hundred years. Long centuries of trial and affliction have made it what it is. Its roots strike deep into antiquity ... And is it not vexatious to hear little assimilating politicians talk about bending and fashioning this ancient tree, as if it were a twig?[143]

Davis's close friend, Daniel Owen-Madden, was at times critical of Young Ireland but he was sympathetic to its defence of Irish national character. He derided English efforts to transpose onto Ireland the entirely alien political culture of Benthamism:

> There is a class of Imperialists who propose to govern Ireland without the slightest regard to local feelings, or to Irish prejudices. They would wish to obliterate Ireland in the map of the Empire, and to substitute West Britain. They would first deride all Irish instincts, malign all Irish character, and then proceed to treat a concursive and semi-celtic population, as if it inherited the individualism and characteristic phlegm of English nature. This school of Imperialists is one made up of Whigs, Whig-Radicals, and Economists, steeped to the lips in the chilling philosophy of Benthamism. Many of them as individuals reject the tenets of the Benthamite creed, but when they deal as politicians with the interests of Ireland, they overlook all the acquired and natural distinctions between the countries, and require the Irish to grovel down in abject and slavish subserviency to England. They would not leave to Ireland a memory, a proud recollection, a generous native impulse, or a single natural character of any kind. They would try and reduce it into being the tame and commonplace copyist of England.[144]

Owen-Madden defended Irish character from the individualistic phlegm of the Benthamites, but it was an established strategy in Britain in general to invoke the idea of national character in attacks on Benthamism. Since Young Ireland drew heavily on these criticisms, it is worth tracing their ideological contours here.

141 *Nation*, 19 April 1845.
142 *Nation*, 5 November 1842.
143 Charles Gavan Duffy, *Thomas Davis: The Memoirs of an Irish Patriot, 1840–1845* (London, 1890), 70.
144 D. Owen-Madden, *Ireland and its Rulers since 1829*, 3 parts (London, 1843–44), 3. 237–38.

If the Jacobins had attempted a revolution in European manners, utilitarians, according to Macaulay, also pretended to be 'revolutionists of the moral world'.[145] Disraeli reiterated this charge and insisted that 'the great object of our new school of statesmen … is to form political institutions on abstract principles of theoretic science'.[146] Burke, as we have seen, had attacked French attempts to establish a science of politics. The straight lines of a scientific method were at odds with the crooked forms of historical society. According to Macaulay and Disraeli, however, utilitarians wanted to transform the study of politics into an objective science — a commitment that accounted for their opposition to received wisdom and to the legitimacy of affect in political deliberation. Utilitarians believed 'sentimentality is synonymous with idiocy', according to Macaulay, a rationalist prejudice that he held responsible for James Mill's virtually unreadable prose.[147] The 'anti-poetic' character of Benthamism was central to Young Ireland's sense of its own literary vocation and the group also subscribed to the prevailing opinion that Benthamites 'laugh at sentiment'.[148]

These charges appear to overlook key features of Bentham's thought; his utilitarian enterprise, after all, was founded on distinctly Epicurean principles in which feelings such as pleasure and pain had a dominant role.[149] Passion was the basis of human motivation, in Bentham's eyes, and works such as The Principles of Morals and Legislation (1789) provided an exhaustive taxonomy of a human agent's dominant sentiments. The passions may have been the ground of Bentham's science, but he also believed they should have no guiding role in inquiry itself. A capitulation to sentiment undermined the objective character of scientific investigation. He therefore criticized the 'sinister bias of the affections' and dismissed the 'principle of sympathy and antipathy' as a criterion for judgement in politics.[150] Presumably, this was the reason why Bentham was condemned for his contempt of sentiment in charges that echoed Burke's criticisms of French rationalism.[151] The passions, for Burke, were an irreducible feature of political life and he deemed it both mistaken and dangerous to deny their importance for both rulers and the ruled. Moral sentiments could not be suspended in the name of a more objective grasp of human affairs, for they were foundational to this knowledge; 'that sort of reason which banishes the affections is incapable of filling their place'.[152] Those who rejected sentiment in the name of objectivity or impartiality attacked the foundations of

---

145 Lively and Rees, eds., Utilitarian Logic and Politics, 195.
146 Disraeli, Vindication, 15.
147 Lively and Rees, eds., Utilitarian Logic and Politics, 106.
148 Nation, 5 November 1842.
149 For the Epicurean origins of utilitarianism, see Rosen, Classical Utilitarianism, 15–28.
150 Jeremy Bentham, A Fragment on Government, ed. J. H. Burns and H. L. A. Hart (Cambridge, 1988), 15; Principles of Morals and Legislation, 13–21.
151 Bentham criticized Burke for his irresponsible appeals to the passions. This was embodied in Burke's use of oratory, which was, for Bentham, 'the art of misrepresentation — the art of misdirecting the judgment by agitating and inflaming the passions'. Quoted in Dinwiddy, Radicalism and Reform in Britain, 268.
152 W & S 8. 129.

moral life. This was the charge Burke brought against the Jacobins, but Macaulay and Disraeli revived it in their criticisms of utilitarianism.

In Disraeli's eyes, Benthamism was part of a profoundly anti-historical disposition that failed to recognize that in human affairs, reason operated within a tradition. Political agents, he suggested, derived their co-ordinates from 'the prescriptive practice of the community' in which they lived.[153] In support of this point, Disraeli reiterated Burke's famous defence of 'national character', convinced that this was 'precisely the quality which the new sect of statesmen, in their schemes and speculations, either deny or overlook'.[154] Even later utilitarians like J. S. Mill acknowledged the truth of these attacks, and his own criticisms of Bentham had a decisive impact on Young Ireland. Mill invoked the notion of 'national character' to isolate a fatal inadequacy in Bentham's thought. What, Mill asked, 'could Bentham's opinion be worth on national character?' Bentham's empirical method, Mill suggested, rendered him insensitive to the historical constitution of political and social institutions. Since a national character was not a physical entity, but a moral space that could not be studied on positivist lines, Bentham had little interest in its value. This was a serious flaw, according to Mill, for a 'philosophy of laws and institutions, not founded on a philosophy of national character is an absurdity'.[155] In an earlier essay, Mill had argued that Bentham's approach precluded any understanding of those 'organic institutions' that formed the basis of 'national character'.[156] For this reason, Bentham was also incapable of appreciating the nature of political obedience. Obedience, Mill argued, was a product of both 'habit and imagination'.[157] With Bentham's radicalism in mind, he added that obedience could not transfer itself easily to new institutions even if these were ostensibly more rational and efficient.

Mill famously chose to contrast Bentham with Samuel Taylor Coleridge. William Wordsworth's poetry had rescued Mill after his breakdown in 1826, but he presented Coleridge as the most exemplary critic of eighteenth-century rationalism. Coleridge's philosophy, according to Mill, 'is ontological, because that was experimental; conservative, because that was innovative; religious, because so much of that was infidel; concrete and historical, because that was abstract and metaphysical; poetical, because that was matter-of-fact and prosaic'.[158] Both Bentham and Coleridge, Mill argued, constituted a set of political antinomies that continued to structure national life and intellectual debate —

153 Disraeli, Vindication, 33.
154 Disraeli, Vindication, 16. Disraeli's contemporaries noticed his indebtedness to Burke. Lord Eliot, for instance, remarked on the similarities between the Vindication and Burke's revolutionary writings: 'Indeed, many passages forcibly recall to my mind parts of the Essay on the French Revolution.' See Jane Ridley, The Young Disraeli (London, 1995), 167, 172.
155 Mill, 'Bentham', in Collected Works, 10. 75–160, 99. Bentham, he also suggested, was something of a recluse; the 'quiet, even tenor of his life' militated against any adequate understanding of individual character, and, by extension, any hope of understanding the character of nations.
156 'Remarks on Bentham's Philosophy', in Collected Works, 10. 3–18, 9.
157 Collected Works, 10. 17.
158 'Coleridge', in Collected Works, 10. 117–63, 125.

'every Englishman of the present day,' Mill declared, 'is by implication either a Benthamite or a Coleridgian'.[159] At the end of his essay on Coleridge, Mill associated Coleridge's philosophy with the Oxford Movement — or what he tended to call 'Puseyism' after one of the movement's most famous members, Edward Bouverie Pusey, regius professor of Hebrew at Oxford. In other essays, Mill associated Puseyism with Young England: both exemplified, it seemed, the Coleridgian spirit in contemporary national life.

Young Ireland was clearly familiar with Mill's arguments and reiterated them at some length in the pages of the Nation. Moreover, the group acknowledged the links between the Oxford Movement and Disraeli's Tory clique. The Nation gently mocked the 'Puseyite elegantes of Young England', but it commended 'their veneration for their national church, and their aspirations for its restoration to pristine zeal and purity'.[160] If Young Englanders were practitioners of Puseyism, Young Irelanders agreed with Mill that Coleridge was their 'first pioneer'.[161] Young Ireland subscribed wholly to Mill's dichotomies and insisted that Puseyism was 'the antagonism to Benthamism'. It was, in other words, a response, 'to the Indifferentism, the frigid Rationalism, and the anti-spiritual Benthamism' that were and remained prevalent in England. The Nation went on to outline — drawing heavily on Mill — the spirit of Puseyism embodied by Coleridge:

> He ministered to the worship of the Fair and Good, after a different fashion from Bentham. Mind-worship, and not Comfort-worship — the spirit of poetry, and not the practice of calculation — the necessity of loving and perceiving the Beautiful, as being auxiliary to the faith that confides in the Eternal, in preference to the sordid philosophy, mundane in its notions, and terrestrial in its desires, that cannot believe in the unseen, and will only believe to sustain the body. Such, as contra-distinguished from Benthamism, was the system of Coleridge.[162]

After its lengthy discussion of 'the spirit of poetry' versus 'sordid philosophy' the Nation declared itself indifferent to both Benthamism and Puseyism, for neither had much to do with Irish politics. This was clearly disingenuous, for Young Ireland had strongly identified with Young England — and the Coleridgian spirit in general — for some time. Collections such as John Manners's England's Trust and Other Poems, (1841), and England's Ballads and Other Poems (1850), or Richard Monckton Milnes's Poetry for the People and Other Poems (1840) or Poems Legendary and Historical (1844) were matched by Young Ireland's

---

159 Collected Works, 10. 121.
160 Nation, 9 September 1843; Nation, 2 September 1843.
161 In 1842 Mill published two articles on Puseyism in the Morning Chronicle. See 'Puseyism [1]' and 'Puseyism [2]', in The Collected Works of John Stuart Mill. Volume 24: Newspaper Writings, ed. A. and J. M. Robson (London, 1986), 811–14; 815–21.
162 Nation, 13 April 1844.

hugely successful collections, *The Spirit of the Nation* and Duffy's *The Ballad Poetry of Ireland* (1843).[163]

Young Ireland's endorsement of the Coleridgian spirit may reflect the 'romantic' character of its nationalism, but this description has tended to obscure its political logic. Against reductive forms of political science, Young Ireland emphasized both the historical and affective nature of political reason on practical — not utopian or romantic — grounds. For similar reasons, Young Ireland condemned the methods of Benthamism and its sister science, political economy. In this context, the group was a modest forerunner of the 'historical school' of economics led by figures such as Cliffe Leslie and John Kells Ingram.[164] Ingram started out as a Young Irelander, and his later criticisms of the 'vicious abstraction' of classical political economy reiterate, on a more systematic basis, the group's attacks on the dismal science.[165] Ingram also subscribed to the by now standard criticism of Bentham that he was 'one of the most unhistorical of writers'.[166] More generally, he criticized the 'too absolute character of the theoretic and practical conclusions of the political economists. It follows ... from their *a priori* and unhistoric method that they arrive at results which purport to apply equally to all states of society.'[167] Against this deductive method, Ingram called for a more historically minded approach to political and economic affairs. Young Ireland had called for this much earlier.

163 Young Ireland voiced its concerns about the lack of 'animal fury' in Young England ballads: 'The Young England men are trying to make up for the want of a ballad history in England. Perhaps they will succeed, but with all due deference, we think they have had too much library training, and too little animal fury and individual vehemence to succeed perfectly.' *Nation*, 16 November 1844.

164 For an account of this school see, Thomas Boylan and Timothy P. Foley, *Political Economy and Colonial Ireland: The Propagation and Ideological Function of Economic Discourse in the Nineteenth Century* (London, 1992). See also Gerard M. Koot, *English Historical Economics, 1870–1926* (Cambridge, 1987).

165 John K. Ingram, *The Present Position and Prospects of Political Economy* (London, 1878), 17.

166 *Present Position*, 24.

167 *Present Position*, 26.

2 Civic Virtue in the Modern World

1 Young Ireland and Civic Republicanism

In their polemical attacks on the 'selfish creed' of Benthamism, Young Ireland helped to develop a tradition of interpretation in which Irish virtue stood opposed to English materialism. 'Romantic Ireland,' Yeats maintained, had higher concerns than the pursuit of self-interest or lucre.[1] Young Ireland's opposition to an 'English' ideology of commerce, however, was not primarily derived from 'romantic' sources, but had a broader classical provenance.[2] When Young Ireland declared that 'there are higher things than money, and there are benefits which political economy prates not about and touching which Utilitarianism is dumb', it was providing a modern articulation of Aristotle's conviction that 'a state's purpose is not merely to provide a living but to make a life that is good'.[3] Davis explicitly derived his politics from the 'fountains of Greece' and made repeated use of classical models throughout his writings.[4] He drew on Cicero to outline the duties of the good citizen — 'non nobis solum nati sumus, ortesque nostri partem vindicat' — and contrasted this with the individualism of modern times.[5] Mitchel

---

1 See 'September, 1913', VP, 289–90.

2 Nineteenth-century commentators such as A. M. Sullivan recognized the group's shared fascination for 'classic models in civic virtue'. A. M. Sullivan, New Ireland, 2 vols. (London, 1877), 1. 147. Bentham, on the other hand, had little time for this kind of politics. See Rosen, Jeremy Bentham and Representative Democracy, 23.

3 Nation, 23 September 1843; Aristotle, The Politics, trans. T. A. Sinclair, ed. Trevor J. Saunders (London, 1981), 196.

4 Nation, 15 November 1845. In 'A Nation Once Again', Davis suggested that his nationalism was inspired by the example of 'ancient freemen', particularly the heroics of the Spartans at Thermopylae. Thomas Davis, The Poems of Thomas Davis, ed. Thomas Wallis (Dublin, 1846), 73.

5 Davis, Essays Literary and Historical, 46. The phrase roughly translates as follows: 'we are not born for ourselves alone, but our country claims a part in our birth'.

spent his time upon a prison-ship translating Plato's *Republic* and repeatedly praised the virtues of classical thought in general. 'Ancient philosophy', he suggested, 'was an earnest striving after spiritual truth and good; it dealt with the supersensuous and nobler part of man; and its aim was to purify his nature'.[6] The Young Irelanders believed that political life should share this moral ambition. Young Ireland, moreover, believed in a direct relationship between the good community and the good citizen. This accounts, in part, for the moral insistence of their rhetoric and their inexhaustible interest in virtuous patriots distributed through history. But the principles of ancient citizenship and the institutional realities of modern politics were not easily reconciled.

Young Ireland did not always draw its politics direct from the ancients but relied on a mediating civic republican tradition. This tradition had its origins in Aristotle, Cicero and other Roman writers, but it was given fresh life by Niccolò Machiavelli's interpretation of republican Rome. Machiavelli had a decisive influence on the English political thinker and commonwealthman James Harrington, who in turn had an enormous impact on Irish patriots such as John Toland, Robert Molesworth and Francis Hutcheson.[7] The vocabularies of civic republicanism played a substantial role in the American and French revolutions and were invoked by Irish patriots throughout this period.[8] Given the long history and extraordinary scope of civic republicanism, its specific political and constitutional implications are inevitably ambiguous.[9] It is best regarded, therefore, as a set of vocabularies or conceptual motifs rather than as a systematic doctrine. This language was often used as a form of protest — against monarchical despotism, corrupt oligarchies and arbitrary rule in general. A key constituent of republican rhetoric was the idea of civic virtue — or an active solicitude for the public good.[10] This, for Young

---

6 Mitchel, *Jail Journal*, 43.

7 John Toland, with the support of Molesworth, produced a commentary on Harrington and an edition of his works in 1700. Harrington, wrote Toland, in *Anglia Libera; or, The Limitation and Succession of the Crown of England Explain'd and Asserted* (London 1701), 59, was 'one of the greatest *Republicans* that ever liv'd in the World' [Toland's emphasis]. Hutcheson was also an enthusiast for Harrington's thought. See Caroline Robbins, *The Eighteenth-Century Commonwealthman* (Cambridge, Mass., 1959), 173–74; Ian McBride, 'The School of Virtue: Francis Hutcheson, Irish Presbyterians and the Scottish Enlightenment', in George Boyce, Robert Eccleshall and Vincent Geoghegan, eds., *Political Thought in Ireland since the Seventeenth Century* (London and New York, 1993), 73–99.

8 Here, according to Jacqueline Hill, 'political debate and even strategy remained embedded in the civic Patriot tradition'. Jacqueline Hill, *From Patriots to Unionists: Dublin Civic Politics and Irish Protestant Patriotism 1660–1840* (Oxford, 1997), 170.

9 The decisively 'republican' features of Bolingbroke's political thought, for instance, are not immediately apparent. His patriot king may have had superficial resemblances to Machiavelli's Romulus or to Sparta's Lycurgus, but he also remained an absolute monarch. According to Montesquieu, on the other hand, republicanism was generally distinguishable from monarchical government.

10 According to Blair Worden, 'it is as a politics of virtue that republicanism most clearly defines itself'. See Blair Worden, 'Marchamont Nedham and the Beginnings of English Republicanism, 1649–1656', in David Wooton, ed., *Republicanism, Liberty, and Commercial Society, 1649–1776* (Stanford, 1994), 45–81, 46.

Ireland, was the supreme end of politics: 'What is it that makes a great people? In one word, it is a great virtue'.[11]

Those who failed to promote the common good, according to Young Ireland, almost invariably fomented faction. This diagnosis, which the group repeated time and time again, revealed the extent of its political classicism. For throughout ancient Greece, faction — or *stasis* — was deemed the greatest and most common of evils.[12] All communities, it was assumed, tended to divide into factions, the most ubiquitous and most intractable being the division between the rich and the poor. The test of good government, however, was the way it overrode faction and promoted the good life.[13] Likewise, Davis and his colleagues condemned sectional interests in the name of a magnanimous patriotism. In a fairly typical assault, Meagher denounced 'the old champions of faction — in whose withered souls all that is pure and generous in our nature has rotted out'.[14] Through the terrible alchemy of faction, the *Nation* maintained, virtue turned into vice:

> For the public virtues — the patience, the courage, the truth — essential to our success cannot live amid petty broils and squabbles. The vile spirit of Faction — the spirit of rivalry and cabal — the spirit of division, would turn our patience into angry vituperation, our truth into the furious and lying howl of party spirit, and our courage into an exaggerated or affected caution, from which true hearts would turn in disdain or despair.[15]

A hatred of faction was also the legitimizing basis for the group's rejection of socialism; such politics destroyed the common good by pitting the interests of one class against another.[16] The years of terror under the French Revolution were for Young Ireland a testament to the evils of class conflict. Duffy always remained convinced that the 'Jacobins at any time were never more than a faction'.[17] Young Ireland also condemned religious sectarianism for its factional nature. 'Better that the *Nation*, and all who contribute to it, were sunk in the Red Sea,' Duffy declared, 'than that they should become the watchword of faction, the pretext of division, the rock whereon to make shipwreck of so noble a cause!'[18]

Figures such as Burke had managed to combine a hatred of faction with a defence of party; it was ridiculous, he believed, to decry 'a body of men united, for promoting by their

---

11 *Nation*, 5 August 1843.

12 On this point see M. I. Finley, *Democracy Ancient and Modern* (London, 1985), 44–48.

13 This was one of the guiding principles, for example, of Aristotle's *Politics*.

14 Meagher, *Meagher of the Sword*, 100.

15 *Nation*, 30 June 1846.

16 Young Ireland also believed that socialism connived against one of the foundations of civil society: private property. 'What is the great objection to Socialism? It appears to us to be this — that it destroys the grand sentiment on which society is based — namely the sentiment of property.' See *Nation*, 3 December 1842.

17 *Nation*, 12 February 1848.

18 Duffy, *My Life in Two Hemispheres*, i. 179.

joint endeavours the national interest, upon some particular principle in which they are all agreed'.[19] The Young Irelanders conceded in the end that the aggressive competition of groups had public benefits, but they initially associated this with the evils of faction. Here they aligned themselves with Burke's old antagonist, Bolingbroke — a figure who had famously presented 'the spirit of party' as the source of his country's corruption. Bolingbroke proposed an inclusive patriotism and civic friendship as a means of transforming 'the narrow spirit of party into a diffusive spirit of public benevolence'.[20] He argued, moreover, that the terms 'Whig' and 'Tory' were defunct. There remained only the Country party — so committed to virtue and the public good that it 'is improperly called party' — and the court — a selfish faction that led to the general corruption of the state.[21] In the 1840s in Ireland, the Nation adapted this line of argument for their purposes, insisting that the 'old parties are broken, or breaking up, both in England and Ireland'.[22] In 1843 the spirit of Bolingbroke — and of wishful thinking — was even more pronounced: 'There is no longer a Whig party in this country,' the Nation declared. 'There is no longer any party, but one for nationality and one against it'.[23]

Against the clamour of faction, Young Ireland promoted the benefits of civic friendship — an advocacy that again testified to their classical outlook on political affairs. In the Nicomachean Ethics, Aristotle suggested that friendship holds polities together, and lawgivers should care more about it than justice. For friendship necessarily implies justice to one's friend. Justice, on the other hand, is a necessary but insufficient condition of the good.[24] The politics of friendship also distinguished itself from a later social contract tradition, because it involved a social bond, equipped with its own sense of obligations that was not the product of interest-governed agreement.[25] Modern politics was generally conducted in less intimate settings than those enjoyed by Aristotle and his contemporaries, but Young Ireland was determined to foster civic friendship throughout Ireland. 'Cultivate the love of your brethren', the Nation preached.[26] Civic affection was central to the well-being of the polity: 'Unless men's efforts for friendship ... increase with their powers — they but rise to ruin.'[27] Throughout the 1840s Young Ireland sponsored a cult of friendship in ways that seemed ridiculous and even 'unmanly' to some of their contemporaries.[28] Duffy's histories of the Young Ireland movement were

19 W & S 2. 317.
20 Bolingbroke [Henry St. John], Political Writings, ed. David Armitage (Cambridge, 1997), 6.
21 Bolingbroke, Political Writings, 37.
22 Nation, 15 October 1842.
23 Nation, 3 June 1843. Convinced that England nurtured Irish divisions, the Young Irelanders celebrated Ireland's apparent recovery of its lost unity. 'Faction and feud are passing away,' the Nation declared on 14 December 1844.
24 Aristotle, The Nicomachean Ethics, ed. and trans. Roger Crisp (Cambridge, 2000), 144.
25 Young Ireland criticized the individualist premise and voluntarist presumption of contractarian theories of government. 'Society is not a choice, but an essential of humanity.' Nation, 28 December 1843.
26 Nation, 13 May 1843.
27 Nation, 31 May 1845.
28 See, for instance, Mermion Savage, The Falcon Family, or Young Ireland (London, 1844).

punctuated by accounts of weekly dinners and Sunday excursions.[29] These accounts of friendship, based on mutual education and improvement, had a typically moral character; its affective basis was a salutary by-product of the pursuit of the good.[30] Through poems and songs, the Young Irelanders advocated friendship on a broader scale with a similar moral orientation towards the good of the patria. The cultivation of national friendship, in Davis's eyes, would make Ireland an invincible force:

And long may last, the friendship fast,
Which binds us altogether;
While we agree, our foes shall flee
Like clouds in stormy weather.[31]

The benefits of friendship might be extolled in sentimental poetry, but they were often difficult to establish in practice. Ireland would never enjoy the kind of patriotic bonhomie envisaged for it in the pages of the Nation. Young Ireland's increasingly bitter struggles with O'Connell suggested that national cohesion was not simply elusive, but that it was also potentially undesirable. Moreover, these spats demonstrated that the idea of 'faction' was often an unhelpfully plastic concept. Young Ireland condemned the sectarian bent of O'Connellite politics, but this critique of faction could easily appear self-refuting. The defender of 'Old Ireland' duly presented his youthful critics as a self-promoting clique and as dangerous sources of discord.

Young Ireland, as a consequence, was forced to reconsider the values of public antagonism and disagreement. The group may have denounced 'division', 'rivalry' and 'cabal', but in their various challenges to O'Connell the Young Irelanders ultimately stressed the public utility of dissent. 'Fear no dissension', Meagher maintained. 'Dissension is good where truth is to be saved'.[32] While the group distinguished Irish politics from an English system 'founded on antagonism', it nevertheless acknowledged the political value of such internal strife. Antagonism, the paper claimed, 'is also the cause of much freedom, much discussion, and intellectual activity'. Civil discord was a condition of the vita activa and 'a safeguard against apathy and social torpor'.[33] The group's advocacy of friendship was Aristotelian, but its defence of antagonism embodied a distinctly Machiavellian strand of the republican tradition: rival groups checked asymmetries of power and promoted a climate of public vigilance that sustained

29 'The writers of the Nation,' he maintained, 'lived much together, and educated each other by friendly discussion on every problem in the Irish case.' Duffy, My Life in Two Hemispheres, 1. 65.

30 Cicero, Laelius, On Friendship and The Dream of Scipio, trans. J. G. F. Powell (Warminster, 1990), 37; 'virtue itself both produces and maintains friendship, nor can friendship exist by any means without virtue'.

31 Nation, 13 May 1843.

32 Meagher, Meagher of the Sword, 99.

33 Nation, 13 April 1844.

liberty.[34] For this reason, Young Ireland finally acknowledged the public utility of a party system. 'Parties in a well-tempered and reasoning community', the *Nation* declared in 1847, 'are as the elements in nature, acting upon and purifying one another, each having its office and its limitation'. Public vigilance, however, remained necessary: 'To prevent public favourites from decaying into public nuisances, and to preserve party from degenerating into faction, a reasonable confidence and a wise watchfulness are equally required from the whole community.'[35] In Ireland's condition, according to Davis, 'suspicion proves zeal'.[36]

This emphasis on vigilance may have struck some contemporaries as paranoid, but for Young Ireland it was a bulwark against corruption. In the republican tradition, corruption implied the erosion of civic virtue through the irrational prioritization of private interests over the public good. A Machiavellian language of corruption was used throughout eighteenth-century Britain to criticize the use of government credit, public debt, and the existence of standing armies. Government patronage, according to its critics, had rendered parliament dependent on the court and led to the 'universal corruption' of the state.[37] Throughout the 1780s and beyond, Irish patriots criticized the way Irish votes and Irish MPs were tied to patronage systems — the Irish Volunteer conventions raised these issues over and over again — and attacked the Hanoverian practice of appointing Englishmen to Irish jobs.[38] Young Ireland also condemned

34 Machiavelli was alive to the benefits of friendship and to the evils of faction, but he also recognized the political value of civil discord. Niccolò Machiavelli, *Discourses on Livy*, trans. Harvey C. Mansfield and Nathan Tarcov (Chicago and London, 1996). He thought the antagonism between plebeians and patricians in ancient Rome was a generally positive force: 'those who damn the tumults between the nobles and the plebs blame those things that were the first cause of keeping Rome free'. For the more complicated role of civic antagonism in his thought as a whole, see Gisela Bock, 'Civil Discord in Machiavelli's *Istorie Fiorentine*', in Gisela Bock, Quentin Skinner and Maurizio Viroli, eds., *Machiavelli and Republicanism* (Cambridge, 1990), 181–201. For Young Ireland's explicit invocation of Machiavelli arrangements for civil defence, see *Nation*, July 1 1848.
35 *Nation*, 8 May 1847.
36 *Nation*, 2 March 1844. In the past, Irish patriots such as William Drennan had praised the political benefits of 'never sleeping suspicion'. William Drennan, *An Address to the Volunteers of Ireland, by the Author of a Letter to Edmund Burke, Esq., Containing Reflections on Patriotism, Party Spirit, and the Union of Free Nations* (Dublin, 1781), 33.
37 Bolingbroke, *Political Writings*, 206, directed his readers to Machiavelli's famous account of a people fallen into a state of 'universal corruption'. A similar fate awaited Britain unless it produced its own *ridurre ai principii* and restored the true spirit of its constitution. The idea of a *ridurre ai principii*, or return to first principles, was central to a neo-Machiavellian tradition of republicanism. It was also recommended by Davis in his article 'First Principles' in the *Nation*, 16 August 1845.
38 Henry Flood in *A Letter to the People of Ireland on the Expediency and Necessity of the Present Associations in Ireland in Favour of Our Own Manufactures with Some Cursory Observations on the Effects of a Union* (Dublin, 1779), 22, condemned the 'scandalous system of corruption and prodigality, in the civil and military establishment'. Grattan explicitly invoked Bolingbroke to denounce the 'arts of bribery and corruption' practised in Ireland. See *Speeches of the Rt. Hon. Henry Grattan*, 2nd edn. (Dublin, 1853), 139. The United Irishmen also railed against 'the whole system under which Venality, Corruption and Tyranny have dared to trample on the Liberties of my country, where emoluments are peculation, and what are called honours a disgrace'. See Arthur O'Connor, *The State of Ireland*, ed. James Livesey (Dublin, 1998), 31.

'the voice and menace of corruption' and criticized the promotion of private interests over public virtue.[39] Criticisms used against eighteenth-century Whig corruption were redeployed against modern-day Whigs and their Irish defenders. As the editors of the *Nation* confessed in June 1844, 'there was a time when we felt for Whig corruption a terror wherewith we never honored the artillery of Wellington'.[40] In these attacks, Young Ireland implicitly criticized O'Connell for his support of the Whigs as well as his own abuse of the patronage systems that accompanied Emancipation. Like many republicans, Young Ireland believed that corruption led directly to public servitude. 'A country must be corrupted', Davis proclaimed, 'before it can be enslaved'.[41]

Davis's concept of collective slavery was by no means new. Swift had baptized Ireland a 'land of slaves' both in derision and in protest.[42] Poynings's Law and the Declaratory Act, according to their critics, impeded Irish constitutional liberties and were interpreted as the legal manacles that sustained Irish slavery.[43] The Declaratory Act of 1720 — which rendered the Kingdom of Ireland subordinate to the King and the Parliament of Great Britain — was denounced by William King as 'the enslaving act'.[44] Grattan also condemned Britain's efforts 'to make Ireland a slave'.[45] Drennan's *Letters of Orellana* were composed by a self-confessed 'Irish Helot' and addressed to 'fellow-slaves'.[46] And Wolfe Tone lamented the 'abject slavery' of Ireland.[47] The broad and often banal nature of these references to servitude can obscure their political significance. To be a slave in a Roman setting, as Quentin Skinner has shown, was 'to be *in potestate*, within the power of someone else'.[48] This condition of servitude did not denote the absence of basic comforts or enjoyments, but it did mean that these benefits were dependent on the will of a master. Collective slavery for Roman writers implied a similar condition of dependency: a civil association was unfree when it was subject to the will of another nation or state. This interpretation was deployed time and time again by Irish patriots to condemn Ireland's dependent condition. Drennan was one of the most articulate

---

39 *Nation*, 2 September 1843.

40 *Nation*, 22 June 1844. The Whigs 'found some corruption in Ireland, and they left more'. *Nation*, 2 March 1844.

41 *Nation*, 17 December 1842.

42 See 'Verses on the Death of Dr. Swift', in Jonathan Swift, *The Complete Poems*, ed. Pat Rogers (London, 1983), 485–98, 496. See Jonathan Swift, *The Drapier's Letters to the People of Ireland against Receiving Wood's Halfpence*, ed. Herbert Davis (Oxford, 1935), 108: '*Freedom consists in a People being Governed by Laws made with their own Consent, and Slavery in the Contrary*' [Swift's emphasis].

43 Grattan, *Speeches*, 41–42: 'I here, in this Declamatory Act, see my country proclaimed a slave! I see every man in this House enrolled a slave!'

44 Robbins, *Eighteenth-Century Commenwealthman*, 147.

45 Grattan, *Speeches*, 44.

46 William Drennan, *Letters of Orellana, An Irish Helot, to The Seven Northern Counties not Represented in the National Assembly of Delegates, Held at Dublin, October 1784, for Obtaining a More Equal Representation of the People in the Parliament of Ireland* (Dublin, 1785).

47 Theobald Wolfe Tone, *The Writings of Theobald Wolfe Tone, 1763–98. Volume 1: Tone's Career in Ireland to June 1795*, ed. T. W. Moody, R. B. McDowell and C. J. Woods (Oxford, 1998), 98.

48 Quentin Skinner, *Liberty before Liberalism* (Cambridge, 1998), 41.

defenders of the principle that a liberty enjoyed on sufferance or trust was no liberty at all. 'Every nation under the sun must be placed in one of two conditions,' he declared.

> It must be free, or enslaved. I make no scruple in affirming that there is *no* medium between those two situations; and if we are deceived into the belief that there is such as an intermediate state, it is by mistaking the prudent moderation of tyrants, the mildness of modern manners, or the gentle but powerful influence of religion for public liberty.[49]

The absence of oppression in Ireland was purely contingent. 'Away with the liberty', he declared, 'that hangs pendulating upon a *perchance!*'[50] Grattan also equated dependency with slavery in his bid for an independent legislature in Ireland and Young Ireland repeatedly quoted his definition of public bondage: '"To depend upon the honour of another country, is to depend upon her will and to depend upon the will of another country, is the definition of slavery." This was the doctrine of Henry Grattan — let it be our motto.'[51]

This certainly became the motto. Some modern commentators had dismissed the language of public servitude as a dangerous form of political hyperbole, but the Young Irelanders never declined opportunities for using such rhetoric.[52] The Irish nation was 'a rightless dependant — an injured slave'.[53] Things had not changed much from the days of Swift: Ireland was still a 'land of slaves'. The country was 'a prison — a province — a thing governed not by its own will, but by its guards, gaoler, and turnkeys'.[54] Ireland's servitude, according to the *Nation*, was not mitigated by the possession of benign masters or just laws: 'What matter whether those masters be kind and indulgent or sullen and imperious — slaves are not less slaves because they are pampered. It is the condition of *receiving laws*, bad or good, at the hands of another, that makes the true description, essence and proper difference of servitude.'[55] This restated the classical republican argument: a state surrendered its liberty when it relied on an agency other than the body of its own citizens. Such dependency may produce ample benefits, but

---

49 Drennan, *Letters of Orellana*, 7 [Drennan's emphasis].

50 Drennan, *Letters of Orellana*, 11 [Drennan's emphasis]. See also his *Letter to Edmund Burke, Esq.; By Birth an Irishman, By Adoption an Englishman, Containing Some Reflections on Patriotism, Party-Spirit, and the Union of Free Nations. With Observations upon the Means on which Ireland Relies for Obtaining Political Independence* (Dublin, 1780), 29: 'concessions of commercial privileges are but titles of servitude, and donative of tyranny'.

51 Meagher, *Meagher of the Sword*, 59. See also *Nation*, 15 July 1848. Grattan made this remark in a speech criticizing the Act of Union. See *Speeches*, 284. The Young Irelanders were hugely enthusiastic supporters of Grattan: 'No other orator has brightened the depths of political philosophy with such vivid and lasting light'. *Nation*, 22 February 1845.

52 William Paley criticized 'those popular phrases which speak of a free people; of a nation of slaves; which call one revolution the aera of liberty, or another the loss of it; with many expressions of a like absolute form'. See *The Works of William Paley with Additional Sermons Etc. Etc.*, 6 vols. (London, 1830), 3. 356.

53 *Nation*, 1 July 1843.

54 *Nation*, 30 September 1843.

55 *Nation*, 25 July 1846 [*Nation's* emphasis].

these were contingent upon another's will. There was, therefore, an arbitrary character to such enjoyments, and true freedom was the opposite of arbitrariness. Again Young Ireland referred to Grattan on this point: 'as Grattan said in College-Green, the country that depends for its liberties on the honor of another, depends on its caprice, and that is the definition of slavery'.[56] Young Ireland pointed out again and again that political servitude corrupted the moral character of the nation. When a country surrenders its independence, Meagher maintained, 'it loses all faith in its own faculties and is soothed and pampered into debasement. The spirit of the freeman no longer acts — the gratitude of the slave destroys it.'[57] If Irish people were not prepared to exercise 'the virtues of freedom', according to the Nation, they should be prepared to 'bear the lot of slaves'.[58]

When Young Ireland extolled 'the virtues of freedom', it seemed to have a distinctive concept of liberty in mind, one which required a life of active citizenship for its existence. 'No man should be idle — no man should be silent', the Nation declared. 'These are startling indications of corruption.'[59] Freedom, for figures like Bentham, was an idea 'purely negative', but the notion implied something more positive for Young Ireland.[60] This reflected the fact that freedom for these patriots was intimately bound up with virtue. This relationship could be viewed across a spectrum in the republican tradition: on the one hand, virtue was a simple condition of freedom: civic virtue, for instance, kept people free from hostile invasion or internal corruption, but it had no intrinsic relationship to this freedom. Here liberty could remain a 'negative' or minimal concept.[61] On the other hand, virtue could be viewed not only as a condition, but as a constituent of freedom. In this 'positive' or teleological account, virtue was a form of self-realization and was internal to the very notion of liberty. But virtue was also a fundamentally practical affair: it had to be practised in order to be enjoyed. 'As in the Olympic Games', Aristotle explained, 'it is not the most attractive and strongest who are crowned, but those who compete ... so in life it is those who act rightly who will attain what is noble and good'.[62] Cicero was equally convinced that virtue was a kind of practice: 'virtue is not some kind of knowledge to be possessed without using it: even if the intellectual possession of knowledge can be maintained without use, virtue consists entirely in its employment'.[63]

---

56 Nation, 14 December 1844.
57 Meagher, Meagher of the Sword, 59.
58 Nation, 13 May 1843.
59 Nation, 25 January 1845.
60 Quoted in Douglas G. Long, Bentham on Liberty: Jeremy Bentham's Idea of Liberty in Relation to his Utilitarianism (Toronto and Buffalo, 1977), 74. To put it in the terms of one modern theorist, freedom, for Young Ireland, was less 'an opportunity-concept' than 'an exercise-concept', which required a life of active citizenship as its condition of realization. Charles Taylor, 'What's Wrong with Negative Liberty?', Philosophy and the Human Sciences: Philosophical Papers 2, 211–19, 213.
61 Virtù, for Machiavelli, was the lived acknowledgement of the relationship between individual freedom and the free state. But his account of freedom itself could remain fairly minimal or largely 'negative'.
62 Aristotle, Nicomachean Ethics, 14.
63 Cicero, On the Commonwealth and On the Laws, ed. James E. G. Zetzel (Cambridge, 1999), 3.

Young Ireland subscribed — with remarkable fidelity — to this classical understanding of virtue. According to the *Nation*, there was 'no such thing as negative virtue ... All virtue must be active'. 'The man who does not fight *for* a truth', the paper continued, 'is as guilty as the man who *violates* it'.[64] Young Ireland's outlook on politics was broadly Aristotelian: it provided a context for the virtues, the exercise of which yielded a unique kind of pleasure. Aristotle regarded politics as a 'master science' because it incorporated all other human goods in the pursuits of its own end. Young Ireland shared a similar perspective. 'Politics', the *Nation* declared, 'the science of government — the art of bestowing the means of happiness on our fellow creatures — is, in reality, the highest sphere for the highest intellect and the highest virtue'.[65] A life of citizenship allowed human beings to express their talents and develop their character. 'I would especially desire the diffusion of civic zeal', Davis declared, 'because in it I see the means, the only means of human improvement'.[66]

Central to Young Ireland's understanding of citizenship was the idea of education.[67] 'Educate, That You May Be Free', Davis famously insisted.[68] The relationship between freedom and education assumed by Davis was a central feature of republican thought and it was a dominant theme in Irish patriot literature. 'Good Learning', Molesworth explained, 'is a great Antidote against the Plague of *Tyranny*'.[69] Young Ireland remained equally convinced of the links between liberty and learning. As Duffy put it, 'the happiness and independence of nations seem everywhere to bear a strict proportion to their moral and intellectual training'.[70] Education was, perhaps, a desirable and necessary feature of any competent administration, but, as Montesquieu explained, it was particularly important in a republican context. Despotic governments, he suggested, survived though the propagation of fear; monarchies appealed to a code of honour that tolerated and even complemented the pursuit of private interests; but republics relied on virtue — a principle which involved 'a renunciation of oneself, which is always a painful thing'.[71] Republican government depended on the love of one's country and of its laws and it was education's role to instil this affection. Davis worried, however, that the 'self-denying virtues are "passing away, passing away"' and he reiterated the need for civic education to reverse this corruption.[72] He hoped that public education would

---

64 *Nation*, 12 February 1848 [*Nation*'s emphasis]. See Jean-Jacques Rousseau, *The Discourses and Other Early Political Writings*, ed. and trans. Victor Gourevitch (Cambridge, 1997), 17: 'In politics, as in ethics, not to do good is a great evil, and every useless citizen may be looked upon as a pernicious man.'

65 *Nation*, 8 May 1847.

66 *Essays Literary and Historical*, 45.

67 According to Duffy, 'education was the agency, without which we could accomplish nothing', *My Life in Two Hemispheres*, 1. 61. In *Young Ireland: A Fragment of Irish History*, 5, he claimed that 'of all revolutionary forces education was the greatest'.

68 *Essays Literary and Historical*, 225.

69 Robert Molesworth, *An Account of Denmark as It was in the Year 1692* (London, 1694), 25.

70 Charles Gavan Duffy, George Sigerson and Douglas Hyde, *The Revival of Irish Literature* (London, 1894), 5.

71 Montesquieu, *The Spirit of the Laws*, 35.

72 *Essays Literary and Historical*, 8.

also overcome the discord of sectarianism and faction in Ireland — although here his proposals for non-denominational colleges often seemed to aggravate the divisions he wished to overcome.

Davis was convinced that popular self-rule demanded an educated citizenry, but he also believed that education was internal to the practice of republican government. Active citizenship, in other words, was intrinsically civilizing; it endowed citizens with responsibilities and duties that broadened horizons and opened minds. 'Practice', Davis maintained, 'is the great teacher'. He tended to believe that national independence would produce a more popular government and provide opportunities for a more active civic life: 'independence', he therefore concluded, 'is the natural and best way for a People to learn all that pertains to freedom and happiness. Our greatest voluntary efforts, aided by the amplest provincial institutions, would teach us less in a century than we would learn in five years of Liberty'.[73] Young Ireland glorified the ancient republics of Greece on precisely this basis. Not only had they enjoyed independence from other states, the strong participatory ethos of these political entities had produced human flourishing. Here citizens were encouraged to pursue excellence and this culminated in a society of supreme distinction. Even the artistic achievements of ancient Greece were intrinsically related to its rich conception of freedom.[74] According to the Nation, the 'liberty of Greece, the "nationality fever" of Athens created its pattern-deeds, its art, its oratory, its deep, pure, unrivalled literature'. [75] Davis lauded the polities of ancient Greece and Rome, but he also regarded the republics of Renaissance Europe as examples of true civilization.[76] The task of modern Ireland was to emulate the achievements of these republics. In order to do so, the nation must be free; this freedom, however, required a life of civic virtue. Education was needed to produce virtuous citizens, but the practice of citizenship was itself an educating force. This was the virtuous circle upon which Young Ireland's politics turned. But an obvious question remained: how would modern political and social structures accommodate these ideals?

2 Ancient and Modern Liberty

The Young Irelanders may have derived their conception of citizenship from classical models, but it was not immediately apparent how the spirit of the ancients could be

---

73 Nation, 5 October 1844.
74 This link between republican liberty and cultural excellence was also asserted by classical authors. Longinus, for instance, reported but did not necessarily endorse a 'well-worn view that democracy is the kindly nurse of great men, and that great men of letters may be said to have flourished only under democracy and perished with it'; 'On the Sublime', in Aristotle/Horace/Longinus: Classical Literary Criticism, trans. T. S. Dorsch (London, 1965), 97–158, 156.
75 Nation, 16 December 1843.
76 'Where, sir, but in the civic republics of Europe [...] where else do you find the cradles of commerce, the preservers of literature, the restorers of art and science? And where but in these free towns and in the little republics [...] was liberty sheltered and saved?' Nation, 24 June 1843.

revived in a modern political setting. Benjamin Constant had outlined the problem in detail in the second decade of the nineteenth century. Constant admired what he called 'ancient liberty', but he judged attempts to revive it for the modern world to be a misguided and potentially dangerous enterprise. The small size of ancient political institutions, he conceded, allowed for 'active and constant participation in collective power'. But modern states were generally larger structures and the individual's political influence was proportionally smaller within this setting. 'Lost in the multitude', Constant explained, 'the individual can almost never perceive the influence he exercises. Never does his will impress itself upon the whole; nothing confirms in his eyes his own cooperation'.[77] This may be an unhappy condition, but it was not removed by abstract incitements to civic activism. Moreover, ancient liberty, as Constant pointed out, was predicated on the institution of slavery, and moderns justifiably baulked at this form of exploitation. The practical demands of making a living in a modern commercial society circumscribed the opportunities for political participation. But even if our time was not so limited, it was legitimate to demur from committing one's life to politics. For commerce, Constant suggested, generated its own set of goods and interests that were not necessarily available to us in a life of political service and it was legitimate to restrict oneself to the pursuit of these private ends. Human beings, for Constant, were not exclusively political animals; politics was not necessarily the master science; and a life of active citizenship was not the only means to human flourishing.

Such views posed a considerable challenge to Young Ireland's vision of citizenship. If in Constant's eyes the exigencies of living meant that few had the time to dedicate themselves to politics, the Famine that ravaged Ireland in the late 1840s made this fact brutally apparent. Against this background, Young Ireland's incitements to a life of civic virtue seemed unhelpfully abstract. The group's elevation of politics over other pursuits meant that their understanding of Ireland's economic hardships were often extraordinarily crude. In the midst of mass starvation in 1847, the *Nation* deemed the Famine 'a national judgment, — a scourge of Heaven for national sin'. This sin was its abdication of political independence to a foreign ruler — 'the deadliest crime a nation can commit'.[78] Even before the extreme scarcity and utter demoralization of the Famine years, Young Ireland was understandably criticized, particularly by the hard-nosed politicos of the O'Connellite movement, as a group of obtuse fantasists.[79]

While there was considerable justice in these attacks, Young Ireland did make efforts to harmonize their ideals with the realities of modern politics. If, as Constant suggested, the large scale of modern states precluded popular participation in government, then

---

77 Benjamin Constant, *Political Writings*, ed. and trans. Biancamaria Fontana (Cambridge, 1998), 316.

78 Until the people repented of this sin, the *Nation* proclaimed that, 'the hand of God shall be heavy on their land: the famine shall waste them and the Pestilence that walketh in darkness shall wear and wither them; — they shall crawl and pine, and whine and beg, *and beg in vain*, until they learn the worth of a man's manhood — the infinite value and virtue of a nation's independence!' *Nation*, 6 February 1847.

79 Sullivan, *New Ireland*, I. 170: 'Their educational propaganda was scoffed at as boyish bubble-blowing.'

Ireland's relatively small size could be seen as a political virtue.[80] Davis argued as much and drew attention to the 'power of small states, resulting from their unity and energy'.[81] Nevertheless, Ireland considerably outsized ancient republics, and collective face-to-face discussion about political affairs was impossible on a national scale. Young Ireland hoped, however, that advances in mass communication would overcome the political difficulties caused by spatial distances in modern states. The newspaper press, in this respect, was the guarantor of ancient liberty and made the resurrection of a classical participatory politics a viable ambition. Young Ireland was not alone in nourishing this hope. J. S. Mill, for instance, maintained:

> The newspapers and the railroads are solving the problem of bringing the democracy of England to vote, like that of Athens, simultaneously in one *agora*, and the same agencies are rapidly effacing those local distinctions which rendered one part of our population strangers to another, and are making us more than ever ... a homogeneous people.[82]

The very title of the Nation reflected its ambition to produce a unified people through the medium of the newspaper. Duffy drew repeatedly on Tocqueville's claim that 'nothing but a newspaper can drop the same thought into a thousand minds at the same moment'.[83] The aim of the Nation was to offer a similar forum for the consolidation of public opinion.

The Young Irelanders cited Tocqueville's judgements on the press, but they also shared his belief that democracy was the imminent political future awaiting Europe. The Nation was convinced of 'the irresistibility of the democratic element'.[84] Young Ireland's endorsement of democracy was arguably an expression of their republican principles, but for many political thinkers there was no necessary relationship between republicanism and democratic rule. Just government, for republicans, operated in the interests of people, but this did not necessarily imply that the people should rule.[85] Nor were figures such as Davis blind to the dangers of democratic rule in Ireland. If democracy in practice was conducted upon majoritarian lines, then this could lead to the oppression of minorities — particularly when these divisions were fuelled by sectarian differences and class hatred. Davis's term for Thierry — a 'Conservative Republican'

---

80 Political thinkers from Montesquieu to Rousseau had maintained that a republican government was only possible in small states. Joseph De Maistre was emphatic on this point; see his *Considerations on France*, ed. and trans. Richard A. Lebrun (Cambridge, 1994), 37: 'the phrase *large republic* like *square circle*, is self-contradictory'.

81 Nation, 24 June 1843.

82 J. S. Mill, 'De Tocqueville on Democracy in America [II]', in *Collected Works*, 18. 165.

83 Tocqueville, *Democracy in America*, Book II, 111.

84 Nation, 24 June 1848.

85 Toland's republicanism, for instance, did not imply 'a pure Democracy, nor any particular Form of Government; but an independent Community, where the Common Weal or Good of all indifferently is design'd and pursu'd let the Form be what it will'. See Toland, *Anglia Libera*, 92.

— matched his own political attitudes; the aim here was to secure the common good and 'to guard against a tyranny over the majority or by the majority'.[86] On another level, however, Young Ireland believed that democratic rule was the best means of enjoying the positive freedom of active citizenship. However, it was impossible to ignore the fact that modern democratic government was a very different creature to the direct democracy enjoyed by the ancients. Moderns may have regarded representative democracy as the only viable synthesis of the principle of popular self-rule with the technical merits of the modern state — or what Tocqueville more pointedly described as the 'compromise between administrative despotism and the sovereignty of the people' — but this also meant that opportunities for political participation were necessarily limited.[87] Indeed, Tocqueville worried that modern democracy would encourage, not civic participation, but a dangerous disengagement from political affairs. The Young Irelanders were haunted by his perceptive account of these possibilities.

One of Tocqueville's key concerns was that modern democracies would provoke 'individualism' to a dangerous degree. Individualism was a distinctly modern vice, but it was structurally similar to the republican idea of 'corruption' in its nature and consequences. Like corruption, individualism was not simply a moral shortcoming, but a failure of political reason; it proceeded, as Tocqueville put it, 'from erroneous judgment more than from depraved feeling'.[88] Above all, it stemmed from an inability to recognize that public and private liberties were co-dependent. Tocqueville recognized, as Constant had, that moderns dedicated themselves through necessity as well as choice to the pursuit of private interests over public affairs.[89] But this preoccupation had particularly dangerous political consequences. A widespread disengagement from politics meant that power was delegated to bureaucratic élites whose activities remained unscrutinized. The jargon of democracy perpetuated this problem, because the people's nominal sovereignty blinded them to the realties of its actual servitude. This prospect troubled Davis and he outlined the consequences of individualism in apocalyptic terms:

> on the shore of democracy is a monstrous danger; no phantasm is it, but alas! too real — the violence and forwardness of selfish men, regardful only of physical comfort, ready to sacrifice to it all sentiments — the generous, the pious, the just (victims in their order), till general corruption, anarchy, despotism, and moral darkness shall re-barbarise the earth.[90]

---

86 *Nation*, 26 November 1842.
87 Tocqueville, *Democracy in America*, Book II, 319.
88 *Democracy in America*, Book II, 98.
89 See *Democracy and America*, Book II, 293: 'Private life in democratic times is so busy, so excited, so full of wishes and of work, that hardly any energy or leisure remains to each individual for public life.'
90 Davis, *Essays Literary and Historical*, 45.

He explicitly invoked Tocqueville's advice that a programme of moral purification was a necessary means of overcoming the corruption intrinsic to modern democracies. This was to reiterate once more the importance of education as a guarantor of virtue. The object of education was to alert citizens to the fact that collective and individual liberties were mutually dependent. But virtue, for Young Ireland, was also an active principle and it was not immediately clear that modern political institutions provided adequate means for its expression. Representative democracy, as we have seen, presupposed a substantial delegation of political agency. Moreover, the centralized nature of modern states constrained opportunities for popular participation in government.

Young Ireland repeatedly criticized the centralized character of modern political institutions. 'Centralisation', the *Nation* maintained, 'obscures the history, dilutes the original tastes and peculiar faculties, weakens the patriotism, corrupts the ambition, and misapplies the resources of the provinces subject to it'.[91] Tocqueville believed that centralization was a general problem in modern states, but it was likely to manifest itself, he suggested, in a dangerously exacerbated form in a democratic setting. The principle of equality, he argued, necessitated 'uniformity of legislation'.[92] However, this uniformity was often won at the expense of historical differences and local institutions such as regional parliaments, guilds, corporations, municipalities, and estates. In democracies these structures were often considered irregular and, therefore, inequitable, not least because they often owed their being to aristocratic power. The dismantling of these mediating institutions, however, led to an undesirable concentration of the state's powers. The individual's sphere of influence was consequently weakened, while the agency of the state grew immense. A heavily centralized democracy, he suggested, was a subtle form of despotism.[93]

Young Ireland shared Tocqueville's concerns about the future of freedom in centralized democracies:

> Democracy has only kept half the promise given by its apostles. Centralization is at least as great a foe to freedom, to spirit, and to prosperity, as aristocracy. In fact, centralization, when there are no independent powers to check it, creates an official despotism, uniting the costliness and faction of an aristocracy with the iron grasp of mere monarchy.[94]

Centralization was both a cause and symptom of individualism. Denied opportunities for political participation, citizens had little choice but to dedicate themselves to their

---

91 *Nation*, 22 June 1844.
92 *Democracy in America*, Book II, 289.
93 *Democracy in America*, Book II, 319: 'Such a power does not destroy, but it prevents existence; it does not tyrannize, but it compresses, enervates, extinguishes, and stupefies a people, till each nation is reduced to nothing better than a flock of timid and industrious animals, of which the government is the shepherd.'
94 *Nation*, 18 March 1843.

private affairs. There were no immediate solutions to this problem, but Tocqueville promoted a policy of decentralization as the best means of restoring meaningful political agency to individuals in a democratic context. Young Ireland sponsored a similar programme. 'Local government,' the *Nation* announced 'is of the essence of democracy.'[95] The newspaper declared itself dedicated to reviving local patriotism and 'banishing centralisation'.[96]

The *Nation* recognized that modern states required some form of centralized authority for their unity and security. 'Some central machinery to prevent the growth of civil feuds, and to make military power more actively defensive', the paper declared, 'seems *desirable* in every nation'.[97] But this structural necessity should not lead to the destruction of mediating institutions and the erosion of local ties. Modern politics, according to Young Ireland, was conducted around a precarious dialectic of unity and diversity. Reversion to either extreme led to the corruption of the polity. Centralized authority was a necessary condition of national unity; indeed, the excessively local character of earlier forms of Irish patriotism, according to Young Ireland, had checked the development of national cohesion and broad-level solidarity: 'Disunion was the fixed character of their nationality, made up of a cluster of clans. It is the evil which appertains to all localism, like a cholera-house beyond the gates of the city.'[98] But if some form of centralized machinery was necessary for a unified state, the group was adamant that unity should not be purchased at the expense of liberty and diversity; indeed, 'the utter absence of such machinery is preferable to systematic centralisation'.[99] A centralized government was particularly effective in times of war, but its long-term retention produced 'universal uniformity' and civic enervation.[100] As the *Nation* put it: 'Centralisation in great crises is more favorable to union than localism; but union in its keeping, degenerates into uniformity, and thence to slavery. It is the problem of the human race to reconcile individual liberty and association.'[101]

By no means, however, could Young Ireland claim to have solved this problem. The group proclaimed local government to be 'the creed of Greece and of nature' and espoused it as a policy for Ireland, but the practical administrative implications of this advocacy remained opaque.[102] Young Ireland insisted that its critique of centralization was also an indictment of the British Empire, and suggested that Irish nationalism was an intrinsically decentralizing force. But the young patriots entirely overlooked the way nationalism itself could lead to the erosion of regional identities and local ties, producing national uniformity at the expense of human diversity.

95 *Nation*, 18 February 1843.
96 *Nation*, 2 September 1843.
97 *Nation*, 22 June 1844 [*Nation*'s emphasis].
98 *Nation*, 11 March 1848.
99 *Nation*, 22 June 1844.
100 Tocqueville, *Democracy in America*, Book II, 332.
101 *Nation*, 11 March 1848.
102 *Nation*, 23 December 1843.

While the constitutional implications of Young Ireland's critique of centralization remained vague, the group proposed other means of promoting active citizenship in Ireland. Davis, in particular, entertained the hope that civic virtue could be revived in Ireland through the creation of a citizen militia. The extravagance of this ambition — which seemed to overlook the basic realities of modern warfare — revealed the extent of his commitment to an older civic republican tradition. Republicans throughout the seventeenth and eighteenth century in Britain and Ireland had advocated the use of citizen militias and had attacked the growth of standing armies. The republic ideal of *virtù* had always implied that the citizen was free to participate equally in all the tasks essential to the well-being of the patria. To pay another to fight on one's behalf was to relinquish a central component of citizenship and to abandon one's unmediated relation to the polity in which one lived. Against this ideological background, a standing army marked a disastrous delegation of civic responsibility. The concentrated power of a standing army not only eroded virtue in the state, but was a threat to the security of its citizens.[103] Molesworth and his circle advanced these arguments to condemn the retention of mercenary forces by William III after the conclusion of peace in 1697. Similar arguments were used against a range of measures, from the use of mercenaries to the introduction of a professional police force, throughout the eighteenth century.[104]

Governmental incursions on the right to bear arms were also condemned on republican grounds. The Gunpowder and Convention Acts of 1793, which abrogated the people's rights to arms and assembly, were condemned, for instance, as an attack on citizenship itself. In 1843, Young Ireland revived these arguments to denounce the Irish Arms Bill — Davis called it 'The Slaves Disarming Bill' — introduced by the government as a check to the increasingly pugilistic stance of the Repeal Movement.[105] In an article entitled 'The Philistine Bill', the Young Irelanders delivered an impassioned defence of the right to bear arms. 'To carry arms', the Nation declared, 'is the first right of man, for arms are the guardians of property, honor, and life'.[106] Mitchel continued the campaign in the United Irishman, insisting 'that every man (except a born slave, who aspires only to beget slaves and die a slave) ought to have arms and to promote their use of them'.[107] Arms were not simply the guarantor of private rights; they were the enabling basis for the practice of civic virtue.[108]

---

103 See J. G. A. Pocock, *The Machiavellian Moment, Florentine Political Thought and the Atlantic Republican Tradition* (Princeton, 1975), 410–13, 419–21, 499.

104 Pitt's attempts to introduce a professional police force in 1785 were widely condemned in Ireland as 'unconstitutional'; it was an attack on citizenship and a lurch towards 'absolute monarchy'. Hill, *From Patriots to Unionists*, 184.

105 *Nation*, 6 May 1843.

106 *Nation*, 1 July 1843.

107 *United Irishman*, 12 February 1848.

108 Arguments of this kind had formed the ideological background to the Volunteer Movement of the late 1770s and 1780s in Ireland. See Stephen Small, *Political Thought in Ireland, 1776–1798: Republicanism, Patriotism and Radicalism* (Oxford, 2002), 83–112. See William Drennan, *Letter to Edmund Burke*, 16: 'The Volunteers

Davis hoped that the re-creation of a citizen militia in Ireland would restore a context in which the connection between public and private freedom was both expressed and defended. In January 1845, for instance, Young Ireland pledged its commitment to a national militia, and advanced the republican argument that a citizen militia 'is the only force which can repel the invader, without endangering the citizen'.[109] A month earlier Young Ireland had called for a militia, appealing to British history to justify the principle of a citizen army. The group reiterated Whig interpretations of the English Civil War, insisting that the immediate quarrel between the parliament and Charles I was for control of the militia. James II, they added, 'was expelled mainly for the offence of a standing army of 30,000'. The article then appealed to the descendants of Cromwell and William to honour the principles of their forefathers and to deliver a citizen militia to Ireland. 'A Militia', the *Nation* concluded, 'is the right of Ireland — to withhold it is unconstitutional, an insult, and a grievance; give us again the Citizen Soldiery — give us a National Militia'.[110] Davis created the '82 Club not only to commemorate the achievements of the Volunteers in 1782, but to restore a citizen militia to nineteenth-century Ireland. Convinced that 'without popular arms, popular liberty' was always unsafe, Davis hoped his new Club would lay the foundations for Irish liberty. The organization, he believed, would help to restore 'the edifice of freedom so ruthlessly and foully overturned in 1800'.[111]

Young Ireland was convinced, therefore, that the practice of martial virtue was a central component of freedom. 'Be it for defence, or be it for the assertion of a nation's liberty', Meagher declared, 'I look upon the sword as a sacred weapon'.[112] War, for Davis, had moral value. His article entitled 'The Morality of War' outlined the different ways in which martial conflict served as an enabling context for the virtues:

> Unjust war is, like all other unjust things, very wicked and condemnable. But a just war is as noble to him who has justice on his side as any other just act — nay, it is more noble; for there is more of self-restraint, more contempt of bodily suffering, more of high impulse, more of greatness achieved for its own great sake — more, in short, of heroism, in war than in almost any other human occupation.[113]

[cultivated] an independence and republicanism of spirit' and succeeded in 'uniting the characters of Citizen and Solider, cementing them together in one common and consistent appellation'; and also in his *Letters of Orellana*, 26–27: 'The military ardour which this institution inspired advanced the civilization of Ireland more in five years than in half a century before, and that merely by connecting the public interest with a kind of personal ambition.' (Quoted in Curtin, *The United Irishmen*, 31.) Davis idealized the Volunteers. See, for instance, his poem, 'Song of the Volunteers of 1782' in *Nation*, 13 May 1843.

109 *Nation*, 4 January 1845.
110 *Nation*, 14 December 1844.
111 *Nation*, 19 April 1845.
112 *Nation*, 1 August 1846. For the context to this remark see John M. Hearne, 'Thomas Meagher: Reluctant Revolutionary', in John M. Hearne and Rory T. Cornish, eds., *Thomas Francis Meagher: The Making of an Irish American* (Dublin, 2006), 67–91.
113 *Nation*, 10 June 1843.

In bellicose poetry and prose, Young Ireland provided a necessarily selective celebration of Ireland's history of martial valour. Davis's 'Battle-Eve of the Brigade', 'Clare's Dragoons', 'Fontenoy' and 'Oh! For a Steed', are four of his more better-known paeans to the warrior virtues.[114] Duffy's notorious 'Muster of the North' was also a fierce poetic commemoration of bloodshed.[115] By far the most pugilistic member of the Young Ireland group was Mitchel. The object of a political community in Mitchel's eyes was not, it appears, to secure peaceful co-existence for its members, but to embody human excellence through the pursuit of virtue. War, for Mitchel, was a forum for the virtues and allowed human beings to realize their highest ends. 'Peace', he declared in America in 1854, 'is often ignoble, corrupt and ignominious. Not peace but war has called forth the grandest, finest, tenderest, most generous qualities of manhood and womanhood'.[116] While figures like Davis glorified the securing of legislative independence in 1782, Mitchel regretted that this victory had not involved bloodshed: 'If Ireland in 82, instead of winning her independence from the coward by the mere flash of unbloody swords, had like America, waded through carnage to her freedom, like America, she had been free this day.' Predictably, Mitchel celebrated the revolutions in 1848 and hoped they would restore virtue to an emasculated and indolent modernity. The year 1848 failed to live up to his hopes, but he continued to believe in the redemptive power of martial struggle. 'Give us war in our time, O Lord!' he famously prayed.[117]

When Young Ireland quarrelled with O'Connell over the relative merits of 'moral' and 'physical' force, the issue was as much a question of ideology as it was of strategy. The group had difficulties in submitting to O'Connell's repudiation of violence, because it seemed to undermine a key constituent of republican citizenship. Initially, however, the group applauded O'Connell's methods.[118] This support may have been a purely contingent policy, but the group's simultaneous endorsement of martial virtue in principle and pacifism in practice led to frequent obfuscation, special pleading and baroque qualification. It culminated in a pusillanimous rhetoric that was extravagantly at odds with the moderate policies the group in fact espoused. Meagher may have declared

---

114 Davis, *Poems*, 147–48, 142–46, 149–53, 11–13. 'A soldier's life's the life for me / A soldier's death, so Ireland's free', he also announced in 'Song of the Irish Militia' (21). In 'A Rally for Ireland – June, 1689' he reiterated his conviction that political freedom presupposes the right to bear arms: 'Laws are in vain, unless swords maintain', *Nation*, 17 June 1843. Only by exercising such a right, he asserted in 'Song for the Volunteers', had his predecessors managed to secure Irish constitutional liberties: 'How vain were words till flashed the swords of the Irish Volunteers', *Nation*, 13 May 1843.

115 *Nation*, 18 November 1843.

116 *Citizen*, 15 July 1854. Dillon spoke for many of the Young Irelanders when he declared that peace was not the ultimate end of politics. Drawing on Tacitus, he announced: 'We value peace much, but we value freedom more — we have no sympathy with those who would "made [sic] a desert and call it peace".' O'Cathaoir, *John Blake Dillon*, 17.

117 Mitchel, *Jail Journal*, 315.

118 *Nation*, 14 October 1843: 'The man who dares to adopt any policy not sanctioned by O'Connell will deserve the deepest execration ...'

the sword a sacred weapon, but those wielded by Young Ireland were usually wooden.[119] Glorifications of war in the *Nation* succeeded hot denunciations of physical force. In an article on 'The Theory of Moral Force' in February 1844, the *Nation* dismissed political violence in robust terms: 'Can anything be more precarious', it asked, 'than the success of revolutions brought about by physical force?'[120] A week later the *Nation* criticized these views, which were, the paper claimed, the largely unrepresentative opinions of an 'occasional contributor'. The newspaper then provided a clarification of its attitude to political violence:

> We have always glorified, and shall ever worship, the brave, profuse of their blood in a good cause. We shall not deny the hero-creed of Greece to flatter the fat and sensual Quakerism of this age. There are worse things than to die or to kill. 'Tis better to slay a man than let him dishonor virtue, destroy the rights of property, crush liberty.[121]

The Young Irelanders eventually split with O'Connell over the question of physical force: the Emancipator's absolute rejection of violence was not simply imprudent; it was, in their eyes, potentially corrupt and undermined a vital component of citizenship.[122] Young Ireland's efforts to accommodate O'Connell's pacifism, on the other hand, had produced considerable bluster and self-contradiction.

These inconsistencies, however, had also an ideological origin and arose from a common nineteenth-century perception that the ethos of martial virtue was an anachronism in a commercial age. Commerce, Constant argued, led to a general softening of manners; it encouraged civilized interaction between peoples and 'placed the interest of societies beyond the frontiers of their own territory'.[123] In this context, the ideal of martial virtue had little value. 'We have finally reached the age of

---

119 Young Ireland was often prepared to abandon swords altogether. See the poem 'We Want No Swords' in *Nation*, 15 October 1842. For a full-blooded endorsement of the sword, see M. J. Barry's poem on that theme in Charles Gavan Duffy, et al., *The Spirit of the Nation: Ballads and Songs by the Writers of "The Nation"* (Dublin, 1845), 170–71. According to Daniel Owen-Madden, Young Ireland's endorsement of violence was largely aesthetic and, therefore, reassuringly impotent on a political level: 'Its songs, its vehement effusions, its ballads, may disturb society and foment angry passions, but assuredly they can achieve nothing further than bestowing a literature on the popular passions of the Irish lower nation.' See Owen-Madden, *Ireland and Its Rulers since 1829*, 3. 245.

120 *Nation*, 24 February 1844.

121 *Nation*, 2 March 1844.

122 In November 1845, Mitchel published a notorious article in the *Nation* outlining tactics for ambushing troops. This was civic education in the old style. When O'Connell protested, Mitchel qualified his position and insisted that 'moral force' remained the best means of securing independence. Both Mitchel and Duffy, however, questioned the wisdom of an abstract rejection of all forms of violence, even if current circumstances made its use unpropitious and undesirable. O'Connell refused to tolerate any qualification and Young Ireland eventually split with him on this issue.

123 Constant, *Political Writings*, 54.

commerce', Constant declared, 'an age which must necessarily replace that of war'.[124] Many subsequent commentators subscribed to this view.[125] Wilhelm von Humboldt, for instance, admired martial virtue, but he was convinced the practice was in terminal decline: 'war seems to be one of the most favourable manifestations for the culture of human nature; and I confess, it is not without regret that I see it disappearing more and more from the scene'.[126] Even the *Nation* entertained this belief. 'Physical force', one commentator declared, 'is now but a boyish dream of the past'.[127] Elsewhere the *Nation* conceded that 'fighting has become as manifestly impossible as flying in the air'.[128] According to one commentator, the use of physical force was a symptom of barbarism: 'That there exists in social man lingering traces of the savage state is proved by nothing more completely than by his alacrity for fighting.'[129] Such savagery, the article maintained, must be put aside in politics and moral force must be adopted in its stead. This may have been a short-term and half-hearted rationalization of policies advocated by O'Connell; as a sociological description and prognosis, it was also wildly mistaken. But this did not necessarily mean that the ethos of the citizen soldier or the political values remained possible in a modern age.

Of particular significance here was the perceived impact of commercial processes such as the division of labour on modern political mores. Here the Scottish Enlightenment constitutes a key context for understanding Young Ireland's political predicament. Adam Smith had provided one of the most penetrating analyses of the tensions between modern commercial practices and classical republican mores in the *Wealth of Nations* (1776). Here he had related increases in production to the division of labour and specification of function in modern societies.[130] Smith regarded the division of labour as an intrinsically civilizing process, but he also recognized the political and moral costs of this development. In Book V of the *Wealth of Nations*, he adopted the vocabularies of a civic republican tradition — which the success of his own political economy would help to marginalize — to decry the corrosion of virtue under the division of labour. Excessive specialization, he maintained, led to 'the almost entire corruption and degeneracy of the great body of the people'.[131]

---

124 Constant, *Political Writings*, 53.

125 Auguste Comte, for instance, juxtaposed military with industrial societies and showed how the values of the latter must triumph. Auguste Comte, *The Positive Philosophy of Auguste Comte*, trans. Harriet Martineau, 2 vols. (London, 1853), 2. 173. On the topic of war, Buckle was convinced that 'this barbarous pursuit is, in the progress of society, steadily declining, must be evident, even to the most hasty reader of European history'. See Henry Thomas Buckle, *History of Civilization in England*, 3 vols. (London, 1869), 1. 90.

126 Wilhelm von Humboldt, *The Sphere and Duties of Government*, trans. Joseph Coulthard (London, 1854; repr. Bristol, 1996), 55.

127 *Nation*, 17 October 1846.

128 *Nation*, 18 July 1846.

129 *Nation*, 24 February 1844.

130 See Istvan Hont and Michael Ignatieff, 'Needs and Justice in the *Wealth of Nations*', in Istvan Hont and Michael Ignatieff, eds., *Wealth and Virtue: The Shaping of Political Economy in the Scottish Enlightenment* (Cambridge, 1983), 1–44.

131 Smith, *Wealth of Nations*, 2. 781.

Confined to the repeated performance of specific tasks, the labourer underwent a physical and intellectual atrophy: it rendered him, 'not only incapable of relishing or bearing a part in any rational conversation, but of conceiving any generous, noble, or tender sentiment'.[132] This destruction of the human character had worrying social costs.

Such concerns were not unique to Smith. Adam Ferguson had already condemned the destructive effects of specialization in his *Essay on the History of Civil Society* (1767). According to Ferguson, 'to separate the arts which form the citizen and the statesman, the arts of policy and war, is an attempt to dismember the human character, and to destroy those very arts we mean to improve'.[133] The division of labour removed the necessary conditions for the practice of virtue in such a way that 'society is made to consist of parts, of which none is animated with the spirit of society itself'. The decline of Athens, he maintained, began with the disastrous specialization of social function: 'the history of this people abundantly shewed, that men ceased to be citizens, even to be good poets and orators, in proportion as they came to be distinguished by the profession of these, and other separate crafts'.[134] Smith may have shared some of these concerns, but he was also convinced that the clock could not be wound back. Only in 'barbarous societies', he argued in Book V of the *Wealth of Nations*, could one hope to be a citizen soldier, producer, and politician at the same time.[135] The structural features of a commercial society — as well as the realities of modern warfare — precluded the republican ideal of a citizen soldier. A direct and immediate relationship between the citizen and the patria eluded the modern world.

This judgement seemed to unhinge a key constituent of Young Ireland's outlook on politics. Davis conceded that his attempts to revive the cult of the citizen soldier might be at odds with 'the scornful spirit of the age'.[136] But the difficulties had less to do with the cynicism of moderns, than with the basic features of their social organization. When Smith presented the division of labour as both the product and precondition of a civilized society, he seemed to underline a fundamental contradiction between the process of civilization and the values that had traditionally pertained to political life. Rousseau had already outlined this dichotomy in the starkest terms. 'The ancient politicians', he declared, 'forever spoke of morals and of virtue; ours speak only of commerce and of money'.[137] If there was a choice between ancient virtue and modern luxury, Rousseau was in no doubt where his commitments lay. Many figures, of course, attempted to transcend this apparent dichotomy by merging a republican ethos with the practices of

---

132 *Wealth of Nations*, 2. 782.
133 Adam Ferguson, *An Essay on the History of Civil Society*, ed. Fania Oz-Salzberger (Cambridge, 1996), 218.
134 *Essay on the History of Civil Society*, 207.
135 *Wealth of Nations*, 2. 689–708; 782–84.
136 *Nation*, 19 April 1845.
137 Rousseau, *Discourses and Other Writings*, 18.

a commercial society. An attempted synthesis of this kind is one of the distinguishing features of Irish patriotism in the eighteenth century.[138]

Grattan's republican defence of Irish freedoms, after all, was initially aimed at securing no more than free trade. If virtue implied the lived acknowledgement of the links between public and private freedoms, Drennan suggested that Irish patriots never lost sight of this connection, recognizing, as they did, that 'a free trade necessarily implies a free constitution'.[139] Young Ireland, in many ways, continued in this tradition. The group hoped to boost Irish trade and berated England for hampering its growth — 'the whole world is stirred up against the insolence and rapacity of the English oligarchy'. Young Ireland's autarkic ideals, however, veered towards protectionism instead of free trade. The group hoped to fuse the spirit of patriotism with economic well-being by encouraging Irish consumption of Irish products. 'Why', the Nation asked, 'does this spirit of self-preference, which animates and unites to this mutual honor and mutual profit the drowsy Germans in the North and the energetic Americans in the West, slumber in our country?'[140] The argument for Irish independence, according to the Nation, was not reducible to economic factors, but the journal insisted that there were 'substantial benefits to be derived from the protection to our trade, and the creation of a manufacture' by an Irish government.[141]

The viability of this economic strategy was open to question, but it also fell short of the group's initial ideal of a community unified in its pursuit of the good. The group had always maintained that the good was not a simple matter of economic advancement. As the Nation put it, the 'conscience of Ireland is not in the purse, nor her soul in her gullet'.[142] Although pledged to increasing Ireland's economic well-being, Young Ireland repeatedly worried about the corrupting effects of commerce. Predictably, this corruption was identified with English social mores.[143] Here Young Ireland's defence of Irish virtue developed a strong primitivist dimension. 'Oh, no! oh, no!', Davis cried, 'ask us not to copy English vice, and darkness, and misery, and impiety; give us the worst wigwam in

138 Small, *Political Thought in Ireland, 1776–1798*, 102: 'One of the achievements of Irish patriot thought was to combine the most useful elements of classical imagery and language with an individualistic recognition that Patriotism must also be based on self-interest, property, and trade.'

139 Drennan, *Letter to Edmund Burke*, 21. However, Drennan also acknowledged 'a certain selfishness of spirit that usually clings to the spirit of commerce' and noted 'that rigid adherence to private interest which forms a part of the mercantile character' (19–20). In *Letter to the People of Ireland*, 5, Flood admitted that the habits of trade 'very much contract the political mind' even while advocating policies aimed at boosting Ireland's commercial fortunes.

140 *Nation*, 29 October 1842.

141 *Nation*, 23 September 1843.

142 *Nation*, 15 February 1845.

143 In England, 'gold is God'. *Nation*, 4 March 1848. The Englishman, Mitchel maintained, in *Jail Journal*, 89, 'worships only money, prays to no other god than money, would buy and sell the Holy Ghost for money, and believes that the world was created, is sustained, and governed, and will be saved by the only one true immutable Almighty Pound Stirling'.

Ireland and a dry potato rather than Anglicize us'.[144] In this context, Ireland's lack of economic development could present itself as a sign of its moral integrity and Spartan virtue. The reasons for this primitivist turn were not hard to fathom. Commercial societies were intrinsically disposed to perpetuate the vice of individualism.

'To the ancient Greek, or the Roman', Adam Ferguson declared, 'the individual was nothing, and the public every thing. To the modern, in too many nations of Europe, the individual is every thing, and the public nothing'.[145] Ferguson was convinced that we owed much to both fields of value and declared that public and private interests were viewed as opposites 'only by mistake'.[146] But it was difficult, nevertheless, to see how public and private interests could be brought into *direct* harmony in a concrete or lived sense in a commercial context. Smith had hoped to resolve the apparent contradiction between public and private values by outlining their indirect connection. Through the action of an 'invisible hand', the pursuit of purely selfish interests contributed to the public benefit.[147] This was not unproblematic even on its own terms — as Smith's attack on the selfish interests of merchants which play havoc with the economy indicated — but when Smith reoccupied the discourse of civic republicanism, public virtue and private interests re-emerged as seeming antinomies. Young Ireland, in turn, occasionally viewed the question of citizenship in strikingly polarized terms. 'We and others differ in theory from Mr. O'Connell', the *Nation* declared, 'as to the relative value of national liberty and individual life. We think scarcely any amount of the latter equivalent to the former. Mr. O'Connell thinks each priceless'.[148]

The Young Irelanders had not set out with this dualism in mind, but had tried to integrate public and private interests in an expansive patriotism. The group sponsored a wide range of measures, such as the institution of democracy, local government, decentralized administration, public education, and citizen soldiery as means of reintegrating individuals in the broader life of the community. Despite these policies, however, the group's incitements to civic activism could still seem forbiddingly abstract. Ironically, a movement that set out to defend both the priority and integrity of politics against the encroachments of political economy began to appear distinctly apolitical. The largely 'aesthetic' quality of Young Ireland's cult of the warrior was itself a testament to a distressing gap between the group's values and the practices of modern life. For this reason, it may be tempting to attribute a 'romantic' or strictly 'cultural' character to Young Ireland's doctrine. But this is at best a blunt evaluation and risks confusing a consequence with a cause. Young Ireland would bequeath to later generations the problem of integrating individual freedom with the collective good. Yeats grappled with

144 Davis, *Essays Literary and Historical*, 75.
145 *Essay on the History of Civil Society*, 57.
146 *Essay on the History of Civil Society*, 141.
147 Smith, *Wealth of Nations*, I. 456.
148 *Nation*, 27 June 1846. Cited in P. S. O'Hegarty, *A History of Ireland under the Union, 1801 to 1922* (London, 1952), 238.

this issue all his life, but his own reflections on the matter led him into an increasingly dissonant relationship with Young Ireland and its legacy.

Part II
Nationalism and Its Discontents: W. B. Yeats

3   Unity and Diversity

1 Unity of Being and Modern Fragmentation

For much of his career, Yeats was inspired by an ideal of communal life that he associated with the ancients. 'I always rouse myself to work', he wrote in 1909, 'by imagining an Ireland as much a unity in thought and feeling as ancient Greece and Rome and Egypt'.[1] These societies had derived their sense of integration from their shared pursuit of cultural excellence and he hoped that modern Ireland would pursue a similar vocation. For this reason, he initially celebrated Young Ireland's vision of a nation; it had restored a moral substance to politics and emphasized the public significance of culture. The group made a shared interpretation of the good life possible by producing a practical forum for public discussion. No national life was viable, in Yeats's eyes, without an ethical structure reflected and sustained by potent symbols:

> You cannot keep the idea of a nation alive where there are no national institutions to reverence, no national success to admire, without a model of it in the mind of the people. You can call it 'Kathleen-ni-Houlihan' or the 'Shan Van Vocht' in a mood of simple feeling, and love that image, but for the general purposes of life you must have a complex mass of images, making up a model like an architect's model. The Young Ireland poets created this with certain images …[2]

Young Ireland had produced a model of the good life for the nation; Yeats hoped to produce a more sophisticated one. His aim was to create a 'Holy City in the imagination,

1   M, 251.
2   M, 183–84.

a Holy Sepulchre as it were, or Holy Grail of the Irish mind'.[3] This would provide Ireland with standards of excellence that would also serve as its conditions of unity. The aim of this chapter is to explore the attractions and difficulties of this ideal.

Recalling Virgil's description of the Romans, Yeats asked in the 1930s: 'What idea of the state, what substitute for that of the toga'd race that ruled the world, will serve our immediate purpose here in Ireland?'[4] Arnold had raised a similar question in the 1860s and his self-consciously Hellenic view of the state's ethical vocation had a decisive influence on the young Yeats.[5] Admittedly, the irredentist strain in Yeats's nationalism made it difficult for him to share Arnold's confidence in the virtue of the state as such, but both believed that communities had a moral vocation.[6] The purpose of a political association, for Arnold, was not merely to satisfy the private interests of its constituents, but to embody an 'ideal of reason and right feeling'.[7] This conviction provided the basis for a positive and demanding conception of collective freedom. 'Nations', he maintained, 'are not truly great solely because the individuals composing them are numerous, free, and active; but they are great when these numbers, this freedom, and this activity are employed in the service of an ideal higher than that of an ordinary man, taken by himself'.[8] Culture was one name for this ideal and for the virtues developed in its pursuit. Yeats shared the same belief. Moreover, the object of culture was to expound, as he put it, 'the ideal hope not of individual life, but of the race, its vision of itself made perfect'.[9] Cultural endeavour was not a question of purely subjective expression or private entertainment; it had a public character and a cognitive substance; 'a right understanding of life and of destiny is more important than amusement'.[10] The role of a nation was to foster this understanding among its members.

Both Yeats and Arnold had hoped that culture would serve as a unifying principle for modern nations, but it was also undermined by the sociological views to which both

3   M, 184. As soon as he outlined this ideal in 1909, he doubted it as a possibility for modern Ireland.
4   E, 377.
5   For a discussion of Arnold's more general impact on Yeats's art, see Ronald Schuchard, 'Yeats, Arnold, and the Morbidity of Modernism', *Yeats: An Annual of Critical and Textual Studies*, 3 (1985), 88–106. See also George Watson, 'Yeats, Victorianism, and the 1890s', in Marjorie Howes and John Kelly, eds., *The Cambridge Companion to W. B. Yeats* (Cambridge, 2006), 36–58, 40–45.
6   Arnold, according to one critic, had 'a strong, almost Roman, sense of the state but little sense of the people'. See Stefan Collini's Introduction to Arnold, *Culture and Anarchy and Other Writings*, ix–xxvi, xxv. The early Yeats, on the other hand, often condemned the state and idealized the people. He admired Shakespeare, 'who cared little for the State', and he later condemned Edmund Spenser as 'the first poet who gave his heart to the State'; see EI, 106, 373. Later, however, he drew on Coleridge to insist that the state had a spiritual vocation, as in E, 335: a 'State must be made like a Chartres Cathedral for the glory of God and the soul. It exists for the sake of the virtues and must pay their price'. But elsewhere he insisted that the state should have no moral *telos*: 'I am not sure that I like the idea of a State with a definite purpose.' See UP 2. 448.
7   Arnold, *Culture and Anarchy*, 15.
8   *Culture and Anarchy*, 14.
9   UP 2. 200.
10   UP 2. 199.

subscribed. Arnold idealized the cultural life of Elizabethan England, when English culture had not yet divorced itself from the mainstream European tradition. Yeats too believed that 'Europe shared one mind and heart, until both mind and heart began to break into fragments a little before Shakespeare's birth'.[11] This fragmentation had complex origins that extended back to the religious quarrels of the Reformation, but Arnold believed it was exacerbated by the modern forces of 'industrialism and individualism'.[12] He did not specify how exactly these two forces were related, but he was certain that they would ultimately lead to 'anarchy and social disintegration'.[13] Yeats also worried about the anarchic tendency of modern times. He was convinced that the 'resolution to stand alone, to owe nothing to the past, when it is not mere sense of property, the greed and pride of the counting-house, is the result of that individualism of the Renaissance which had done its work when it gave us personal freedom'.[14] An increasingly exorbitant emphasis on an ill-considered version of liberty ultimately culminated in 'individualistic anarchy'.[15]

Yeats struck many poses in this broken world. Early in his career, he craved the kind of social integration that preceded the Renaissance:

> If Chaucer's personages had disengaged themselves from Chaucer's crowd, forgot their common goal and shrine, and after sundry magnifications became each in turn the centre of some Elizabethan play, and had after split into their elements and so given birth to romantic poetry, must I reverse the cinematograph?

Here the poet insisted that ethical communities had a teleological structure; the solidarity they historically enjoyed was not the affective outcome of spontaneous interaction or the possession of a common domicile, but of the pursuit of a 'common goal'. Social life, for Yeats, was a kind of shared pilgrimage. He also believed that Chaucer's journey might be resumed, that a 'nation or an individual with great emotional intensity might follow the pilgrims, as it were, to some unknown shrine, and give to all those separated elements … a symbolical, a mythological coherence'.[16] The ambiguity of Yeats's prose reflected the difficulty of the task: a 'mythological coherence' acknowledged the unifying power of myth, but it also suggested that this ideal of unity was potentially a mere illusion.

The attempt to foster social coherence through the stipulation of a common purpose or shared good was for many of Yeats's contemporaries a dangerously misguided

---

11 A, 191. Also see EI, 110: 'Shakespeare wrote at a time when solitary great men were gathering to themselves the fire that had once flowed hither and thither among all men, when individualism in work and thought and emotion was breaking up the old rhythms of life, when the common people, sustained no longer by the myths of Christianity and of still older faiths, were sinking into the earth.'

12 Arnold, *Culture and Anarchy*, 88.

13 *Culture and Anarchy*, 89.

14 EI, 353.

15 A, 556. This conclusion was partly responsible for his desire to curb individual freedom. In 1924, he recommended 'not the widening of liberty, but recovery from its errors'. *Irish Independent*, 4 August 1924.

16 A, 193.

enterprise. For Weber, for instance, life was a question of rival values and there was no transcendental access to some ultimate end. From the perspective of human immanence, life was inescapably polytheistic. Human beings were always faced with the following question: 'Which of the warring gods should we serve?'[17] Weber found no answer to this question; Yeats wrestled with its implications all his life. As he searched for 'Unity of Being' he repeatedly encountered the problem of competing goods.[18] This bore sharply on his own sense of his vocation as an artist, for within the chaotic polytheism of the modern world, art and politics appeared as rival gods.

Yeats sometimes maintained that art should remain distinct from politics — 'that even patriotism is more than an impure desire in an artist'.[19] To conflate them both, he suggested, was to undermine the integrity of each.[20] He criticized the Young Irelanders for their insensitivity to this fact and distinguished between 'our new movement, who judged literature by literary standards, and a number of people, a few of whom were writers, who judged it by its patriotism and by its political effect'.[21] But he also recognized that an overzealous defence of the purity of art deprived it of its social significance; in this respect, he remained haunted by the achievements of Young Ireland:

> The alliance of politics and literature that marked the ''48 movement' resulted in so great a popularity for the poets and prose writers who taught the doctrine of nationality that we are accustomed ever since to think of those years as our one period of literary activity. The writers who came after, lacking the great wind of politics to fill their sails, have lived and wrought almost forgotten of the nation.[22]

Early in his career, Yeats was passionately committed to resuscitating art as a public force and this, he sometimes suggested, demanded a restoration of its political character. He yearned in his youth for a lost era in Ireland when art seemed to possess a quasi-miraculous political force, when a simple 'satire could fill a whole country-side with famine'.[23] In *The King's Threshold*, for instance, he exemplifies this position in the figure of

17 Weber, *From Max Weber: Essays in Sociology*, 153.
18 A, 190: 'I thought that in man and race alike there is something called "Unity of Being", using that term as Dante used it when he compared beauty in the *Convito* to a perfectly proportioned human body'. In 1919, he attempted to 'begin another epoch by recommending to the Nation a new doctrine of unity of being'; see E, 280.
19 EI, 4.
20 In a letter to *United Ireland* in 1893, he adopted a more qualified position: 'I did not say the man of letters should keep out of politics ... but only that he should, no matter how strong be his political interests, endeavour to become a master of his craft, and be ever careful to keep rhetoric, or the tendency to think of his audience rather than of the Perfect and the True, out of his writing.' UP 1. 307.
21 W. B. Yeats, *Prefaces and Introductions*, ed. William H. O'Donnell (Houndmills, Basingstoke, and London, 1988), 223. Hereafter cited as PI.
22 UP 1. 215–16.
23 UP 1. 164.

the poet Seanachan who protests against his exclusion from political decision-making in the court by going on hunger strike.

But Yeats seemed increasingly to recognize that his holistic understanding of culture strained against some of the structural features of modern social organization. He was obsessed with the social ramifications of the specification of labour and of function in the modern world and was convinced that the reign of 'the specialists' presupposed the death of culture.[24] Authentic art, on the other hand, thrived in largely unspecialized settings:

> All great poets — Dante not less that Homer and Shakespeare — speak to us of the hopes and destinies of mankind in their fullness; because they have wrought their poetry out of the dreams that were dreamed before men became so crowded upon one another, and so buried in their individual destinies and trades, that every man grew limited and fragmentary.[25]

The division of labour destroyed 'Unity of Being' and eroded the conditions for the production of great art. Horrified by the way civilization seemed to replicate itself 'by division like certain low forms of life', he claimed that the modern world had deprived itself of a holistic understanding of being.[26] He derided the abstract nature of modern civilization, 'meaning by abstraction not the distinction but the isolation of occupation, or class of faculty'.[27] This atomizing process destroyed social cohesion. 'A conviction that the world was now but a bundle of fragments', he admitted in *Autobiographies*, 'possessed me without ceasing'.[28]

His criticisms of specialization owed something to the influence of William Morris.[29] Like Morris and Marx before him, Yeats believed that specialization destroyed human character.[30] Through the division of labour, individuals 'live in a portion of themselves, become professional and abstract'. 'The specialist's job', he insisted, 'is anybody's job, seeing that for the most part he is made, not born'.[31] Yeats wanted to restore a unified character to human beings and to resurrect, 'the normal, passionate, reasoning self, the

---

24 E, 432.
25 UP 2. 124.
26 A, 194.
27 A, 190.
28 A, 189.
29 Reflecting on his youth, Yeats admitted to 'having turned Socialist because of Morris's lectures and pamphlets'. He required no 'original thought to discover, being so late of the school of Morris, that machinery had not separated from handicraft wholly for the world's good, nor to notice that the distinction of classes had become their isolation'. See A, 146, 192; Peter Faulkner, *William Morris and W. B. Yeats* (Dublin, 1962).
30 Marx had argued that the division of labour estranged individuals from themselves; here 'each man has a particular, exclusive sphere of activity, which is forced upon him and from which he cannot escape'. Karl Marx and Friedrich Engels, *The German Ideology*, ed. and trans. S. Ryanskaya (Moscow, 1964), 44. William Morris, *Collected Works. Volume 23: Signs of Change, Lectures on Socialism* (London, 1915), 277.
31 E, 433.

personality as a whole'.[32] He set himself a task — for which he was not, perhaps, naturally well equipped — of becoming 'that forgotten thing, the normal active man'.[33] He admired this ideal in others and championed, for instance, Robert Gregory's integrated personality. 'Soldier, scholar, horseman, he', Gregory had magnificently transcended the overspecialized character of his times.[34] Yeats craved this personal wholeness, but his father dismissed it as an impossible dream: 'You are haunted by the Goethe idea, interpreted by Dowden, that a man can be a complete man. It is a chimera — a man can only be a specialist'.[35] This rebuked the poet's plans for his own development, but it also challenged his vision of a unified culture in Ireland.

Yeats may have lamented the modern 'fall into division', but not everyone shared his conviction that the division of labour destroyed social unity.[36] Several advanced the argument that the specification of labour and function produced new forms of connection, even as it displaced older forms of solidarity. The specialized nature of modern life, according to Emile Durkheim, meant that each individual depended on the activities and competence of others for the satisfaction of their most basic needs. This network of dependency produced what he provocatively called 'organic solidarity' — a structure of feeling that established a sense of connection while preserving difference.[37] Yeats also hoped to square the circle by establishing unity in difference, but he remained pledged to a form of social cohesion that Durkheim termed 'mechanical solidarity' or 'solidarity by similarities'.[38] This was a traditional social bond based around shared beliefs or a collective consciousness. Yeats was often inclined to think of social experience in terms of a collective mind; he regarded it as axiomatic for his work that 'many minds can flow into one another, as it were, and create or reveal a single mind, a single energy'.[39] He also believed that some minimal consensus about values was a prerequisite for national well-being. 'You can only create a model of a race which will inspire the action of the race as a whole,' he insisted, 'if you share with it some simple moral understanding of life.'[40]

32 EI, 272.

33 A, 492.

34 'In Memory of Major Robert Gregory', VP, 323–28, 327.

35 J. B. Yeats, Letters to His Son W. B. Yeats and Others 1869–1922, ed. with a Memoir by Joseph Hone (London, 1944), 97. Dowden's Goethe searched for unity, but this did not preclude a sense of focus; it demanded 'that we should give unity to our lives by devoting them with hearty enthusiasm to some pursuit, and that the pursuit is assigned to us by Nature through the capacities she has given us'. Edward Dowden, New Studies in Literature (London, 1895), 144.

36 A, 502.

37 Emile Durkheim, The Division of Labour in Society, trans. H. D. Halls (Houndmills, Basingstoke and London, 1984), 68–175.

38 See Durkheim, Division of Labour in Society, 31–67. Much of A Vision is taken up with the question of establishing unity through diversity; Yeats criticizes an 'abstract synthesis' which negates difference and sponsors instead a unity that can accommodate particularity. See V, 161.

39 EI, 28.

40 M, 184. Even Durkheim ultimately acknowledged the necessity of 'mechanical solidarity' in all stages of society and he based his later search for a civic religion on this.

Without the guidance of a common framework or shared tradition, he maintained, 'we are broken off and separate, some sort of dry faggot'.[41]

Yeats hoped that art would produce this common framework. Figures before him had claimed that art could overcome the painful ruptures of an overspecialized world, but they often tended to overlook the possibility that art might become subject to the very forces of division it was supposed to redress.[42] Yeats remained both fascinated and appalled by the specialized nature of modern artistic practice.[43] His schoolfriend and intellectual colleague, John Eglinton, always maintained that Yeats was committed to a highly esoteric form of artistic practice: 'The notion of "schools" of poets, abhorrent to most poets, is congenial to him and indeed, if he could have his way, I think he would make of the whole profession of literature one vast secret order.'[44] This captured something of Yeats's fascination for arcane knowledge and for the intimacy and exclusivity of clubs. But it also ignored his repeated criticisms of the esotericism to which he was simultaneously disposed. He recognized that an overspecialized art became a rarefied form of communication between experts. He insisted, therefore, that 'it is needful that the populace and the poets shall have one heart — that there shall be no literary class with its own way of seeing things and its own conventions'.[45] This desire for integration even led him to attempt the healing of division within the arts, by investing in '"the applied arts of literature", the association of literature, that is, with music, speech and dance'. Through such a fusion he hoped to effect an even greater synthesis that would transcend or incorporate all specialized fields of endeavour so that 'all, artist and poet, craftsman and day-labourer would accept a common design'.[46] The problem with Yeats's project of unification, however, was that it seemed to run counter to some of the basic mechanics of modern social development. His pursuit of 'unity of culture' in Ireland developed, therefore, a self-consciously primitivist dimension.[47] Marx entertained the improbable hope that the division of labour would be

---

41 EI, ix.

42 Schiller had advanced one of the most powerful accounts of the unifying role of art in an overspecialized society. See Friedrich Schiller, *On the Aesthetic Education of Man in a Series of Letters*, ed. and trans. Elizabeth M. Wilkinson and L. A. Willoughby (Oxford, 1967).

43 This reflects, perhaps, the influence of Morris. According to Morris, the 'division of labour, which has played so great a part in furthering competitive commerce, till it has become a machine with powers both reproductive and destructive, which few dare to resist, and none can control or foresee the result of, has pressed specially hard on that part of the field of human culture in which I was born to labour. That field of the arts, whose harvest should be the chief part of human joy, hope, and consolation, has been, I say, dealt hardly with by the division of labour ...' William Morris, *Collected Works. Volume 22: Hopes and Fears for Art, Lectures on Art and Industry* (London, 1914), 82.

44 John Eglinton [pseud. for William Magee], *Irish Literary Portraits* (London, 1935), 24.

45 UP 1. 147.

46 A, 194.

47 For a good account of the influence of comparative science on Yeats's primitivism, see Sinéad Garrigan, *Primitivism, Science, and the Irish Revival* (Oxford, 2004). See also Gregory Castle, *Modernism and the Celtic Revival* (Cambridge, 2001).

abolished in a society of the future; Yeats dreamed that the answer to the problem would be derived from the communities of the past.[48]

2 Primitive Simplicity and Modern Complexity

In his pursuit of wholeness, Yeats often presented Ireland as a glorious exception to general laws of social development and drew on modern sociological theories in his efforts to account for Ireland's anomalous character. Herbert Spencer, one of the most renowned social scientists of the nineteenth century, played a significant role in this aspect of Yeats's thought. According to Eglinton, the young Yeats surprised his schoolfellows by declaring himself an 'evolutionist' and proclaimed that 'no-one could write an essay now except Herbert Spencer and Matthew Arnold'.[49] Eglinton, himself a keen evolutionist, niggled Yeats with his earlier Spencerian pronouncements, presumably conscious of the fact that Spencer seemed to stand for everything Yeats abhorred: Spencer's evolutionary science seemed totally opposed to Yeats's glorification of the imagination and contempt for scientific method; Spencer's shrill advocacy of 'individualism' in politics appeared at odds with Yeats's more communitarian vision; Spencer's contempt for the barbaric past — at least on a political level — seemed to contradict Yeats's glorification of the old. But Eglinton failed to recognize, or deliberately ignored, the fact that Yeats drew on Spencerian categories only to reverse their normative thrust. In Spencer's eyes, 'the law of all progress' dictated a move from simplicity to complexity, 'from the homogeneous to the heterogeneous'.[50] Yeats subscribed to a similar law and outlined on several occasions how societies resembled biological organisms in their movement from simple and homogenous states to ever more complex forms of organization.[51] Ireland, he suggested, however, remained an exception to this general rule of development.

He explicitly invoked Spencer in 1886 to sanction the 'barbarous truth' of Samuel Ferguson's poetry. These poems, he claimed, were told 'with such simplicity and sincerity that we seem to be no longer in this modern decade, but listening to some simple and

---

48 In *German Ideology*, 45, Marx declared that 'in communist society, where nobody has one exclusive sphere of activity but each can become accomplished in any branch he wishes, society regulates the general production and thus makes it possible for me to do one thing today and another tomorrow, to hunt in the morning, fish in the afternoon, rear cattle in the evening, criticise after dinner, just as I have a mind, without ever becoming hunter, fisherman, shepherd or critic'.

49 Quoted in Foster, *Apprentice Mage*, 32. Charles Johnston also remembered Yeats's interest in evolution. As he recalled, 'many a delightful afternoon we spent roaming over the Dublin hills, or the cliffs of Howth, Yeats holding forth on evolutionary botany, while I listened, commented, and at the end of ends, declared myself still unconvinced'. 'He had just discovered Darwinism', Johnston noted, 'and was brimful of the Descent of Man'. W. B. Yeats, *Interviews and Recollections*, 2 vols., ed. E. H. Mikhail (London and Basingstoke, 1977), 1. 13, 7. Hereafter cited as IR 1 and IR 2.

50 Herbert Spencer, *Essays: Scientific, Political, and Speculative*, 2 vols. (London and Edinburgh, 1883), 1. 3.

51 In a public lecture in 1893, for instance, Yeats outlined a general law of development, which moved from relative homogeneity to increasing heterogeneity. See 'Nationality and Literature', in UP 1. 266–75.

savage old chief telling his companions round a forest fire, of something his own eyes have seen'.[52] This celebration of 'simplicity' — a recurrent term of praise in Yeats's early work — drew upon Spencer's sociology, while inverting its values. 'In complexity', Spencer had argued, 'our large civilized nations as much exceed primitive savage tribes, as a vertebrate animal does a zoophyte'.[53] Yeats, on the other hand, despised 'all that sterile modern complication' and glorified a savage simplicity lost to 'us moderns with our complex life'.[54] He was convinced that the task of 'all culture is certainly a labour to bring again the simplicity of the first ages'.[55] Yeats deplored the corrupting effects of the differentiation of function, but Spencer celebrated its civilizing effects. Indeed, the laws of political economy possessed ontological significance for Spencer. He used the laws of biological science to describe the social organism, but he also inverted this method and presented social norms as natural principles. Spencer's account of the 'physiological division of labour' was a stark example of a process in which contingent human practices were converted into general biological laws.[56] To violate these norms was to transgress the immutable laws of nature.

Yeats insisted, however, that modern life was overspecialized: 'Man is like a musical instrument of many strings, of which only a few are sounded by the narrow interests of his daily life; and the others, for want of use, are continually becoming tuneless and forgotten.' He contrasted modern dissonance with the harmony enjoyed by primitive man. He insisted that the residue of primitive art still survived in Ireland and could redeem individuals from their alienated condition. 'Heroic poetry', Yeats explained, 'is a phantom finger swept over all the strings, arousing from man's whole nature a song of answering harmony. It is the poetry of action, for such alone can arouse the whole nature of man'.[57] Heroic art or 'the poetry of action' even seemed to bridge the divide between thought and deed — the most rudimentary separation, according to Marx, from which all subsequent division of labour followed.[58] Primitive art involved no 'narrow specialism'.[59] An absence of differentiation characterized even the style of primitive poetry; its 'beauty lies in great masses — thought woven with thought — each line the sustainer of his fellow'. Because of this perfect integration, no line of his poetry could be removed from its context and objectified: 'Take a beauty from that which surrounds it

---

52 UP 1. 90–91.
53 Spencer, *Essays: Scientific, Political, and Speculative*, 1. 397.
54 A, 152; UP 1. 84.
55 EI, 167.
56 For Spencer, 'the analogy between the economical division of labour and the "physiological division of labour" is so striking, as long since to have drawn the attention of scientific naturalists'. See *Essays: Scientific, Political, and Speculative*, 1. 408.
57 UP 1. 84.
58 Marx, *German Ideology*, 43: 'Division of labour only becomes truly such from the moment when a division of material and mental labour appears ...'
59 UP 1. 291.

— its colour is faded, its plumage is ruffled — it is dead.'[60] Ferguson's art distinguished itself from modern poetry, which is written by experts for experts:

> Almost all the poetry of this age is written by students, for students. But Ferguson's is truly bardic, appealing to all natures alike, to the great concourse of the people, for it has gone deeper than knowledge or fancy, deeper than the intelligence which knows of difference — of the good and the evil, of the foolish and the wise, of this one and of that — to the universal emotions that have not heard of aristocracies, down to where Brahman and Sudra are not even names.[61]

By reflecting on this gloriously undifferentiated world, Yeats was convinced that one could win immunity 'from that leprosy of the modern — tepid emotions and many aims. Many aims, when the greatest of the earth often owned but two — two linked and arduous thoughts — fatherland and song'.[62] The good was simple and multiplicity, it seemed, was error. By negating the plural character of the modern era, Yeats managed to retain his faith in a tradition of patriotism bequeathed to him by Young Ireland. Here the pursuit of a shared good remained viable, because the good retained its unified character; it was reducible to two interconnected principles: poetry and patriotism.

Not all of Yeats's contemporaries, however, believed that this tradition of patriotism had a future in Ireland. Eglinton, for instance, dismissed patriotism as a destructive anachronism in the modern age. His method and argument had a strong Spencerian resonance; indeed, he explicitly endorsed 'evolutionary philosophy' for the way it vanquished all metaphysical speculation in a 'blaze of commonsense'.[63] According to Eglinton, the 'apparent loss of the patriotism which builds up a state is one of those irreparable natural facts, like death, or the mingling of a stream with the sea, against which our philosophy is tasked to discover what solace it may, or to what new factor the displacement of the old is due'.[64] Eglinton was fairly vague about this 'new factor' but he was convinced that the old patriotism had outlived its conditions of possibility. He derived this conclusion from an extended meditation on the impact of specialization on modern social mores. The differentiation of function was constitutive of modern civilization and a 'wise sociology' must look this fact in the face:

> In a highly civilized period wisdom, or the fully awakened human consciousness, is resolved like light through a prism into its constituents, so that in whatsoever place a man labours the full-blended beam does not light his task, but this one sees

---

60 UP 1. 92.
61 UP 1. 101.
62 UP 1. 104. For an account of Yeats's conception of the primitive past as conflict rather than unity, see Garrigan, *Primitivism, Science, and the Irish Revival*, 57–58.
63 John Eglinton, *Pebbles from a Brook* (Dublin, 1901), 55.
64 *Pebbles from a Brook*, 67.

nothing but physical fact, another only metaphysical truth, another utilitarian, another aesthetic, and so forth, and it is hard to find a spot exempt from these variegated effects, or at last to trust one's eye-sight.[65]

This, in a sense, was Weber's 'warring gods' thesis presented in lacquered prose. Eglinton used this argument to criticize features of classical patriotism: shrill commitments to the common good overlooked the plural nature of modern values.

If patriotism was anachronistic, it was also coercive: its commitment to the moral and social coherence of the polity overruled the basic rights and diverse interests of individuals. Modern social development, in Eglinton's eyes, was bound up with the rise individual freedom. While Spencer tended to present the individual as both the origin and goal of the evolutionary process, Eglinton accepted that society was ontologically prior to the individual.[66] The nation, he suggested, was 'like an aged mother', bringing the individual into being and into communion with others.[67] Nevertheless, he regarded the consolidation of individual autonomy as the proper function or *telos* of all public and private institutions. 'When individuality is hatched', the state had served its proper end; indeed, the truly civilized state was one that recognized its own redundancy. 'When a state has grown to its full stature and become fully conscious of itself,' Eglinton suggested, 'individuals begin to fall away from it, because the individual aspiration is no longer incorporated with the social instinct but has emerged, and individualist experiments of all kinds become the outlet of the higher activities; not patriotism, wars and politics'.[68] The consequences for patriotism were clear. An immediate identity between public and private interests in the practice of civic virtue was no longer possible in a specialized society. 'Patriotism, in fact, in the old sense', Eglinton declared, 'is only possible when the whole life-interest of the individual is comprised within that of the patria'.[69] This form of solidarity was, he suggested, a characteristic of only the most primitive societies.

Either patriotism was dead or it must be reinvented to suit the needs of individuals who have transcended the confines of their respective states. Eglinton gestured vaguely to a future that seemed to combine elements of Spencer's fantasy of free-market anarchy and a notional world republic in which a shared respect for the freedom and equality of the individual operated as a kind of collective consciousness. It was hardly surprising that Yeats considered Eglinton to have turned from 'all National ideas'. In an article published in the United Irishman in November 1901, Yeats committed himself to a hot rebuttal of Eglinton's views. Eglinton's

---

65 *Pebbles from a Brook*, 37.
66 Eglinton seemed to resemble Durkheim more than Spencer in regarding the individual as a social construction rather than as something natural or primary. 'In fact, if in lower societies so little place is allowed for the individual personality,' Durkheim argued, 'it is not simply that it has been constricted or suppressed artificially, it is quite simply because at that moment in history it *did not exist*.' See Durkheim, *Division of Labour in Society*, 142 [Durkheim's emphasis].
67 *Pebbles from a Brook*, 72.
68 *Pebbles from a Brook*, 42.
69 *Pebbles from a Brook*, 73.

individualism, he suggested, was antithetical to Ireland's largely communitarian view of the world. Yeats spelt out the political implications of these differences:

> that which has made John Eglinton turn from all National ideas and see the hope of the world in individual freedom, in 'the individual grown wiser than his institutions', has made me a Nationalist and has made me see the hope of the world in re-arrangements of life and thought which make men feel that they are part of a social order, of a tradition, of a movement wiser than themselves.[70]

Eglinton's individualistic ethos was the expression of an ideology of commerce that had distinctly English origins. 'The truth is', Yeats declared, 'that John Eglinton is too preoccupied with English literature and civilisation to remember that the decadence he has described is merely the modern way, because it is the English way, because it is the commercial way'.[71] Here Yeats returned to his old belief that Ireland retained a primitive virtue which other countries had surrendered to the march of commerce.

3 Military Civilization in the Age of Commerce

Patriotism continued to thrive among the Irish, Yeats maintained, because 'Ireland cannot put from her the habit learned from her old military civilization'.[72] Here the poet again deployed the vocabularies of nineteenth-century sociology to account for Ireland's distinctive character. The basic juxtaposition of military and commercial cultures had its origins in the eighteenth century; versions of this schema appeared in a range of thinkers from Adam Ferguson, to Kant, to Constant to Saint-Simon to Comte. By the time Herbert Spencer enlisted the opposition, it had become a kind of sociological orthodoxy. Military civilization, according to Spencer, was a largely defunct and invariably despotic social system. In a reductive synthesis of established arguments, he argued that military societies were fixed hierarchical structures in which the interests of the individual were sacrificed to the practicalities of the community's defence. However virtuous, ancient societies, he suggested, lacked even a minimal concept of personal freedom. 'In ancient Greece', according to Spencer, 'the citizen belonged neither to himself nor to his family, but belonged to his city'.[73] Industrial society, on the other hand, distinguished itself from this rigid social structure through its relatively spontaneous form of social co-operation, which was largely achieved through the collective pursuit of private interests. Here individual liberty was deemed the supreme good. Anything that seemed to infringe upon this liberty — which included almost all kinds of state intervention — was either

---

70 UP 2. 257.
71 UP 2. 259.
72 A, 101.
73 Herbert Spencer, *Political Writings*, ed. John Offer (Cambridge, 1994), 103.

anachronistic or barbaric.[74] Indeed, Yeats may have based his conviction that ancient Ireland was 'above all things democratic and communistic' on Spencer's denunciation of such barbarism.[75]

Yeats was only briefly attracted to socialism, but the general communitarian values of his youth were wholly at odds with Spencer's uncompromising individualism. He lauded Young Ireland's attempt to combat the social atomism of the modern world by promoting a life of civic virtue and public friendship. But the group's patriotism could also seem anachronistic in a modern commercial setting: here, after all, rational self-interest appeared to have replaced the civic virtues and the *homo economicus* had superseded the *zoon politikon*. Even if one continued to glorify a patriotic commitment to the public, the specialized nature of modern life precluded opportunities for its proper exercise. In the light of nineteenth-century sociology, Young Ireland's patriotic ethos, organized around a cult of martial virtue, could seem like a dangerous return to the values of Spencer's military civilization. Yeats enthusiastically embraced this possibility, however, and was adamant that Ireland's military culture remained in operation; 'the trappings of the warrior ages', he insisted, 'has not passed away'.[76] The social cohesion of Ireland's military civilization produced a flourishing culture. 'Behind Ireland fierce and militant', he proclaimed, 'is Ireland poetic, passionate, remembering'.[77] By insisting that Ireland's military civilization was substantially intact, Yeats also attempted to suggest that Young Ireland's tradition of patriotism continued to flourish. In the eighteenth century Smith concluded that the 'heroic spirit is utterly extinguished'; but over a century later, Yeats was convinced that it remained alive and well in Ireland.[78] The Irish still enjoyed a 'world of selfless passion in which heroic deeds are possible and heroic poetry credible'.[79] He rejected the cliché that the practice of martial virtue was in irreversible decline in

---

74 Spencer believed that 'the liberty, which a citizen enjoys, is to be measured, not by the nature of the governmental machinery he lived under whether representative or other, but by the relative paucity of the restraints it imposes on him'. See *Political Writings*, 77. He regarded Gladstone's Irish land reforms as a deplorable violation of the rights of property and the individual liberties they sustained. This act of state-sponsored confiscation, he suggested, was akin to socialism and the latter was indistinguishable from barbarism in its sacrifice of the individual for collective well-being. According to Spencer and many of his liberal contemporaries, Ireland suffered from a Malthusian problem of overpopulation and underproduction. Its problems would be best solved by the institution of free trade, where the iron laws of political economy — which Spencer tended to present as the rationalization of natural law — would ensure that wealth was distributed to those most fitted for its use, while society was simultaneously cleansed of its unproductive elements. State intervention in the form of welfare for the poor merely short-circuited this evolutionary logic, ensuring, as he put it, the 'survival of the unfittest'. For a good account of Spencer's political thought see M. W. Taylor, *Men versus the State: Herbert Spencer and Late Victorian Individualism* (Oxford, 1992).

75 UP 1. 165.

76 UP 1. 165.

77 UP 1. 147.

78 Quoted in Hirschman, *The Passions and the Interests*, 101.

79 UP 1. 104.

the West; nor did he accept that the emasculated values of politeness had everywhere supplanted the warrior virtues of patriotism.[80]

Ireland maintained its military civilization and this was expressed in a virtuous hatred of its enemies. Yeats ultimately condemned Ireland's 'great hatred', but he initially applauded its unifying power. 'All movements', he insisted, 'are held together more by what they hate than by what they love'.[81] His defence of ancient enmities may be dismissed as no more than the romantic atavism of a misguided poet, but political theorists such as Carl Schmitt — a robust critic of the romantic outlook — also insisted that a basic friend–enemy distinction was a fundamental principle of political life.[82] By enlisting this stark dualism, Schmitt was attempting to reassert the priority of politics over the secondary values of civil society. He condemned ideologues of the age of commerce — particularly Constant and Spencer — for circulating a set of 'demilitarized and depoliticalized concepts' in a general bid to supplant politics with economics.[83] This was a form of political bad faith, as deluded as it was deluding, for the basic concept of the political, the unappeasable rift between friend and enemy, would always reintroduce itself in a sublimated form.[84] Yeats, of course, never provided a thesis so brutally systematic, but his high regard for the ethos of a 'military civilization' was also an attempt to promote the patriotic virtues over the milder values of 'industrial civilisation'. He exercised a patriotic contempt for le doux commerce and its seemingly attendant values of cosmopolitan tolerance, refinement and moderation. 'It is one of our illusions that education, the softening of manners, the perfection of law — countless images of a fading light — can create nobleness and beauty.'[85] He dreamed of 'enlarging Irish hate' until it rejected the values of a commercial age; 'were we not', he asked, 'a poor nation with ancient courage, unblackened fields and a barbarous gift of self sacrifice?'[86]

Yeats rejected the liberal conviction that the optimal goal of social life was peaceful co-existence. Indeed, in later life he applauded the virtues of violent conflict in ecstatic terms:

---

80 Constant was an influential proponent of this view; see Political Writings, 54; '... the spirit of the age triumphs over the narrow and hostile spirit that men seek to dignify with the name of patriotism'. Republicans had long predicted that the emasculated values of politeness would supplant the warrior virtues of patriotism. See Rousseau, Discourses, 8: 'National hatreds will die out, but so will the love of Fatherland.'

81 EI, 250. For a study of the theme of hatred in Yeats, see Joseph M. Hassett, Yeats and the Poetics of Hate (Dublin, 1986).

82 Carl Schmitt, The Concept of the Political, trans. George Schwab (Chicago and London, 1996), 67: 'Political thought and political instinct prove themselves theoretically and practically in the ability to distinguish friend and enemy.' Yeats championed hatred on a general level, but Schmitt believed that political enmity was different to private hatred. For Schmitt's critique of romanticism, see Carl Schmitt, Political Romanticism, trans. Guy Oakes (Cambridge, 1986). For a brief comparison of Yeats and Schmitt, see McCormack, Burke to Beckett, 366–71.

83 Schmitt, The Concept of the Political, 71.

84 According to Schmitt, The Concept of the Political, 79, 'this allegedly non-political and apparently even antipolitical system serves existing or newly emerging friend-and-enemy groupings and cannot escape the logic of the political'.

85 UP 2. 199.

86 UP 2. 211.

Dear predatory birds, prepare for war, prepare your children and all that you can reach, for how can a nation or a kindred without war become that 'bright particular star' of Shakespeare, that lit the roads in boyhood? Test art, morality, custom, thought, by Thermopylae; make rich and poor act so to one another that they can stand together there. Love war because of its horror, that belief may be changed, civilisation renewed. ... Belief is renewed continually in the ordeal of death.[87]

Just as Schmitt had deployed his friend–enemy distinction against the 'neutralizations and depoliticalizations' of liberalism, Yeats also declared that his vision of conflict was inimical to 'British liberalism and all its dreams'.[88] His hostility to 'damned liberalism' was emphatic in later life but it was also implicit in the attitudes of his 'savage youth'.[89] He rejected a Spencerian liberalism, at any rate, when he refused to regard the individual as either the origin or goal of social and moral life. He was also dismissive of liberal myths of progress.[90] 'When I was a boy,' Yeats reported, 'everybody talked about progress, and rebellion against my elders took the form of aversion to that myth. I took satisfaction in certain public disasters, felt a sort of ecstasy at the contemplation of ruin, and then I came upon the story of Oisin in Tir nà nOg [sic] and reshaped it into my *Wanderings of Oisin*.'[91] This heady mixture of *Schadenfreude* and revolt reflected a very Yeatsian paradox; it based a rejection of one's elders on the superior wisdom of one's forefathers.

The Wanderings of Oisin, as Yeats suggests, was a product of this rebellion and celebrated the virtues of an earlier age. The poem merits detailed discussion, for it not only celebrates the virtues of 'military civilisation', it demonstrates more emphatically than any of Yeats's other pronouncements in prose that these values cannot be restored to the modern world.[92] The poem is both a paean to a heroic civilization and a tragic *ubi sunt*. It celebrates the martial valour of the ancient Fianna, but it also acknowledges that these warriors have been supplanted by lesser creatures — a 'small and feeble populace stooping with mattock and spade'.[93] Yeats's derisive account of this community of labourers is part of a more general attempt to salvage a more primordial virtue against the secondary values of civilized society. Oisin, the famous

---

87 V, 52–53. He had proposed a more ambiguous policy in 1901, E, 83: 'We wish to grow peaceful crops, but we must dig our furrows with the sword.'

88 Schmitt, *The Concept of the Political*, 69; Sturge Moore, *W. B. Yeats and T. Sturge Moore: Their Correspondence, 1901–1937*, ed. Ursula Bridge (London, 1953), 154.

89 Frank O'Connor, 'The Old Age of a Poet', *Bell*, 1, 5 (1941), 7–18, 12; E, 451.

90 According to W. J. McCormack, 'Edmund Burke, Yeats and Leo Frobenius: "The State a Tree"?', in Seán Patrick Donlan, ed., *Edmund Burke's Irish Identities* (Dublin, 2007), 226–62, 243: 'Yeats's attitude to British liberalism needs little comment. His rejection of its moral earnestness, its complicity in empire, its consequent hypocrisy, and its groundless optimism can be verified through any of a dozen major texts in prose and poetry.'

91 E, 392.

92 In Harold Bloom's estimate, *The Wanderings of Oisin* was also 'Yeats's most underrated major poem', a judgement that probably still remains true. Harold Bloom, *Yeats* (New York, 1970), 87.

93 VP, 58.

Fenian *émigré*, is one of civilization's discontents. He repudiates the menial and craven practices of modern civilization and vows to 'dwell in the house of the Fenians, be they in flames or at feast'.[94] The primitivist dimension of these values is clear; and it is both identified and denounced by St. Patrick early in the poem:

> Boast not, nor mourn with drooping head
> Companions long accurst and dead,
> And hounds for centuries dust and air.[95]

Oisin's identification with the past is also a shrill rejection of the present. But the hero remains trapped in a world he despises. His plight reveals the difficulty involved in advocating values that have seemingly outlasted their contexts of use. In this regard, *The Wanderings of Oisin* is a strikingly patriotic poem, which simultaneously acknowledges the fraught nature of the patriotism it espouses. Even Oisin dissents from the patriotic values he ostensibly embodies. Superficially, the hero's stridently anti-Christian attitude reflects his firm commitment to the Fenian fatherland over the *Civitas Dei*. For almost two millennia in Europe, patriots had frequently regarded Christianity with suspicion and even derision.[96] It was a religion that encouraged a widespread disengagement from politics by elevating the eternal life over the temporal world; it emasculated citizens by privileging contemplative experience over the active life. Oisin duly denounces the 'lying clerics' of Christianity who lure us from a life of heroic virtue with 'barren words and flatteries of the weak'.[97] His allegiances, he maintains, lie with the 'mightier masters of a mightier race'. Christianity's cult of suffering and its ethics of the weak finds its pathetic object in 'a milk-pale face / Under a crown of thorns and dark with blood'.[98] But under Oisin's anti-Christian histrionics, there resides a less confident attitude and a more ambivalent patriotism.

This ambivalence issues from Oisin's fraught relationship to time. For classical patriots, the vagaries of *fortuna* necessitated a life of political activism. The cycle of a society moving from prosperity to decline could never be halted, perhaps, but the process could be delayed through public vigilance and civic virtue. Politics, therefore, attempted to provide continuity in a world of change, and searched for order within the temporal. This, however, did not amount to a flight from the temporal order as such, for such transcendence would remove the very source and ground of politics. But Yeats's early poetic career features a variety of imaginative attempts to escape time

---

94 *VP*, 63.
95 *VP*, 11.
96 Most famously, perhaps, Machiavelli's *Discourses on Livy*, 6, 131, subordinated religion to politics and denounced 'the weakness into which the present religion has led the world'.
97 *VP*, 42.
98 *VP*, 38.

altogether.[99] Oisin's journey to the Country of the Young, where he 'mocked at Time and Fate and Chance', is a particularly striking example of this bid for transcendence.[100] Christianity, as he suggests, may have devalued temporal experience in the name of an eternal realm, but Oisin is also an amphibious creature scuttling between dichotomous worlds. His wanderings through eternity lead to a depreciation of political virtue, to an empty re-enactment of martial glory abstracted from the time-bound contexts that gave it meaning. Here the mortal significance of battle is entirely repressed or forgotten: 'a century there I forgot / How the fetlocks drip blood in the battle, when the fallen on fallen lie rolled'.[101]

If Oisin's patriotism is compromised by his search for transcendence, it is also undermined by more worldly matters. He remains an ambiguous figure, appearing both as the embodiment of ancient virtue and as a particular example of the acquisitive *homme bourgeois*. He is bribed out of a life of heroic virtue. He abandons the rigours of military civilization for Niamh's promise of luxury, security and comfort:

> And there I will give you a hundred hounds;
> No mightier creatures bay at the moon;
> And a hundred robes of murmuring silk,
> And a hundred calves and a hundred sheep
> Whose long wool whiter than sea-froth flows,
> And a hundred spears and a hundred bows,
> And oil and wine, honey and milk,
> And always never-anxious sleep.[102]

But the price paid for this 'never-anxious sleep' is political lassitude. In the classical — and generally sexist — tradition of patriotism this lax condition was often associated with effeminacy. Woman, as the metonym for the private or domestic sphere, was used to characterize the prioritization of private interests over the public good.[103] Effeminacy was both the symptom and cause of the pursuit of idleness and comfort over strenuous citizenship and martial valour.[104] Moreover, to pursue luxury was to be a victim of dangerous passions; this form of incontinence was traditionally regarded as a female

---

99 He acknowledged the problem of contingency as precisely such in his aptly titled poem 'To the Rose upon the Rood of Time'. The poem entitled 'He mourns for the Change that has come upon Him and His Beloved, and longs for the End of the World' is also a repudiation of the temporal world in the name of the absolute. VP, 100–01, 153.

100 VP, 20.

101 VP, 52.

102 VP, 8.

103 Cf. G. W. F. Hegel, *Phenomenology of Spirit*, trans. A. V. Miller (Oxford, 1977), 288.

104 In 1888, Yeats spoke approvingly of those 'protests against that life of domestic ease and public indifference that most men wish for'. UP 1. 124.

failing. Judged in this context, Oisin seems to be both a subject and object of dangerously feminine passions. He is seduced away from the Fenian polity by the beautiful Niamh:

> And then I mounted and she bound me
> With her triumphing arms around me,
> And whispering to herself enwound me.[105]

Oisin is subjugated by Niamh's 'triumphing arms' — the obvious play on 'arms' bolsters the suggestion that the limbs of love are victorious over the tools of war. Love has supplanted martial valour and erotic idleness has replaced the muscular exercise of citizenship. When Oisin subsequently reasserts himself in martial conflict it is for largely private ends. He protects ladies from sea-monsters and concerns himself with chivalric niceties such as disposing of the monster's body 'Lest Niamh shudder'.[106] Violence is devoid of political significance, and the largely private interests of Romance have displaced more public or political concerns. Ultimately, Oisin becomes the citizen of a kind of inverted state, characterized by the complete reversal of the principles of active citizenship. This is the Island of Forgetfulness, inhabited by Yeats's community of sleepers. No martial valour here — the bodies of these sleepers are 'long warless' — but absolute idleness.[107] This is no longer heroic poetry. Yeats had defined such verse as 'the poetry of action', but what we discover here is the poetry of supreme indolence. Yeats's Island of Forgetfulness is an anti-political polity; its social bond is predicated on a total negation of a common purpose or shared goal. There is no *res publica* or recognizably public thing, only the supreme privacy of sleep.[108]

Arguably, *The Wanderings of Oisin* ultimately affirms patriotism even while it describes its inversion. Oisin seems to realize that time is a condition of meaning and value, and that his flight from the temporal has deprived his life of significance. His initial wandering from the Fenian polity culminates in a brave attempt to return to it. The poem's narrative trajectory, therefore, enacts a classic 'patriot' recovery: it tracks a bold return to first principles in the face of effeminacy and corruption. But the poem is also a testament to the impossibility of return and an implicit repudiation of its own seemingly anachronistic vision of the virtuous polity. The poem ends with Oisin's shrill negation of a fallen present he cannot escape. *The Wanderings of Oisin* is distinguished by a patriotic nostalgia that is internally acknowledged as such. Nevertheless, Yeats would still insist that Ireland possessed the social preconditions for a vibrant patriotism and heroic art. 'Alone, perhaps, among the nations of Europe', he declared, 'we are in our epic or ballad

---

105 *VP*, 9.
106 *VP*, 41.
107 *VP*, 49.
108 According to Bloom, *Yeats*, 89, Oisin's search for the sublime is 'impossible to distinguish from an absolute solipsism'.

age'.[109] Here he again argued that Ireland enjoyed a simplicity and coherence that was at odds with the atomized nature and lyrical tendency of modern times.

4 Epic Unity and Lyrical Modernity

Yeats appeared to derive his distinction between epic and lyric forms from Arthur Hallam's essay on Tennyson, but Hallam's discussion owed much to earlier aesthetic debates. Hegel, for instance, had strongly distinguished between epic and lyric forms and he related both to a more fundamental opposition between classical and romantic values. The epic form had outlived the classical epoch, but it found its apotheosis in that period; the lyric, on the other hand, had its origins in the classical past, but it received its fullest expression in the romantic age.[110] Because the differences between classicism and romanticism, for Hegel, were as much political as they were aesthetic, I want to draw on his account to examine Yeats's treatment of epic and lyric values. Yeats and Hegel, for all their differences, expressed a similar kind of ambition: both had hoped to bring a unifying principle to a divided modernity, and to restore a collective significance to an atomized social life. In elaborating this ambition, both men were haunted by the apparent unity of ancient civilizations. Hegel, in particular, was awed by the beautiful coherence of classical Greek life. The Greek state, he believed, was itself a kind of aesthetic unity, and was organized around the perfect integration of law and custom, individual and community. Here life was aesthetically lived and society resembled an artwork in its beautiful unity and perfect balance.[111] However, he grew ever more resigned to the fact that this particular form of unity was not to be recuperated in modern times. For the defining feature of modernity, Hegel believed, was the discovery of a particular form of autonomy and freedom — a principle that won scant recognition, according to him, in the Greek polity.[112] Yeats also came to acknowledge — both as its radical advocate and hostile critic — a principle of subjectivity which he identified with modernity. His

109 UP 1. 273.

110 G. W. F. Hegel, *Hegel's Aesthetics: Lectures on Fine Art*, trans. T. M. Knox, 2 vols. (Oxford, 1975), 2. 1093, 1152: 'Epic's mode of presentation ramifies into numerous species and collateral species and occurs extensively in many epochs and amongst many peoples, but we have come to know it in its perfect form as epic proper and found epic proper actualized in the most artistically adequate way by the Greeks.' In the romantic era, 'lyric poetry is of such overwhelming importance that its principle is asserted, far more profoundly than was possible in the case of the Greeks and Romans'.

111 G. W. F. Hegel, *Hegel and the Human Spirit: The Jena Lectures on the Philosophy of Spirit of 1805–6*, trans. Leo Rauch (Detroit, 1983), 159–60: 'In ancient times the common morality consisted of the beautiful public life — beauty [as the] immediate unity of the universal and the individual, [the polis as] a work of art wherein no part separates itself from the whole, but is rather this genial unity of the self-knowing Self and its [outer] presentation.' See Gillian Rose, *Hegel Contra Sociology* (London, 1981), 123–30.

112 G. W. F. Hegel, *Elements of the Philosophy of Right*, ed. Allen W. Wood, trans. H. B. Nisbet (Cambridge, 1991), 151: 'the right of *subjective freedom* is the pivotal and focal point in the difference between *antiquity* and the *modern age*' [Hegel's emphasis].

attitude to this subjective ethos remained forever volatile, but its ubiquity in modern times gradually undermined his hopes for epic unity in Ireland. This conclusion had significant repercussions on his nationalism.

Yeats subscribed to the view — powerfully articulated by Hegel, but shared by many others — that history was defined by its increasingly subjective character. He outlined this process in a variety of ways and on several occasions, but he produced one of his most cogent formulations of the issue in a lecture in 1893, entitled 'Nationality and Literature'. Here he suggested that the historical development of art was distinguished by two related phenomena: the rise of the autonomous individual and the decline of art as a public force. In an epic age, art was fully integrated with national life; in a lyrical era, on the other hand, poetry stood aloof from its broader social context and ceased to be a public power.[113] Under the aegis of lyrical values, 'poetry steps out of the market-place, out of the general tide of life and becomes a mysterious cult, as it were, an almost secret religion made by the few for the few'.[114] Yeats's account of art's retreat from the agora embodied at times the 'lyrical' values it described, because it appeared to overlook the wider social basis for aesthetic change.[115] However, he acknowledged in the end that the shift from epic 'simplicity' to lyric 'complexity' reflected a broader social pattern:

> Granted fit time and fit occasion, I could apply the same law of division and sub-division and of ever increasing complexity to human society itself … and show you how in the old civilizations an endless sub-division of society to trades and professions and of human life to habits and rules, is making men every day more subtle and complex, less forcible and adaptable.[116]

Here Yeats returned to the old chestnut of the division of labour and its socially enervating effects. He believed that the specialization of culture was related to its increasing subjectivism, although he remained uncertain whether it did so as cause, symptom or as dialectical partner.

For both Yeats and Hegel, the epic was the supreme form of national art and it flourished during a nation's youth.[117] The beautiful unity of Greek life, according to Hegel, found one of its earliest and most powerful expressions in the epic form. Here we discover

> a world hovering beautifully between the universal foundations of life in the ethical order of family, state and religious belief, and the individual personal character;

---

113 In UP 1. 269. Yeats also suggested that there was an intermediate 'dramatic' phase between epic and lyric eras.

114 UP 1. 271.

115 UP 1. 268.

116 UP 1. 272.

117 Yeats insisted that Ireland remained a 'young' nation in which a genuinely national art remained possible. UP 1. 273. For Hegel, epic embodies 'a unity which in its original and undisrupted character occurs only in the earliest periods of poetry and a nation's life'. Aesthetics, 2. 1046.

between spirit and nature in their beautiful equipoise; between intended action and external outcome; between the national ground of undertakings and the intentions and deeds of individuals ...[118]

Yeats's epic age enjoyed a similar kind of integration or 'simplicity'. In this period, the individual's relation to his community, the goods internal to this form of life, and the relation between this society and nature itself found its ultimate articulation and synthesis in epic art. This art was so part of social life that it was, perhaps, difficult to delimit it as an artistic practice as such. There was no abstract division between aesthetic attributes and epistemic or ethical values, between the principles epic set down for itself and the beliefs immanent in everyday life. The concord that he attributed in later life to ancient Byzantium — where 'religious, aesthetic and practical life were one' — was in his youth a feature of epic culture in general.[119] Epic art embodied the 'national character' and revealed no rift between public and private values.[120] In epic, as Hegel explained, the individual 'stands in the midst of a whole nation whose aim and existence in a widely correlated inner and outer world provides the immovable and actual foundation for every individual'.[121] The loss of this unity marks the decline of the epic form. Gradually, the individual abstracts itself from the life of the nation and commits itself to its own private vision of the world. This is a defining feature of romanticism, according to Hegel, and it finds its ultimate expression in the lyric form.[122]

Yeats's lyrical period is characterized by a similar inward turn. By this time, 'the human spirit has begun to look in upon itself with microscopic eyes and to judge of ideas and feelings apart from their effects upon action'. Removed from the world it surveyed, the lyrical ego was faced with the impossible task of attributing meaning and significance to its environment, while remaining aloof from the actual contexts in which these values inhered. For Yeats as for Hegel, the external world is no longer an adequate object for the lyrical artist; 'poets no longer can take their inspiration mainly from external activities and what are called matters of fact, for they must express every phase of human consciousness no matter how subtle, how vague, how impalpable'.[123] The individual, it seems, has turned his back on his concrete environment, which the subjective outlook has reduced to a cluster of 'external activities' or 'matters of fact'.[124] The world now presents itself as resolutely external, while values seem to be a wholly internal or private matter. The lyrical soul, therefore, directs its gaze inward to furnish itself with meaning. Confined to its own interiority, the ego has difficulty affirming itself through action in

118 *Aesthetics*, 2. 1098–99.
119 V, 279.
120 UP 1. 269.
121 Hegel, *Aesthetics*, 2. 1070.
122 See *Aesthetics*, 1. 519, 528.
123 *Aesthetics*, 2. 1078.
124 *Aesthetics*, 2. 1046.

what was now an alien world. The epic for both Yeats and Hegel was a poetry of action; the lyric, however, was not so. Here, according to Yeats, the 'vast bulk of our moods and feelings are too fine, too subjective, too impalpable to find any clear expression in action'.[125] Fundamentally estranged from the world, the lyrical artist struggled to lend his private vision a concrete or communicable form. The lyric, for Yeats, necessarily culminates in 'obscurity'.[126] The romantic poet faced a similar problem in Hegel; here 'the inner, so pushed to the extreme, is an expression without any externality at all'.[127] Ultimately, this art lacks any suitable means of manifesting itself in the world.

Yeats believed that the lyrical artist turned his back on tradition and its attendant benefits. Intrinsic to a tradition, Yeats suggested, were core values and narrative structures that gave pattern to our lives. Within these frameworks human beings were both socialized and individualized at the same time. He reflected back on an undamaged tradition, where 'one could have all the subtlety of Shelley, and yet use no image unknown among the common people, and speak no thought that was not a deduction from the common thought'.[128] Here one could be creative in language without paying the price of esotericism. The contents of tradition, he insisted, were 'made by no one man, but by the nation itself through a slow process of modification and adaptation, to express its loves and its hates, its likes and its dislikes'.[129] All individual creation, therefore, was in some sense derivative. 'No conscious intention', he explained, 'can take the place of tradition', because all creative acts ultimately depended on this rich resource.[130] However, the modern subject generally refused to acknowledge the priority of tradition and regarded itself as the origin and ground of meaning in the world. This attitude was responsible for the romantic cult of originality, which Yeats often professed to despise. 'Talk to me of originality', he declared late in life, 'and I will turn on you with rage'.[131] A romantic poetics that reduced all art to a purely subjective operation was a hubristic outlook, and lent a false priority to individual genius. 'Genius and talent', he concluded, 'have torn Europe to pieces'.[132] Rather than treating his poetry as a creation *ex nihilo*, Yeats often regarded his own work as a redescription of an established structure of meaning. Tradition was the supreme artist that stood behind his own second-order artistry.[133]

Yeats initially hoped to escape what Hegel termed bad particularity and subjective mannerism by committing himself to a shared tradition. Artists like Samuel Ferguson, he suggested, had no mannerisms; their art had its 'roots in no personal idiosyncrasy,

---

125 UP 1. 271.
126 UP 1. 274.
127 *Aesthetics*, 1. 527.
128 EI, 296.
129 UP 1. 273.
130 UP 1. 83.
131 EI. 522.
132 EI. 468.
133 Here Eliot's assessment of the aesthetic credo of Yeats was acute: 'Art was greater than the artist'. T. S. Eliot, *Selected Prose of T. S. Eliot*, ed. Frank Kermode (London, 1975), 249.

but in Irish character and Irish history'.[134] Ferguson's poetry enjoyed an impersonal quality through its integration in a tradition. This anonymity was a defining feature of epic, according to Hegel; in this context, the 'art-work is its own minstrel' and the author has entirely disappeared.[135] Yeats aimed for a similar impersonality and hoped 'to create once more an art where the artist's handiwork would hide as under ... half-anonymous chisels'.[136] He spoke admiringly of an undisturbed folk-life in which schoolboys 'hand their story-books to one another without looking at the title-page to read the author's name'.[137] Art, therefore, was less a subjective act than a form of collaboration; as Yeats suggested: 'works of art are always begotten by previous works of art, and every masterpiece becomes the Abraham of a chosen people'.[138] Art, like the language from which it derived, was irreducibly social. He was convinced that old symbols provided a rich testimony of the way meaning was shared and intersubjectively constituted across time:

> It is only by ancient symbols, by symbols that have numberless meanings beside the one or two the writer lays an emphasis upon, or the half-score he knows of, that any highly subjective art can escape from the barrenness and shallowness of a too conscious arrangement, into the abundance and depth of Nature.[139]

A symbol discloses a whole vista of meaning of which its user may remain largely unaware.

By presenting tradition as the bedrock of meaning in life and art, Yeats hoped to curb the destructive hubris of the modern subject. Romanticism, for Hegel, was a supreme manifestation of this kind of subjectivism. Considering itself as the source and ground of the universe it surveys, the romantic ironist lacked any viable basis for agency in the world. To take a stand within a context would be to spoil the abstract sense of possibility which ironists identified with freedom.[140] These romantic figures were bereft of value and meaning because they failed to commit themselves to the contexts in which such blessings arise. By contrast, the Roman Cato, according to Hegel, derived his freedom from his full participation in the life of the res publica. He did not live in abstraction from his world, but could 'live only as a Roman and a republican'.[141] This form of commitment was not a restriction of Cato's freedom, but was the basis of its realization. According to

---

134 UP 1. 404. Cf. Hegel, *Philosophy of Right*, 49: 'When great artists complete a work, we can say that it had to be so; that is, the artist's particularity has completely disappeared and no *mannerism* is apparent in it. Phidias has no mannerisms; the shape itself lives and stands out. But the poorer the artist is, the more we see of himself, of his particularity and arbitrariness' [Hegel's emphasis].

135 *Aesthetics*, 2. 1049.

136 A, 150.

137 A, 217.

138 EI, 352.

139 EI, 87.

140 See *Aesthetics*, 1. 64–69.

141 *Aesthetics*, 1. 68.

Hegel, this concrete freedom was also a feature of epic art; individuals lived in harmony with their world and reflected 'national character' in their own personalities.[142] For Yeats too, character in epic society was also embedded in its social environment; 'characters like Macbeth and Lear, like Oedipus and Agamemnon, cannot be separated ... from the world about them'. The general trend of culture, he believed, was to become 'more and more interested in character for its own sake'.[143] But the individual's attempt to transcend its social contexts ultimately produced 'the abstract poet, living nowhere, a man wandering in the void, in the indefinite, a philosopher and scholar, a saint, even, anything you will, but not a man full of passions, not incarnate life'.[144]

Romantic art, Hegel suggested, ultimately imploded because it could not lend its extreme, subjective vision a communicable form. At this point, 'art annuls itself and brings home to our minds that we must acquire higher forms for the apprehension of truth than those which art is in a position to supply'.[145] Yet the great achievement of romanticism, he suggested, was its recognition of a particular form of subjective freedom — a principle that it repeatedly misrepresented but which served, nevertheless, as its animating spirit.[146] Hegel refused to abandon subjective freedom as a fundamental component of his own philosophy: his task in the *Philosophy of Right*, for instance, was to discover how this freedom is produced and maintained through the intersubjective contexts and communicative infrastructures of the modern state. For this reason, he was critical of ancient societies and epic values. For all the beautiful unity of the classical world, it failed to accommodate sufficiently a principle of personal freedom. Because ancient states were organized round the subject's unreflective identification with the polis, they 'could not withstand the division which arose within the latter as self-consciousness became infinitely reflected into itself'.[147] Plato, he suggested, had the distinction of recognizing this. According to Hegel, Plato constructed his 'purely substantial state' in opposition to the principle of subjective freedom, which he recognized as a threat to the beautiful unity of the polis.[148] This, however, was neither possible nor desirable in a modern context. For it was reason's wont to lend itself a subjective form and to think its way out of received social forms.

142 *Aesthetics*, 2. 1068.

143 UP 1. 270.

144 W. B. Yeats, 'Four Lectures by W. B. Yeats', ed. Richard Londraville, in Warwick Gould, ed., *Yeats Annual No. 8* (Houndmills, Basingstoke, Hampshire and London, 1991), 78–122, 91.

145 *Aesthetics*, 1. 529.

146 Romantics such as Friedrich Schlegel had promoted a doctrine of personal freedom that was indistinguishable from pure arbitrariness. Hegel understood freedom in Kantian terms as rational self-determination; it was not the empty lawlessness that Schlegel promoted, but the will's absolute accordance with the law of reason. For a comprehensive discussion of Hegel's concept of freedom, see Paul Franco, *Hegel's Philosophy of Freedom* (New Haven and London, 1999) and Allen Wood, *Hegel's Ethical Thought* (Cambridge, 1990).

147 Hegel, *Philosophy of Right*, 222.

148 *Philosophy of Right*, 223.

Yeats also recognized that the development of the modern subject had largely eroded the beautiful unity of the epic era. In his nostalgia for this kind of integration, he often regarded subjectivity as a destructive principle. Self-consciousness was indistinguishable from social estrangement and the pursuit of inwardness culminated in isolation. Unsurprisingly, therefore, we frequently encounter in Yeats's early poetry an overwrought subjectivity seeking to transcend itself through a series of limit experiences. Oisin, for instance, seems to regard erotic love as a reprieve from the self, while the Island of Forgetfulness affords similar opportunities for self-oblivion. Unfortunately, Oisin wakes up. So, too, does O'Driscoll, the dreamer, who is restored to the agony of self-consciousness after sleep in 'The Host of the Air'.[149] Consciousness, it seems, merely confirms the ultimate 'vanity of Sleep'.[150] Yeats gradually recognized, however, that the problems of an overburdened subjectivity would not be overcome by the simple rejection of self-consciousness. He also believed that 'epic society' would not survive this inward turn. For it was central to the life of the subject, as a rational and moral agent, to query the forms of life in which it participated. This is a conclusion presented in a late poem, 'Meru':

> Civilization is hooped together, brought
> Under a rule, under the semblance of peace
> By manifold illusion; but man's life is thought,
> And he, despite his terror, cannot cease
> Ravening through century after century,
> Ravening, raging, and uprooting that he may come
> Into the desolation of reality:
> Egypt and Greece, good-bye, and good-bye, Rome![151]

The joys of civilization are ambiguous: the peace it affords may be a simple delusion or it may be a real benefit derived from benign 'semblance'. Life appears to derive coherence from 'manifold illusion', although the impression of a prior manifold may be an illusion itself. Nevertheless, if civilization is predicated on fiction, truth seems to require the destruction of both. 'Ravening through century after century', rational inquiry is a destructive and even barbaric process. While the dialectic of reason culminated, for Hegel, in absolute knowledge, Yeats's end of history is considerably darker.[152] The 'desolation of reality' towards which we strive may simply be an ultimate knowledge in

---

149 *VP*, 43–145.
150 *VP*, 154.
151 *VP*, 563.
152 See George Mills Harper, ed., *Yeats and the Occult* (London and Basingstoke, 1975), 221. With Marxism most probably in mind, Yeats claimed that 'Hegel's Philosophy of History dominates the masses, though they have not heard his name, as Rousseau's philosophy did in the nineteenth and later eighteenth centuries, and has shed more blood'. *EI*, 468–67.

which all distinctions between subject and object disappear.[153] But absolute knowledge may also reveal the fundamental emptiness of the world as well as the futility of this final wisdom. But whatever the status of this knowledge, we cannot stall its development — a fact brought home by the inexorable quality of rhyme and rhythm in 'Meru'. Reflection is a condition of life and to deny its exercise is to oppose existence itself. This reflective attitude is fated to contest and to undermine the values around which our various social orders have been organized. Yeats must say goodbye, therefore, to the ancient civilizations of Egypt, Greece and Rome. And while he insisted in 1893 that Ireland remained an epic culture, he was forced in the end to bid farewell to this kind of unity.[154] This would also mean relinquishing the patriotic ideals of Young Ireland.

4 Young Ireland and the Lyrical Principle

From an early stage in his career Yeats regarded Young Ireland as representatives of an Irish epic or ballad age. He included Davis and Mangan in a list of nineteenth-century Irish poets, all of which are 'either ballad or epic writers, and all base their greatest work ... upon legends and upon the fortunes of the nation'.[155] Indeed, the Young Irelanders had invoked these aesthetic categories themselves. In his Preface to the fourth edition of the *Ballad Poetry of Ireland*, Duffy declared the ballad to be the supreme form of public art. Duffy insisted — just as Yeats would also argue — that Ireland was a comparatively youthful nation, and that it had the prerequisite public spirit for successful ballad-making. He commended Wordsworth for outlining the profound significance of the ballad, but hinted that the English poet remained alienated from the culture in which the ballad thrived:

> It was the great achievement of Wordsworth to wed philosophy to the ballad, and to put a high moral purpose and large intellectual development into his ballad stories; but the ages that required only the simple passion and the obvious truth were ages of great faith, worth and heroism. Let us rejoice if we have not yet passed out of them.

Duffy distinguished — as Yeats would later do — between a poetry of action and a poetry of reflection. The latter was characterized by the enervation of public feeling

---

153 In 'Fergus and the Druid', he had glorified an absolute identity between the knower and the known; here Fergus discovers himself 'grown nothing, knowing all'. VP, 104.

154 Yeats's late poem 'The Statues' is a testament to the difficulty of absolute goodbyes. Here he hopes to emulate the achievements of the Greeks who had installed the discipline of form on 'vague immensities'. Ireland has been wrecked by the 'filthy modern tide', but it may yet restore an epic integrity and coherence to the world. See VP, 610–11.

155 UP 1. 273.

and civic virtue; 'the poetry of action and passion, and faith and noble sentiment are still common. Poetry of reflection succeeds in a lower state of public feeling.'[156] Duffy organized his praise of Samuel Ferguson around this dichotomy. Ferguson's ballads, he suggested, 'appeal to the imagination and passions, not to the intellect'. These ballads were inseparable from the social contexts that produced them and were suffused with 'a living and local interest'. Duffy suggested that a modern ethos of reflection alienated us from our social environment and this was reflected by the decline of the ballad in the modern world. He deemed it probable that 'Mr. Ferguson holds ballad poetry to have been vitiated by the excesses of reflection over incident'.[157] Duffy maintained, however, that the ballad was alive and well in Ireland.

Duffy's description of Ireland's balladic character, grounded in public passion and action, was clearly consonant with his more general patriotic vision. Young Ireland, as we have seen, extolled a neo-classical view of citizenship, where the citizen affirmed himself as a political being through his active identification with the life of the community. This identification, as it appeared to many figures in the nineteenth century, was immediate, and was not a matter of reflection or rational choice. Hegel insisted that Greek citizenship was not a matter of conscience, because this subjective faculty did not exist as such:

> Of the Greeks in the first and genuine form of their Freedom, we may assert that they had no conscience; the habit of living for their country without further [analysis or] reflection, was the principle dominant among them. The consideration of the State in the abstract — which to our understanding is the essential point — was alien to them. Their grand object was their country in its living and real aspect; — this actual Athens, this Sparta, these Temples, these Altars, this form of social life, this union of fellow-citizens, these manners and customs. To the Greek his country was a necessary of life, without which existence was impossible.[158]

By insisting that Ireland possessed a balladic character, Duffy was attributing a similar notion of citizenship to the Irish. Here the individual's identification with the polity was also immediate; it was not a product of reflection, but was largely intuitive. Nor did the Irish consider their country in the abstract, but, as everyone was repeatedly reminded, their patriotism was 'racy of the soil'.

Yeats also suggested that Ireland's epic character provided for the citizen's immediate identification with the life of the patria. Irish public-spiritedness distinguished itself from the English preoccupation with private interests. This individualism, according to Yeats, was reflected in the ponderous egotism of English poetry:

---

156 Duffy, *Ballad Poetry of Ireland*, 17.
157 Duffy, *Ballad Poetry of Ireland*, 30.
158 G. W. F. Hegel, *Philosophy of History*, trans. J. Sibree (New York, 1902), 334 [Hegel's emphasis].

The Saxon is not sympathetic or self-abnegating ... He is full of self-brooding. Like his own Wordsworth, most English of poets, he finds his image in every lake and puddle. He had to burthen the skylark with his cares before he can celebrate it. He is always a lens coloured by self.[159]

In his essay on Ferguson, Yeats stated that most modern art is damagingly solipsistic: 'At once the fault and the beauty of the nature-description of most modern poets', he declared, 'is that for them the stars, and streams, the leaves, and the animals, are only masks behind which go on the sad soliloquies of a nineteenth century egoism'.[160] Schiller had argued that the acute self-consciousness of moderns made their investment in nature sentimental; the Greek, on the other hand, possessed a naïve love of nature and 'does not cling with inwardness, with emotion, with sweet sorrow to her as we moderns do'.[161] Yeats liked to suggest that the Irish enjoyed a similarly transparent relationship with nature. He presented John Todhunter's poems, for instance, as a representative case of Irish sympathy; these poems were antithetical to the spirit of English poetry: 'because there is no egotism in them there is no gloom'. Any sadness that existed in these poems 'is nature's, not man's — a limpid melancholy'.[162]

Over time, however, Yeats's account of Irish simplicity and intuitiveness became ever more qualified. Although he praised Irish poetry for its simple, unreflective quality, he drew an interesting distinction at one point between the 'primitive poetry ... of Gaelic Ireland and Scotland' and the verse written by Young Ireland and other nineteenth-century writers. These more modern figures produced poetry which was 'half-cultivated, half-instinctive'.[163] Although the Nation writers were affiliated to an older tradition of Irish poetry, their verse was also marked by a higher level of self-consciousness. Already, then, the 'lyrical' principle was beginning to obtrude, auguring the destruction of epic unity. As Yeats moved through the early years of the twentieth century, he hardened his conviction that Young Ireland writers repressed this lyrical tendency in their commitment to an epic coherence that was increasingly unreal. The political implications of this aesthetic appraisal are obvious: the Young Irelanders appeared to stifle individual freedom for the sake of an outdated notion of social coherence. They resembled, in other words, Plato's guardians in their suppression of the subjective principle on behalf of the beautiful polity. Yeats increasingly distanced himself from this political vision and was sceptical about the possibility and desirability of the subject's full immersion in the life of the polis.

---

159 W. B. Yeats, Letters to the New Island (Houndmills, Basingstoke, and London, 1989), 89. Hereafter cited as LNI.
160 UP 1. 103.
161 Friedrich Schiller, On the Naïve and Sentimental in Literature, trans. Helen Watanabe O'Kelly (Manchester, 1981), 33. Yeats spoke of Ferguson's 'epic vastness and naïveté' and contrasted this with 'the subtlety of feeling, the variety of cadence of a great lyric poet'. PI, 106.
162 LNI, 89.
163 UP 1. 412.

Indeed, the word 'citizen' developed an increasingly negative purchase in Yeats's work. 'A poet', he insisted in 1909, 'is a good citizen turned inside out'.[164] Disdain for the law-abiding citizen in an Irish context was often indicative of a more strenuous patriotism, one that embraced the idea of violent revolution. Yeats retained these revolutionary associations for the artist, while contesting, on the other hand, the primacy of the patriotic virtues. Young Ireland's civic ideals, he was convinced, impeded the cultivation of subjective freedom. Even Yeats's own paean to epic values, *The Wanderings of Oisin*, seemed to acknowledge that the subjective principle had emerged as a challenge to epic unity. Yeats's Oisin is not the last representative of an epic integrity but is the living embodiment of its demise. The Christian doctrine of the soul, according to Hegel, prepared the way for the modern subject, but the pre-Christian Oisin is already oppressed by a subjectivity he cannot transcend. He resembles, at best, Hegel's 'unhappy consciousness' and is committed to ideals he can neither validate nor attain. He suffers from a curiously modern form of alienation and is consistently estranged from the communities in which he lives. Participation in the life of a community, for Oisin, is a distinctly liberal matter of individual preference or choice-making. Estranged from the Islands of Dancing and of Victories, he craves for the Island of Content, but fails to recognize that such contentment is never recognizable from the outside. Oisin ultimately tries to escape the torment of self-consciousness and seeks oblivion on the Island of Forgetfulness, but this only brings temporary relief. He is ultimately restored to the agony of subjective awareness and to the recognition that Ireland's epic cohesion has disappeared.[165]

In his diaries of 1909, Yeats ultimately conceded that modern Ireland no longer possessed an epic form. 'The soul of Ireland', as he put it, 'has become a vapour and her body a stone'.[166] In other words, the integration of the life of the spirit and the stuff of the world, which had characterized epic culture, no longer existed in Ireland. The rise of subjectivity or the lyrical principle was both the symptom and cause of a gap between private and public values. Whatever the ultimate reasons for these divisions, they would not be overcome, according to Yeats, by shrill injunctions to unite. He now appeared convinced that Young Ireland's ideal of the moral community must be relinquished as a naïve and dangerous kind of political fantasy. Modern states, he suggested, were not communities of sentiment or belief. Nor did they have the ethical substance or coherence of a monastic order. Modern Ireland could never articulate a shared conception of the good through the forum of art because it lacked the social conditions for this vision:

> One cannot have a national art in the Young Ireland sense, that is to say an art recognized at once by all as national because obviously an expression of what all believe and feel,

---

164 M, 140–41.
165 Indeed, *The Wanderings of Oisin* is a version of what Hegel called a 'romantically-epic poetry'. Despite its epic tone, this poetry has a strong lyric character. Cf. *Aesthetics*, 2. 1092.
166 M, 178.

though one can have an imitation, because no modern nation is an organism like a monastery by rule and discipline, by a definite table of values understood by all, or even, as the Western peasants are, by habit of feeling and thought.[167]

Modern states were too large and too differentiated to allow for anything more than the most minimal agreement on the content of the good. To insist upon anything more substantial was either reductive or authoritarian — it either overlooked or overruled the plural nature of modern societies. 'Young Irelandism, because a condescension, a conscious simplification', Yeats concluded, 'could only perish or create a tyranny'.[168] Young Ireland's ideal of the harmonious community was an outdated and illiberal fantasy: it purchased unity at the expense of private freedoms and individual differences. This kind of synthesis produced 'a mob held together not by what is interior, delicate and haughty, but by law and force which they obey because they must'.[169]

Yeats's Young Ireland pursued unity as an end in itself, and foisted a wholly artificial conception of an integrated community upon a richly differentiated life-world. The ancients may have believed that a community derived its cohesion from a shared view of the good life, but to confuse the good with such unity was a dangerous inversion of priorities. Young Ireland had made this mistake. Yeats arguably exaggerated the case. Young Ireland, after all, had a Tocquevillian horror of uniformity, whether expressed as imperialism or centralization. Nevertheless, the group was also zealously committed to an ideal of national unity, and castigated the vice of faction in scores of articles and speeches. But the young patriots often failed to consider on a systematic basis the dangers — not to mention the performative contradictions — of this high-minded attitude. Young Ireland appealed to a notional unity to criticize injustice, but its moralizing rhetoric failed to treat the structural basis of social problems; systematic inequalities were transcended rather than addressed by the abstract call to friendship. 'Whenever', as the Irish socialist Frederick Ryan put it, 'anyone calls for a cessation of the political warfare and a "union of all classes," we know at once that he is a reactionary, well-meaning or otherwise'.[170] It was a charge that easily applied to Young Ireland.

Alive to the shortcomings of Young Ireland's rhetoric of fraternal sentiment, Yeats queried its holistic concept of the nation and suggested that its model of citizenship was drawn from and directed towards the middle class.[171] This charge was not unjust. Both Duffy and Davis regarded the middle class as the heart and mind of the nation. In January 1845, the Nation echoed Abbé Sièyes's rapturous assessment of the third

---

167 M, 251.
168 M, 250–51.
169 M, 251.
170 Frederick Ryan, *Criticism and Courage and Other Essays* (Dublin, 1906), 11.
171 UP 2. 185: 'The writers who made this literature or who shaped its ideals, in the years before the great famine, lived at the moment when the middle class had brought to perfection its ideal of the good citizen.'

estate when it declared that the middle classes 'are emphatically the nation'.[172] Yeats criticized Davis's tendency to exaggerate moral coherence and national unity for political purposes: it resulted in a tired 'apologetics'. Yeats gradually came to see 'the world as a continual conflict', but Davis seemed to regard internal hostilities as a threat to the life of a community.[173] His patriotism could seem, therefore, not only abstract, but strangely apolitical, for it overruled the antagonism that was the *sine qua non* of politics. Human conflict, as Rousseau suggested, was the fundamental condition of politics and made it an intelligible art.[174] Over time, Yeats stressed the virtues of conflict and rejected the idea of unity as a sufficient basis for a vigorous national life:

> England sometimes taunts us with our divisions, divisions that she has done her best to foment; as if she herself was ever united, as if it was natural for any country to be united. No land lives out a wholesome life, full of ideas and vitality, that is not fighting out great issues within its own borders. It is part of the sacrifice we have had to make for our national existence that from time to time the whole of Ireland has to be gathered into one great party. But let us not forget the sacrifice. When all Ireland was so marshalled, we had no individuality of thought.[175]

Like many of his contemporaries in late nineteenth-century Ireland, Yeats attempted to restore the agon to Irish public life in what amounted to an implicit attack on the principles of the Young Ireland movement. In the early years of the Abbey he delighted in 'contraversy [sic]', and promoted his theatre as 'a wise disturber of the peace'.[176] As his contemporary, D. P. Moran, observed, a commitment to political unity had divested Ireland of its capacity for self-critique. Young Ireland appeared to be his implicit object of criticism when he complained of the 'unceasing and spirit-wearying flow of romances about '48, '98, and other periods, in all of which, of course, Ireland was painted spotless white'.[177] Eglinton called boldly for the 'de-Davisisation of Irish literature'.[178] Young Ireland's rigidified narratives and impoverished vocabularies, he suggested, had produced a kind of symbolic bondage from which Ireland needed to escape. Yeats may have shared these views, but he also condemned Eglinton's criticism of patriotism and his individualism.

---

172 *Nation*, 25 January 1845. A week later the journal declared that Ireland will only be redeemed by the middle classes. See *Nation*, 1 February 1845.

173 *V*, 144.

174 Jean-Jacques Rousseau, *The Social Contract and Other Later Political Writings*, ed. and trans. Victor Gourevitch (Cambridge, 1997), 60: 'If there were no different interests the common interest would scarcely be sensible since it would never encounter obstacles: everything would run by itself, and politics would cease to be an art.'

175 'Four Lectures by W. B. Yeats', 78–122, 105.

176 *CL* 3. 118.

177 D. P. Moran, 'The Battle of Two Civilisations', in Augusta Gregory, ed., *Ideals in Ireland* (London, 1901), 23–41, 32.

178 John Eglinton, *Bards and Saints* (Dublin, 1906), 36–43.

In this, he reaffirmed his commitment to nationalism and to a tradition 'wiser' than the individuals over which it reigned. Yeats, however, never resolved the tension between the communitarian values that he sponsored here and the vigorous individualism expressed in much of his subsequent work. He struck an aggressively individualistic attitude when he condemned the rigid pieties and herd-mentality of public life in Ireland, but he also worried about the fragmented character of 'our individualistic age'.[179] This fragmentation was regrettable, but he was convinced that 'Unity of Being' could not be restored on Young Ireland lines. If the patriotism of Young Ireland was dead, Yeats, as we shall see, was even more sceptical of the nationalism that arose in its wake.

179 A, 547.

4 Reflections on Revolution

1 Yeats and the Counter-Revolutionary Tradition

Writing in 1904, Yeats extolled 'the aristocracy of the artists, the only aristocracy which has never oppressed the people and against which the people have never arisen'.[1] But, by 1907, it appeared that the people *had* arisen in a furious protest against *The Playboy of the Western World* and the aristocratic triumvirate of J. M. Synge, Lady Gregory and W. B. Yeats that controlled the Abbey. In his reflections on contemporary Ireland two years later, Yeats maintained that the 'democratic envy and jealousy' of modern Ireland had rendered it incapable of accepting 'the pre-eminence of one or two writers'.[2] He used Lady Gregory's work as an example of that pre-eminence, but he might easily have chosen the plays of Synge. An abstract sense of equality — whose real origin was a rancorous jealousy — had extirpated all sense of real value in Ireland. Yeats's understanding of a transformed Ireland was particularly indebted to a discourse of counter-revolution originating in the thought of Edmund Burke, and incorporating a range of other figures from De Maistre to Taine to Nietzsche. Yeats shared Burke's negative assessment of the French Revolution, but he also believed it had particularly unfortunate results in Ireland.[3] 'The influence of the French Revolution', he complained in 1934, 'woke the peasantry from their medieval sleep, gave them ideas of social justice and equality, but prepared

1   UP 2. 324.
2   M, 168–69.
3   McCormack, in 'Edmund Burke, Yeats and Leo Frobenius: "The State a Tree"?', 229, argues convincingly that 'Burke for Yeats was the author of *Reflections on the Revolution in France* (1790), and related polemics on the issue of Jacobinism. Any interest in Burke's earlier career was subordinated to a high-frequency transmission of arguments against radical change, of defences provided for tradition, of justifications of custom against calculation'.

for a century disastrous to the national intellect.'[4] Yeats was convinced that modern Irish nationalism epitomized this damage. His critique of nationalism also developed into a more general indictment of modern democracy; both, he believed, were dangerous abstractions that overlooked the concrete realities of social and political life.

The conditions of intelligibility for these criticisms can be found in a counter-revolutionary tradition of politics that contains many internal differences and contradictions, but gets its general shape from a strong distrust of abstraction. The word 'abstraction' derives from the Latin term *abstrahere*, meaning 'to draw away or to remove (something from something else)'.[5] Burke denounced the 'hocus-pocus of *abstraction*' that had worked such devastation in Europe.[6] De Maistre also condemned the disastrous effects of a 'chimerical system of deliberation and political construction by abstract reasoning'.[7] Taine derided, in turn, the abstraction of revolutionary doctrine. A reductive rationalism, he suggested, was the by-product of a degraded classicism:

> To pursue in every research, with the utmost confidence, without reserve or precaution, the mathematical method; to derive, limit and isolate a few of the simplest generalized notions; and then, setting experience aside, comparing them, combining them, and, from the artificial compound thus obtained, deducing all the consequences they involve by pure reasoning is the natural process of the classical spirit.[8]

The anti-historical disposition of classicism, Taine argued, had disastrous political effects when adopted by the mediocre men who led the French Revolution. Armed with general principles gleaned largely from Rousseau, these revolutionaries had undermined the historical foundations and established government of France.[9]

Yeats shared Taine's distrust of abstract method. He also chose to relate the abstractions of a decadent classicism to revolution. 'Classical morality in its decay', he argued, 'became an instrument in the hands of commonplace energy to overthrow distinguished men'.[10] Since the first flourishing of classicism during the Renaissance, the tendency of classical thought, he claimed, was to become ever 'more formal and empty until it

---

4   VP, 833.
5   Michael Inwood, A Hegel Dictionary (Oxford, 1992), 29.
6   W & S 9. 50 [Burke's emphasis].
7   De Maistre, *Considerations on France*, 60. For Burke's influence on De Maistre, see Yves Chiron, 'The Influence of Burke's Writings in Post-Revolutionary France', in Ian Crowe, ed., *Edmund Burke: His Life and Legacy* (Dublin, 1997), 85–93, 88–89. According to Chiron, 93, Burke had an 'overwhelming influence' on Taine's account of the Revolution.
8   Hippolyte Taine, *Les Origines de la France Contemporaine: The Ancient Regime*, trans. John Durand, 3 vols. (London, 1876), 1. 201.
9   Hippolyte Taine, *Les Origines de la France Contemporaine: The Revolution*, trans. John Durand, 3 vols. (London, 1878–85), 3. 1; 2. 20.
10 M, 181.

became ignoble in our time'.[11] Whether or not Yeats's views are the result of direct or even indirect exposure to Taine's account of the French Revolution, the highly political nature of his critique of abstraction is clear; it made 'possible the stimulation and condonation of revolutionary massacre and the multiplication of murderous weapons by substituting for the old humanity with its unique irreplaceable individuals something that can be chopped and measured like a piece of cheese'.[12] These criticisms were themselves fairly abstract and were applied with little reference to particular historical circumstances; but for Yeats, English Puritanism, French republicanism and Russian communism were all open to this lethal charge of abstraction.[13]

But it was Ireland that in particular served as the staging-ground for Yeats's quarrel on this score. He complained bitterly in 1909 that 'Ireland is ruined by abstraction'.[14] This had happened because of the radicalization of nationalist politics. In a somewhat idiosyncratic version of recent nationalist history, he recorded how

> a movement, first of poetry, then of sentimentality, and land hunger, had struggled with, and as the nation passed into the second period of all revolutions given way before a movement of abstraction and hatred; and after some twenty years of the second period, though abstraction and hatred have won their victory, there is no clear sign of a third, a *tertium quid*, and a reasonable frame of mind.[15]

It is not difficult to appreciate why Yeats, so conscious of his Anglo-Irish descent, would feel he was witnessing something akin to a social revolution in Ireland.[16] From the time of his birth in 1865 to his death in 1939, he experienced the haemorrhaging of political, social and economic power away from the Anglo-Irish Ascendancy to an increasingly assertive, Catholic middle class. Franchise reform — or what Yeats's compatriot W. E. H. Lecky denounced as 'the degradation of the Irish suffrage' — did much to undermine the political power of the Ascendancy, while Gladstonian land reforms and the Balfour and Wyndham Land Acts of the Conservative regime effectively obliterated its economic base.[17] Many Ascendancy figures chose to regard this change as revolutionary. According to Lecky, for instance, Gladstone's land reform of 1881 was 'an attack on the principle of

---

11   M, 180.

12   E, 436.

13   E, 277. After the Russian Revolution, Yeats was convinced that the political equivalent of religious fundamentalism had once again gripped Europe: 'Logic is loose again, as once in Calvin and Knox or in the hysterical rhetoric of Savonarola … and because it must always draw its deductions from what every dolt can understand, the wild beast cannot but destroy mysterious life.'

14   M, 186.

15   A, 360.

16   As Yeats put it in 1934: 'Lady Gregory, John Synge and I were in some sense typical of an Ireland that was passing away. The Ireland of what historians call "the Protestant Ascendancy".' See W. B. Yeats, 'The Irish National Theatre', ed. David R. Clark, in Warwick Gould, ed., *Yeats Annual No. 8* (London, 1991), 144–54, 148.

17   Lecky, *Democracy and Liberty*, 1. 24.

property more radical than any measure of the French Revolution, or even of the Reign of Terror'.[18] By guaranteeing Irish farmers the three Fs — fair rent, fixity of tenure and freedom of sale — the government, Lecky argued, had undermined key elements of British liberty, such as the right to property and the freedom of contract. It was an act of state-sponsored class warfare that competed with the worst outrages of Jacobin France. Reflecting on the Land League campaign in Ireland, Thomas Webb, a professor of law at Trinity, insisted that Parnell's followers, with Gladstone's blessing, 'have proclaimed a war of extermination against the landlords, as ruthless as that proclaimed against the French proprietors by the Jacobins of France'.[19] Yeats's early mentor, Standish O'Grady, also denounced the 'sucking, whirling maelstrom of agrarian and national revolution' and explicitly compared the plight of the Irish aristocracy with the 'French noblesse' during the Revolution.[20] He berated the Anglo-Irish aristocracy for their passivity in the face of their own demise, and he invoked the forbiddingly exotic term *égalité* to outline the extent and quality of the danger they faced as a class in Ireland:

> If you are satisfied to see all the worth, virtue, personal refinement, truth and honour which you know to be inherent in your own order wiped, as with a sponge, out of Ireland — may be with a bloody sponge — then travel that way. If you wish to see anarchy and civil war, brutal despotisms alternating with a bloody lawlessness, or on the other side, a shabby, sordid Irish Republic, ruled by knavish, corrupt politicians and the ignoble rich, you will travel the way of *Egalité*.[21]

Anarchy, civil war, despotism and sordid republics — all the motifs basic to the counter-revolutionary tradition are deployed here. 'The day of absolute democratic power in Ireland draws nigh,' O'Grady predicted, 'the day of reckoning and vengeance'.[22]

Yeats ultimately concluded that this day of reckoning had come. In 1907, the year of the *Playboy* riots, he suggested that modern nationalism had a distinctly Jacobin aspect, being both democratic in theory and tyrannical in practice:

> Some seven or eight years ago the National movement was democratised and passed from the hands of a few leaders into those of large numbers of young men organised in clubs and societies. These young men made the mistake of the newly

---

18 Lecky, *Democracy and Liberty*, I. 163–64.
19 Thomas E. Webb, *The Irish Question: A Reply to Mr. Gladstone* (Dublin, 1886), 18. Frank Hugh O'Donnell later restaged these arguments and condemned Parnell's endorsement of 'agrarian Jacobinism' at the expense of Home Rule. See his *A History of the Irish Parliamentary Party* (London, 1910), 346. O'Donnell insisted, nevertheless, that Parnell at heart was an 'Irish Whig' not a 'Green Robespierre' (450–51).
20 Standish O'Grady, *Selected Essays and Passages* (Dublin, 1917), 229.
21 *Selected Essays and Passages*, 228.
22 Standish O'Grady, *The Crisis in Ireland* (Dublin, 1882), 31.

enfranchised everywhere; they fought for causes worthy in themselves with the unworthy instruments of tyranny and violence.[23]

But the violence of the Playboy riots was small beer in the face of subsequent events. The Rising of 1916, the War of Independence and the Civil War effected a thoroughgoing revolution in Irish politics. Yeats's response to these events was complex and even contradictory, but it was mediated through a set of established discourses that owed much to Burke. Yeats's debts to Burke have been frequently noted, but his repeated violation of Burke's thought has been examined in less detail.[24]

Yeats did not begin to read Burke's works on a systematic basis until 1918.[25] Until then, he had been either lukewarm about, or dismissive of, Burke. Accused by Clement Shorter in 1904 of exaggerating the achievements of Lady Gregory against those of writers such as Swift, Burke and Goldsmith, Yeats described this as the expression of a typically 'modern' interest in figures 'who hardly seem ... to have come out of Ireland at all'.[26] But he had already begun to deploy in his work motifs that he would later explicitly identify with Burke. A 'nation is like a great tree', he insisted in 1904, long before he attributed this form of political botany to Burke.[27] It may be that the extraordinary popularity of Burke in late Victorian Britain introduced Yeats to motifs and images that he would only later explicitly attribute to him. Liberal disillusionment with democracy in the wake of franchise reform appears to have fostered a veritable cult of Burke among Victorian political thinkers.[28] Burke's attacks on 'enthusiasm' could be applied to Nonconformists and the newly enfranchised alike, while his concept of 'national character' offered the solace of an ostensibly secure identity in a period of enormous political change. In addition, Burke was for some a utilitarian before his time. For others, his attacks on

23 Yeats, UP 2. 351.
24 W. J. McCormack has exposed, however, the dissonance between Yeats's praise of the Ascendancy and Burke's excoriating criticisms of the influence of Protestant oligarchs in Ireland. See McCormack, *From Burke to Beckett*, 49–93. For a more general account of Burke's influence on Yeats, see Donald Torchiana, *W. B. Yeats and Georgian Ireland*, 2nd edn. (Washington, 1992). Torchiana's discussion remains informative, but it tends to overlook the tensions between Burke's professed opinions and the uses Yeats made of them. Torchiana accepts Yeats's attempts to harmonize his later authoritarian and anti-liberal views with Burke's criticisms of democracy. This, however, is an untenable position.
25 Torchiana, *W. B. Yeats and Georgian Ireland*, 169.
26 UP 2. 328.
27 UP 2. 323. Yeats repeatedly claimed that Burke compared the state to a tree, but, W. J. McCormack has argued, there is little in Burke's writings and speeches to warrant it. See McCormack, 'Edmund Burke, Yeats and Leo Frobenius: "The State a Tree"?', 236–37. Alistair MacIntyre, 'Poetry as Political Philosophy: Notes on Burke and Yeats', in *Ethics and Politics: Selected Essays, Volume 2* (Cambridge, 2006), 159–71. Yeats account of the state, according to MacIntyre, exposes the 'imaginative poverty not of a particular regime, but of the structure of every modern state' (171).
28 J. W. Burrow, *Whigs and Liberals: Continuity and Change in English Political Thought* (Oxford, 1998), 15. H. S. Jones, *Victorian Political Thought* (London and Basingstoke, 2000), 65: 'Burke was the universal hero of the Victorian political mind, cherished by Whigs, conservatives, and modern-minded liberals alike ...'

metaphysical politics allowed him to be reread as a positivist in the style of Comte.[29] Moreover, Burke could be made to appear curiously modern by the melding of his 'organic' metaphors into a proto-Darwinian discourse.[30] Yeats was also greatly taken by Anglo-Irish interpreters of Burke. Lecky and Dowden, for instance, repeatedly invoked him to condemn the injustices of land reform in Ireland and to defend the integrity of the empire against the advocates of Home Rule.[31] Gladstone, on the other hand, appealed to Burke's writings to sanction his Irish policies, triggering, in turn, furious counter-interpretations.[32]

These controversies seem to have equipped Yeats with anti-revolutionary arguments and imagery long before he turned to Burke's work for explicit confirmation of positions he had already adopted. For instance, in 'J. M. Synge and the Ireland of His Time', an essay published in 1910, Yeats already echoed Burke's famous denunciation of the French assignats — the paper currency which the government had issued against the security of confiscated Church lands — to criticize the rigidities of Irish nationalism.[33] Nationalist politics, Yeats maintained, resembled 'some State which has only paper money, and seeks by punishments to make it buy whatever gold can buy'.[34] Ignoring his mentor's passionate attacks on the Irish Protestant Ascendancy, Yeats presented their modern-day successors, pre-eminently himself, as the 'people of Burke' — a minority that had contributed most to the 'modern literature' and 'political intelligence' of Ireland.[35]

The political intelligence that Yeats brought to his reading of Burke was uneven and idiosyncratic. For instance, his beliefs that Burke was a Whig who hated Whiggery or that Whiggery itself was a 'levelling, rancorous, rational sort of mind' were peculiar to himself.[36] Moreover, although by 1925 Yeats had enlisted Burke as a precursor of

29 John Morley, Edmund Burke: A Historical Study (London, 1867), 24.

30 Burrow, Whigs and Liberals, 14.

31 McCartney, W. E. H. Lecky, 111–12. 'What was happening in Ireland, Lecky felt, was a violent revolt against a political and social order sanctioned by God, history and Edmund Burke; and, as in the case of Burke in the 1790s, Lecky's world was threatening to topple about his ears.'

32 Edward Huggesson [Baron Brabourne], Facts and Fictions in Irish History: A Reply to Mr. Gladstone (Edinburgh and London, 1886), 3, 42. H. de F. Montgomery also challenged Gladstone's use of Burke; H. de. F. Montgomery, Correspondence with Mr. Gladstone and Notes on the Pamphlet (Dublin, 1887). A. V. Dicey, New Jacobinism and Old Morality (London, n.d.), 18, claimed Burke was fundamentally opposed to the 'new Jacobinism' that reigned in Ireland. George Douglas Campbell [Duke of Argyll], in Irish Nationalism: An Appeal to History (London, 1893), 265–67, also drew on Burke to condemn nationalism and defend the Union.

33 For an account of Burke's criticisms of the assignats, see J. G. A. Pocock, 'The Political Economy of Burke's Analysis of the French Revolution', in Virtue, Commerce, and History: Essays on Political Thought and History, Chiefly in the Eighteenth Century (Cambridge, 1985), 193–212.

34 EI, 314. Yeats drew once more on his condemnation of French revolutionary finance in A, 231. Here he attacked the levelling tendency of modern politics, with its 'mill of argument grinding all things down to mediocrity'. 'If, as I think, mind and metals correspond,' he concluded, 'the goldsmiths of Paris foretold the French Revolution when they substituted steel for that unserviceable gold in the manufacture of the more expensive jewel work'.

35 SS, 99.

36 VP, 486.

the anti-democratic tradition then represented in the writings of Péguy, Claudel, and Maurras, and in Mussolini's fascism, this was effective only as caricature. In that year, Yeats explicitly endorsed Burke's 'organic' concept of the state — 'no mechanism to be pulled in pieces and put up again, but an oak tree that had grown through centuries' — apparently oblivious to the fact that this also constituted a rebuke to the fascist revolution that had won his strong approval.[37] He was at this time fond of quoting Mussolini's remarks on 'the decomposing body of the Goddess of liberty', and disregarded the fact that Burke's anti-revolutionary writings were offered as a defence of what Hume called 'civil liberty' against a particular form of political fundamentalism.[38] Burke's *Second Letter on a Regicide Peace* could easily be read as an indictment of fascist Italy:

> Individuality is left out of their scheme of Government. The state is all in all. Everything is referred to the production of force; afterwards everything is trusted to the use of it. It is military in its principle, in its maxims, in its spirit, and in all its movements. The state has dominion and conquest for its sole object; dominion over minds by proselytism, over bodies by arms.[39]

Yeats saw in fascism a solution to the problem of modern individualism.[40] Burke's anti-revolutionary writings were also critical of an individualist political philosophy; instead of a 'solitary, unconnected, individual, selfish Liberty', Burke had always championed a '*social* freedom'.[41] But his writings also provided a liberal defence of the individual against the encroachments of an absolute state. Burke finally could not be assimilated into Yeats's political project. Yeats acknowledged as much when he used Burke's criticisms of fanatical politics to characterize his own zeal for totalitarian government; he presented his authoritarian interests as a 'new fanaticism' which was comparable to that which 'the people have made of the political thought of the eighteenth century'.[42] While he would continue to decry fanaticism in Ireland — 'Down the fanatic, down the clown' — he was also forced to acknowledge that he himself possessed 'a fanatic heart'.[43]

So, although the charge rebounded upon himself, Yeats repeatedly condemned the fanaticism of Irish nationalism in Burkean terms. There was an obvious irony in

---

37 UP 2. 459. Elizabeth Cullingford, *Yeats, Ireland and Fascism*, 154–57, notes the contradiction between Burke's concept of a state and fascist doctrines. She suggests that Yeats's endorsement of Burke amounted to an implicit disavowal of Mussolini. But his passion for Burke did not seem to diminish his interest in fascism.

38 For Yeats's remarks, see Richard Ellmann, *Yeats: The Man and the Masks* (London, 1979), 249.

39 W & S. 9. 288.

40 Yeats also claimed, however, that fascism represented the rise of the individual man as against what he considered 'the anti-human party machine'. Quoted in Cullingford, *Yeats, Ireland and Fascism*, 148.

41 Edmund Burke, *The Correspondence of Edmund Burke. Volume 6: 1789–91*, ed. Alfred Cobban and Robert A. Smith (Cambridge and Chicago, 1967), 42 [Burke's emphasis].

42 Ellmann, *Yeats: The Man and the Masks*, 249.

43 VP, 506.

this manoeuvre because key strands of Irish nationalism — such as the patriotism of Young Ireland — themselves had a clear Burkean provenance. Burke had successfully harnessed the idea of a 'national character' to resist the corrupting effects of foreign doctrines that had a cosmopolitan or universalizing ambition. Nationalists such as the Young Irelanders repeatedly used the same notion to contest the legitimacy of English structural impositions on local Irish social systems. Nevertheless, Yeats derided Young Ireland's appeal to history; it was, he claimed, in itself ahistorical and supplanted a complex past with a simple-minded caricature.[44] In addition, he maintained that a new nationalism — different (and worse) in its nature and methods from Young Ireland — arose after the fall of Parnell. This recent school of patriotism was dominated by an assertive middle class, those parvenus who had no understanding of the past:

> I could not foresee that a new class, which had begun to rise into power under the shadow of Parnell, would change the nature of the Irish movement, which, needing no longer great sacrifices, nor bringing any great risk to individuals, could do without exceptional men, and those activities of the mind that are founded on the exceptional moment. John O'Leary had spent much of his thought in an unavailing war with the agrarian party, believing it the root of change, but the fox that crept into the badger's hole did not come from there. Power passed to small shopkeepers, to clerks, to that very class who had seemed to John O'Leary so ready to bend to the power of others, to men who had risen above the traditions of the countryman, without learning those of cultivated life or even educating themselves, and who because of their poverty, their ignorance, their superstitious piety, are much subject to all kinds of fear. Immediate victory, immediate utility, became everything, and the conviction ... that life is greater than the cause, withered ...[45]

The teachings of O'Leary's 'school' of patriotism, itself distinct from Young Ireland's, had now been undone by an upstart generation. Conveniently, O'Leary had died in 1907 and — even though Yeats had failed to his attend his funeral — he incorporated the dead Fenian into his growing pantheon of serviceable heroes. O'Leary was a constitutional monarchist, opposed both to republican nationalism and to the universalization of the franchise; he 'hated democracy', Yeats noted, 'with more than feudal hatred' and based his patriotism on an 'aristocratic dream'.[46] If O'Leary's Ireland was dead and gone, it was because the country had experienced something akin to a *bourgeois* revolution. Even if one places an extreme emphasis on Burke's denunciation of a 'monied interest', in order to enhance the anti-bourgeois class element in his attack on the French Revolution, Yeats's account of the nineteenth-century Irish revolution was considerably more class

44 EI, 316–17.
45 EI, 259–60. In 'September 1913' Yeats also contrasted the spirit of O'Leary with the ignorance, piety and materialism that dominated Ireland. VP, 289–90.
46 A, 211; EI, 510.

conscious than that of his much-adapted mentor. The Revolution, for Burke, involved its factions and cabals, but it was not the product of a specific class; it also reflected capitalism's mismanagement more than its immanent development. According to Yeats, however, the source and symptom of the Irish Revolution was an acquisitive and overreaching middle class. Lacking the guiding wisdom of an established tradition, the ideals of this group were necessarily abstract.

2 Abstract Hatred and Irish Nationalism

In his attacks on nationalism, Yeats seized upon a fundamental Burkean principle: the conditions for meaningful political inquiry are necessarily derived from our established social framework. To abstract one's claims from their enabling context is to move beyond meaning. The 'aëronauts of France' had attempted this kind of experiment and it led, Burke concluded, to confusion and error.[47] In their pursuit of moral certainties, the French left behind them the only things that could have given them orientation in the world — namely the values and understandings that were internal to historical forms of life. Revolutionaries engaged in a disastrous form of inversion when they prioritized abstract theory above the concrete practices of everyday social experience. In presenting theory as a foundational discourse — an account of the world that set the terms for everything else — these figures forgot that the theoretical attitude was itself a derivative mode of access to reality. The revolutionary desire for an absolute beginning was as irrational as it was hubristic; it was a self-inflating fantasy that overlooked the social and historical foundations of reason itself.

Yeats repeatedly attacked Irish nationalism on these grounds. The problem with the Irish, he declared in the Senate, was that 'we are all theory mad'.[48] Yeats may have had in mind the often technical and theoretical character of the debates about sovereignty that followed the Treaty in 1921, but his sweeping meta-theories had been in operation well before this. Since, at least, the time of Synge's death in 1909, he had convinced himself that Ireland was in thrall to a destructive form of logical purism. This form of understanding was both inhumane and unforgiving, for the straight lines of logic were fundamentally at odds with the crooked character of human life. In his essay on Synge in 1910, he denounced the 'churlish logicians' of modern Ireland. Here he insisted that the Ireland cherished by nationalists was an abstraction and the values they championed were artificial and empty. The implicit recognition that 'what is so unreal needs continual defence' made nationalists 'bitter and restless'.[49] In 1918 — the year he spent immersed in Burke's writings — he lamented the fact that 'logic-choppers rule the town'.[50] He

47 W & S 8. 293.
48 SS, 35.
49 EI, 313.
50 'Tom O Roughley', VP, 337–38, 337.

retained this conviction for the rest of his life. 'This country', he told Oliver Gogarty, 'is ruined by transcendentalism. It has been ruined by dreams — vague, objectless, unrealisable dreams'.[51]

But Yeats had previously applauded this transcendentalism as a powerful and distinctly Irish virtue. He had initially believed that the Irish passion for the abstract had deep historical roots: 'I used to think that the French and Irish democracies follow, as John O'Leary used to say, a logical deduction to its end, no matter what suffering it caused, because they were Celtic.'[52] Yeats's early understanding of 'Celtic' character was in some respects an inversion of Burke's account of Englishness; Burke had contrasted the natively pragmatic English with the theoretically minded French. According to the young Yeats, the Irish resembled the French in their passion for abstraction. Burke had criticized the French advocacy of abstract rights in his counter-revolutionary writings, but Yeats, in his earlier years, endorsed Ireland's commitment to these principles:

> To me it has always seemed that the passion for abstract right, which has made the letters to the press, the occasional speeches, and above all the conversation of Mr. John O'Leary so influential with the younger generation, is the Celtic passion for ideas, intensified by that mistrust of the expedient which comes to men who have seen the failure of many hopes.[53]

These comments were offered in commemoration of the 1798 rebellion, which drew much of its inspiration from the French Revolution. Yeats downplayed the differences between the Irish and the French in his general commendation of 'the Celtic peoples'. He also linked a Celtic passion for 'abstract right', 'abstract law', 'abstract ideas', and 'abstract emotion', with a series of other well-established tropes representing this apparently Irish virtue. The Irish love of abstraction merged with an Irish 'mistrust of the expedient' so typical of the English utilitarian attitude.[54] Arnold had famously commended a Celtic idealism that pitched itself against the 'despotism of fact'; Yeats's Celts also refused to be bound by the rigours of the sensible world.[55]

The enabling background to Yeats's youthful endorsement of Irish abstraction was a Platonic conception of time and reality. Plato's distinction between true and apparent worlds, or supersensuous and sensuous realities, dominated Yeats's early work and

---

51   Oliver St. John Gogarty, *Going Native* (New York, 1940), 10. Quoted in Torchiana, *W. B. Yeats and Georgian Ireland*, 213.

52   M , 209.

53   UP 2. 36. Rights, Burke insisted, existed within an established political structure and did not belong to individuals living in a state of nature. In other words, rights were a product of political society; they were not its legitimizing condition. When the French presented the rights enjoyed by pre-political individuals as the necessary and sufficient condition of political legitimacy they displayed, he felt, a destructive ignorance of the real foundations of political obligation.

54   UP 2. 36–37.

55   UP 2. 36.

allowed him to depict a turn from the material world as an ascent into truth. Yeats later rejected the nihilistic quality of Platonic thought in Nietzschean terms. Plato, as he put it, 'prepares the Christian desert and the Stoic suicide' when he separated the Ideal from the sensuous world.[56] The early Yeats, however, was Plato's disciple; basic features of Platonism were available to him in the Christian tradition; in the writings of his beloved Shelley; and in more esoteric practices such as symbolism. The temporal vision that emerged under this influence was one whereby history featured as a kind of degeneration, a fall from a primordial state of purity or true being. This view of history as decline allowed Yeats to take his Plato with his primitivism. Ireland, he suggested, was home to an older or more primordial civilization that possessed a basic familiarity with a true being that antedated the fall into history. As he put it in 1898, 'that sense of abstract ideas, of abstract law ... the Celtic peoples have preserved, together with a capacity for abstract emotion, longer than more successful and practical races'.[57] By taking Ireland as its object, Yeats suggested that European civilization could initiate a kind of collective anamnesis and restore itself to its primordial truth. His task, as he put it, was to express 'the idealism of the common people, who still remember the dawn of the world'.[58]

Even in the midst of his praise for Irish abstraction, he acknowledged its destructive aspects. 'The very inhumanity of Irish journalism and of Irish politics', he claimed in his '98 Centenary article, 'comes from a tendency to judge men not by one another, not by experience of the degree of excellence one may hope to meet in life and in politics, but by some abstract standard'.[59] Significantly, as the poet's disenchantment with nationalist politics grew throughout the subsequent decade, he amplified his criticisms of the inhumane features of Irish abstraction. He thus began to sponsor an experiential and circumstantial wisdom over any formal appeal to an absolute and overarching standard. Moreover, he was careful to insist that the 'French and Irish democracies follow ... a logical deduction to its end, no matter what suffering it caused', not because of some inherent racial attribute or because of their fortunate proximity to some Platonic ideal, but rather because of their fatal severance from history.[60]

In saying this, Yeats had re-evaluated his previous notion of history. Time's passing was no longer a forgetting of being, as it was under the Platonic schema, but was an altogether more Burkean affair: it was a slow and incremental accretion of human wisdom. Truth was no longer a property that existed before or outside of history, but was something internal to a set of established traditions and practices. Crucially, he believed that Irish nationalists had alienated themselves from these historical frameworks. In

---

56 M, 271. He also claimed that Plato was the 'First Christian'. See V, 263. According to MacNeice, *The Poetry of W. B. Yeats*, 130, Yeats hoped to avoid in his own system 'the split, the *chorismos*, in Plato's between the worlds of Being and Becoming'.

57 UP 2. 37.

58 UP 2. 196.

59 UP 2. 37.

60 M, 206.

their apparent pursuit of the 'aëronauts of France' Irish patriots had lost contact with ordinary human life. Yeats, therefore, repeatedly juxtaposed the myriad complexity of 'life' with the nihilistic features of nationalist principle: reality failed to measure up to fixed ideals and was rejected on this basis. 'They no longer love', he declared in 1910, 'for only life is loved', and the Irish had supplanted 'life' with a rigid logic.[61]

He was careful to suggest that the rebels of 1916 suffered from an 'excess', rather than a lack, of love, but he also implied that their ideals were at odds with the dynamic and temporal character of life itself:

> Hearts with one purpose alone
> Through summer and winter seem
> Enchanted to a stone
> To trouble the living stream.[62]

The idées fixes of nationalism, it seems, 'trouble the living stream'; the half rhyme of 'one' and 'alone' enacts an insistent singularity of purpose, while the 'stone' embodies its barren result. 'Enchanted', things may be, but lacquered fantasies of liberty seem to produce, rather than redeem, a brutal world.

'Easter 1916' is considerably more complex than an outright indictment of rebellion. Despite his addiction to counter-revolutionary jargon, the Rising in Ireland provoked a genuine ambivalence in the poet. Yeats admired and envied men of action and he often worried that his own contemplative life lacked in comparison both substance and commitment.[63] Moreover, Yeats's genuine man of action was not abstract but wholly concrete; his deeds were their own justification. This was the explicit theme of 'Sixteen Dead Men'; the rebels communicate 'bone to bone' and it is their critics who are lost to an anaemic 'logic'.[64] A similar interpretation could arguably be applied to the Rising itself. It was a foundational moment and its violence could not be condemned by the civilization that it made possible; such criticisms were anachronistic and ultimately incoherent. Judged in this context, the 'stone' of 'Easter 1916' may be seen to stand as a symbolic foundation for a new order. From this perspective, the Rising is the source of a new set of norms, but it is not derived from, or subject to, these norms. The stone of revolution is, therefore, the 'total exception'; it stands outside the general flux of life, but it is the still point from which life gains pattern and significance.[65] Pure contingency,

---

61 EI, 314. In his *Reflections* Burke had defended life from political hatred; the French, he avowed, 'can entertain no sensation of life except in a mortified and humiliated indignation'. *W & S* 8. 100.

62 VP, 393.

63 This is a repeated theme of *Meditations in Time of Civil War*. Here, for instance, a republican soldier provokes envy and self-recrimination in the poet. See VP, 423–24.

64 VP, 395.

65 For this theory of the exception, see Carl Schmitt, *Political Theology: Four Chapters on the Concept of Sovereignty*, trans. George Schwab (Chicago and London, 1985). Schmitt invoked the idea of the exception to defend the authority of the state, but the same theory could easily be used to support the legitimacy of violent

often indistinguishable in the poem from eternal repetition — 'Minute by minute they change' — is thus transformed into a meaningful process.

Yeats was attracted to the idea of a foundational violence and explored the theme in detail in 'The Second Coming', 'Leda and the Swan' and later poems; however, in 'Easter 1916' he remains troubled by its implications.[66] The title and theme of the poem pointed to the redemptive potential of sacrifice, but the poet also suggests that redemption has its limits: 'Too long a sacrifice / Can make a stone of the heart'.[67] Once more, an image of petrifaction emphasizes the inhumane qualities of unrelenting principle. Readers such as Maud Gonne were alert to the negative implications of the poem's core metaphors. Gonne was adamant that 'sacrifice has never yet turned a heart to stone though it has immortalised many'. She strongly rejected the implication that the rebels exemplified the pathology of idées fixes: 'you could never say that MacDonagh & Pearse & Conally [sic] were sterile fixed minds'.[68] Yeats's thoughts about the rebel leaders may have been ambivalent, but he was convinced that Gonne embodied the sterility of fixed principles.

He had arguably Gonne in mind when he compared Ireland in 1910 to a 'hysterical woman who will make unmeasured accusations and believe impossible things, because of some logical deduction from a solitary thought which has turned a portion of her mind to stone'.[69] He was strangely convinced that women were more prone to this fanaticism than men and produced a biological explanation of this unfortunate predilection.[70] This was a curiously literal interpretation of an old trope that associated revolutionary fervour with female hysteria. Since the famous march of the poissardes to the Royal Palace in Versailles on 5 October 1789, women had come to symbolize a dangerous form of political enthusiasm.[71] Yeats's highly politicized accounts of women continue in this

revolution. James Connolly, for instance, emphasized the exceptional character of revolution in 1915: 'We believe in constitutional action in normal times; we believe in revolutionary action in exceptional times. These are exceptional times.' James Connolly, Collected Works, 2 vols. (Dublin, 1988), 2. 117.

66 For a discussion of these themes in 'The Second Coming' and 'Leda and the Swan', see Deane, Strange Country, 172–81.

67 VP, 394.

68 Maud Gonne MacBride, The Gonne–Yeats Letters, 1893–1938: Always Your Friend, eds. Anna MacBride White and A. Norman Jeffares (London, 1992), 384.

69 EI, 314. This image of female hysteria was derived from Goethe's account of religious enthusiasm in Wilhelm Meister. Here, as Yeats described it, 'a saintly and naturally gracious woman, who, on getting into a quarrel over some trumpery detail of religious observance, grows — she and all her little religious community — angry and vindictive'. VP, 818–19. Yeats was not the first to associate religious enthusiasm with modern forms of political fanaticism. Jacobinism resembled Puritanism, Burke had argued, in its proselytizing zeal and uncompromising absolutism. On this point, see J. G. A. Pocock, 'Edmund Burke and the Redefinition of Enthusiasm: The Context as Counter-Revolution', in François Furet and Mona Ozouf, eds., The French Revolution and the Creation of Modern Culture. Volume 3: The Transformation of Political Culture, 1739–1848 (Oxford, 1989), 19–43. In A Vision, Yeats condemned 'the declamatory religious sects and controversies that first in England and then in France destroy the sense of form'. V, 296.

70 'Women,' he maintained, 'because the main event of their lives has been a giving themselves and giving birth, give all to an opinion as if it were some terrible stone doll'. A, 504.

71 See Deane, Strange Country, 117–22. Burke condemned the antics of those 'furies of hell, in the abused shape of the vilest of women' and a host of subsequent writers looked back upon the Amazons of

tradition. In 'Easter 1916' the redemptive power of sacrifice is extended to all the male rebels — even John MacBride — but the political activities of Con Markievicz are wholly corrupting. Her misplaced benevolence and querulous disposition lead to aesthetic — and presumably moral — disaster. The poem 'On a Political Prisoner' made the same point in greater length. Here fanaticism has turned the mind of the countess into 'a bitter, an abstract thing'.[72] The dangers of revolutionary hysteria were evident in a later and damning account of Markievicz and her sister:

> The older is condemned to death
> Pardoned, drags out lonely years
> Conspiring among the ignorant.
> I know not what the younger dreams —
> Some vague Utopia — and she seems,
> When withered old and skeleton-gaunt,
> An image of such politics.[73]

Both women, Yeats suggested, were committed to an impossible politics opposed to all possible worlds — an early draft of the poem denounced their 'Abstract humanitarian dream'.[74] This political idealism, he suggests, conspired against all actual forms of community, and even against the embodied self, for all kinds of determination detracted from the purity of absolute ideals. The search for Utopia, therefore, was ultimately self-destructive, as Yeats's cruel portraiture makes clear.[75] Time and time again Yeats emphasized the negative character of utopian aspiration. 'Capable of nothing but an incapable idealism', he maintained, this politics was wholly negative.[76]

From the beginning, it was precisely the negativity of French revolutionary ideals upon which its critics seized. De Maistre's interpretation of French nihilism was Augustinian: the Revolution was the epitome of evil and the latter was a form of non-being; evil, he declared, 'has nothing in common with life; it cannot create, since its power is purely negative'.[77] The negativity of the Revolution, for Burke, however, arose more from its metaphysical and utopian character: against its exorbitant idealism, all human life was found wanting. Hegel defended aspects of the Revolution, but he also

---

revolution in fascination and fear. Burke, W & S 8. 122. Carlyle deemed Europe 'hag-ridden' since the French Revolution. Thomas Carlyle, *Critical and Miscellaneous Essays*, 6 vols. (London, 1872), 6. 138.

72 VP, 397.

73 VP, 475.

74 Jon Stallworthy, *Between the Lines: Yeats's Poetry in the Making* (Oxford, 1963), 169.

75 Yeats qualified this charge in later years: 'In the lines of the poem which condemn her politics I was not thinking of her part in two rebellions but of other matters of quarrel. We had never been on the same side at the same time.' Quoted in Foster, *Arch-Poet*, 436.

76 V, 138.

77 De Maistre, *Considerations on France*, 38.

denounced its extreme negativity. In the revolutionary desire to isolate the rational will from all determinations, the rational merely degenerated into an empty formalism. Reason could not supply a concrete content to its own willing, and distinguished itself solely by its abstract negation of life. To be a specific will, attached to a particular body, immersed in an established community, was to have lent oneself a determination that was indistinguishable from a forfeiture of freedom. The 'fury of destruction' that accompanied the Revolution, according to Hegel, was a natural by-product of this excessively negative view of freedom, for 'only in destroying something does this negative will have a feeling of its own existence'.[78] For Nietzsche, the French Revolution was largely a product of *ressentiment* and this was also a fundamentally negative disposition; it 'says "no" on principle to everything that is "outside", "other", "non-self": and this "no" is its creative deed'.[79]

Yeats drew on this complex heritage in his own criticisms of Irish negativity and rancour. He provided a playful account of this negative temperament in his poem 'The Three Beggars'. The beggars, it seems, suffer from a crippling *ressentiment*, while King Guaire practises the gay science. He offers a thousand pounds to the first beggar who manages to fall asleep '"before the third noon sounds"'.[80] Predictably, the beggars fail. First, they exchange utopian projections of contentment — 'exorbitant dreams of beggary, / That idleness had borne to pride' — and then try to succeed by depriving each other of sleep.[81] This wholly negative disposition, fuelled by fictions of well-being and a more concrete distrust, eventually culminate in violence. The beggars maul and bite each other through day and night, until King Guaire discovers them 'commingling lice and blood'.[82] This is offered, perhaps, as a primordial example of revolutionary internecine strife.

The dangers of internecine conflict are considerably more menacing in the poetic cycle, *Meditations in Time of Civil War*. The poems appear to include Irish nationalism in their general condemnation of a fanatical idealism. Irish ideals, Yeats suggests, are as destructive as they are empty:

> We had fed the heart on fantasies,
> The heart's grown brutal from the fare;
> More substance in our enmities
> Than in our love ...[83]

---

78 Hegel, *Philosophy of Right*, 38.
79 Friedrich Nietzsche, *On the Genealogy of Morality*, ed. Keith Ansell-Pearson, trans. Carol Diethe (Cambridge, 1994), 21 [Nietzsche's emphasis].
80 VP, 295.
81 VP, 296.
82 VP, 297.
83 VP, 425.

In 'I see Phantoms of Hatred and of the Heart's Fullness and of the Coming Emptiness' he again criticized the dangerous vacuity of revolutionary aspiration. The pedigree of the 'rage-driven, rage-tormented and rage-hungry troop' might be traced to the fourteenth century or to the French Revolution, but it also reflects Yeats's criticisms of modern Irish nationalism.[84] The poem's repetitive lexis enacts an obsessive fixity of purpose. The soldiers plunge 'towards nothing, arms and fingers spreading wide / For the embrace of nothing' — the poem's repeated 'nothings' again emphasize the extreme negativity of fundamentalist zeal.[85] Yeats returned to the same image of barren aspiration in 'A Crazed Moon', where lunatic fingers are once again spread wide to 'rend what comes in reach'.[86]

The poet's campaign against 'abstract hatred' marked yet another reversal of earlier attitudes.[87] He had entertained high hopes for hatred in his youth and had 'dreamed of enlarging Irish hate, till we had come to hate with a passion of patriotism what Morris and Ruskin hated'.[88] Hatred, he suggested elsewhere, would produce its own infinity in its ability to negate every kind of determination and every limit to its own passion.[89] But it was precisely the bad infinity of 'abstract hatred' that he denounced in later life.[90] He recoiled from Ireland's 'whirlpool of hatred', insisting in his poetry that 'Great hatred, little room, / Maimed us at the start'.[91] Yeats even worried that his own writing risked being undermined by 'a kind of Jacobin rage'.[92] In a series of poems, he warned his friends and loved ones about the corrupting effects of logical fundamentalism. Of all types of rancour, an 'intellectual hatred is the worst'.[93]

Yeats believed that such hatred was also sterile; it was incapable of recognizing anything positive outside of its own furious, negating energy.[94] As minds in Ireland grew

---

84 These troops seek vengeance for the murder of Jacques de Molay, Grand Master of the Templars, who was burned at the stake in 1314. Here Yeats appeared to endorse the influential thesis of Abbé de Barruel, in which Masonry was presented as a cause of the French Revolution. In an explanatory note to the poem, Yeats observed that the burning of Jacques de Molay 'is said to have been incorporated in the ritual of certain Masonic societies of the eighteenth century, and to have fed class hatred'. VP, 827.

85 'You will never create anything following the path of nothingness,' De Maistre warned, and Yeats seems to repeat the warning. De Maistre, *Considerations on France*, 86.

86 VP, 488.

87 VP, 482.

88 EI, 248.

89 EI, 181.

90 VP, 482.

91 Quoted in Foster, *Arch-Poet*, 214; VP, 506.

92 M, 157.

93 VP, 405. In an early version of the poem, he admitted that his 'own mind of late / Has grown half barren from much hate'. See Stallworthy, *Between the Lines*, 35. He duly craved for protection from the enervating effects of logic in 'A Prayer for Old Age': 'God guard me from those thoughts men think / In the mind alone'. VP, 553.

94 As Hannah Arendt remarked in a discussion of the French Revolution, 'rage is not only impotent by definition, it is the mode in which impotence becomes active in its last stage of final despair'. Hannah Arendt, *On Revolution* (London, 1990), 211.

ever more formal and empty, their destructive effects paradoxically seemed all the more visceral:

> Hatred as a basis of imagination, in ways which one could explain even without magic, helps to dry up the nature and makes the sexual abstinence, so common among young men and women in Ireland, possible. This abstinence reacts in its turn on the imagination, so that we get at last that strange eunuch-like tone and temper. For the last ten or twenty years there has been a perpetual drying of the Irish mind, with the resultant dust-cloud.[95]

Yeats's critique of abstract hatred seems to present itself as a liberal plea for tolerance in the face of a virulent form of political fundamentalism. And one can argue that his use of counter-revolutionary rhetoric amounts to precisely this. But Yeats's denunciation of the illiberal features of nationalist abstraction is also linked to his repudiation of modern democracy. Of course, these positions were not necessarily inconsistent. Many nineteenth-century commentators regarded liberal values and democratic practices as fundamentally opposed.[96] If Irish nationalism was illiberal, this was partly a function of its democratic character.[97] But Yeats's criticisms of democracy went further than this and eroded the foundations of his more liberal views.

3 Nationalism and Democracy

Yeats had once made the proud boast about Ireland that no 'country could have a more natural distaste for equality'.[98] Under the influence of a democratically minded nationalism, however, the country soon acquired artificial tastes. As far as Yeats was concerned, democratic equality was a dangerous fiction that suppressed the real qualities and distinguishing features of human beings. He read and underlined Nietzsche's denunciation of equality — the principle, according to the philosopher, was 'a self-contradiction, an art of self-violation, a will to lie at any price, a repugnance, a contempt

---

95 M, 177.

96 According to Lecky, for example, 'a tendency to democracy does not mean a tendency to parliamentary government, or even a tendency towards greater liberty. On the contrary, strong arguments may be adduced, both from history and from the nature of things, to show that democracy may often prove the direct opposite of liberty'. Lecky, *Democracy and Liberty*, 1. 217.

97 Yeats was convinced that it was not just nationalists who possessed dangerous fantasies and grasping fingers. 'Personality', he claimed, 'is everywhere spreading out its fingers in vain, or grasping with an always more convulsive grasp a world where the predominance of physical science, of finance and economics in all their forms, of democratic politics, of vast populations, of architecture where styles jostle one another, of newspapers where all is heterogeneous, show that mechanical force will in a moment become supreme.' V, 296.

98 A, 231.

for all good and straightforward instincts!'[99] Yeats's own critique of equality was equally robust: it reduced all life to 'Muck in the yard'.[100] He also believed that the principle of equality was essentially despotic. Since equality can never be found in the actual world, the principle had to be artificially installed through a ruthless suppression of individual differences. As he noted wistfully late in life: 'Instead of hierarchical society where all men are different, came democracy.'[101]

Yeats remained committed, therefore, to Burke's critique of 'mathematical equality' and championed the virtues of hierarchical societies.[102] In his edition of Burke's works, one finds an earmarked section in which the necessary condition of property is its unequal distribution: 'The characteristic essence of property, formed out of the combined principles of its acquisition and conservation is to be unequal.'[103] Whether or not these were Yeats's markings remains uncertain, but the passage certainly accords with his expressed views. 'Landed property,' he suggested in 1930, 'gets its fascination from its inequality: divide it up into farms of equal size or fertility and it would still retain its inequality, no field or hedge like another.'[104] Hierarchical society had, it seemed, nature's sanction.

As a famous sponsor of equality, Rousseau was a particular object of the poet's ire.[105] Yeats was just one of a host of modernist writers who rounded on Rousseau as both the source and epitome of modern depravity.[106] These polemics were as crude as they were extreme and Yeats's criticisms represented little advance in sophistication or restraint. Late in life he presented Swift as a prophet and critic of Rousseauvian values: he 'foresaw

---

99 Yeats owned the Thomas Common edition of Nietzsche's works. See the National Library of Ireland, 1444.

100 VP, 547.

101 E, 435.

102 VP, 481.

103 Yeats owned the Bohn edition of Burke's works. See the National Library of Ireland, 306.

104 E, 313.

105 Here Yeats was clearly outmatched — and perhaps influenced — by Nietzsche. Rousseau, for Nietzsche, was the 'first modern person, idealist and rabble rolled into one; who needed moral "dignity" in order to stand the sight of himself'. Nietzsche despised, above all, the egalitarian features of Rousseau's doctrine. Friedrich Nietzsche, The Anti-Christ, Ecce Homo, Twilight of the Idols and Other Writings, eds. Aaron Ridley and Judith Norman, trans. Judith Norman (Cambridge, 2005), 221.

106 In the New Age in 1910, Allen Upward condemned Rousseau's 'Religion of Humanity'. New Age, 3 January 1910. In 1914, Blast declared its opposition to all 'ROUSSEAUISMS'. Wyndham Lewis, ed., Blast, 1 (1914). According to Lewis, 'there was truly a principle of disintegration, a nihilism, in Rousseau that accounted for all the instinctive hatred of him'. Wyndham Lewis, The Art of Being Ruled (London, 1926), 359. T. E. Hulme despised romanticism, claiming that 'all Romanticism springs from Rousseau'. T. E. Hulme, The Collected Writings of T. E. Hulme, ed. Karen Csengeri (Oxford, 1994), 249. T. S. Eliot was also a critic of romanticism and Rousseau. In a set of lectures in 1916, he presented Rousseau as an individualist who downgraded thought in the name of feeling and entertained a naïve faith in human goodness. See Ronald Schuchard, 'Eliot as an Extension Lecturer', Review of English Studies, 25, 98 (1974), 165–66. Eliot was an admirer of Irving Babbitt who also derided Rousseau. See Irving Babbitt, Rousseau and Romanticism (Boston and New York, 1919) and Irving Babbitt, Democracy and Leadership (Boston and New York, 1924), 70–96.

the ruin to come, Democracy, Rousseau, the French Revolution'.[107] Here Yeats endorsed the contention that Rousseau provided the fuel for the terror and insisted that the values of the *First Discourse* culminated in 'the *sans-cullotes* [sic] of Marat'.[108] Rousseau, he maintained, promoted a dangerous cult of the savage, but this was a misrepresentation of the philosopher's true position. Unlike Yeats himself, Rousseau had always dismissed both the viability and desirability of a return to a savage state.[109] Human beings may have relinquished a natural innocence and simplicity for their incorporation into civil society, but this transition was also ennobling, converting, as it did, a 'stupid and bounded animal' into an 'intelligent being'.[110] Only in civil society, moreover, was true virtue possible; savage man, on the other hand, was not properly a moral being at all.[111]

Yeats was mistaken, therefore, when he associated Rousseauvianism with a naïve faith in humanity's primordial goodness. Many figures in the counter-revolutionary tradition, however, had adopted such a line. Rousseau's apparent faith in human goodness, according to Nietzsche, was a bad sublimation of Christian values.[112] Péguy and Claudel, on the other hand, championed the Christian doctrine of original sin as a bulwark to ideas of natural goodness, which they attributed to Rousseau. Yeats gave explicit approval to these French writers in his essay 'If I were Four and Twenty'.[113] A simple-minded faith in the good man, according to Yeats, weakened the works of Shelley and Ruskin; it also damaged Wordsworth, who was an obvious 'descendant of Rousseau'. The strength of Shakespeare, Villon, Dante and Cervantes, on the other hand, derived from their shared 'preoccupation with evil'.[114] Here he was keen to insist that the people of Ireland 'believed from our cradle in original sin' and were, therefore, suspicious of philanthropic schemes involving cosmopolitan benevolence.[115]

---

107 E, 350.

108 E, 363. Yeats followed Burke in assuming that Rousseau's writings had fomented the French Revolution. In the 1790s, Burke suggested that if Rousseau was alive and 'in one of his lucid intervals, he would be shocked at the practical phrenzy of his scholars, who in their paradoxes are servile imitators; and even in their incredulity discover an implicit faith'. Burke, W & S 8. 219. For a more sceptical assessment of Rousseau's impact on the Revolution, see Joan McDonald, *Rousseau and the French Revolution, 1762–1792* (London, 1965).

109 In a debate triggered by his *First Discourse*, he proclaimed that a return to humanity's first equality was impossible. Such an attempt 'would only plunge Europe back into Barbarism and morals would gain nothing from it'. Rousseau, *Discourses*, 50.

110 Rousseau, *Social Contract*, 53.

111 Civil society constituted a 'moral freedom' that was denied to us in a state of nature; here individuals escaped the bondage of animal appetite and lived under self-prescribed and rational laws. Rousseau, *Social Contract*, 54.

112 Nietzsche professed to despise Rousseau's 'good man'. Friedrich Nietzsche, *The Will to Power*, ed. Walter Kaufmann, trans. Walter Kaufmann and R. J. Hollingdale (New York, 1968), 529. According to Nietzsche, Rousseau's concept of nature was 'still a cult of Christian morality fundamentally'. *Will to Power*, 186. Nietzsche did, however, juxtapose Rousseau's doctrine with 'Pascal's logic' which emphasizsed the significance of original sin. Nietzsche, *Will to Power*, 190.

113 E, 265–66.

114 E, 275.

115 E, 276.

But the Irish were less immune to a destructive rationalism, which Yeats also related to Rousseau. In his *Memoirs*, he wondered whether or not a 'popular thinker' like a Rousseau, Voltaire, or Wesley was not a misfortune; such men were 'too clever, too logical, too definite'.[116] Overlooking Rousseau's frequent attacks on a one-dimensional reason, Yeats maintained that Rousseau had banished the Christian God and had erected the idol 'Reason' in its place. Rousseau was unable to distinguish between an abstract reason and a more experiential wisdom or 'prudence to judge of acts and their consequences'. Everyone possesses an equal, abstract capacity for reason, Yeats suggested, but not everyone exercises prudential wisdom, because this is shaped by experience. 'All have "reason"', he argued, 'but not all have "the means of exercising it and the materials, the facts and ideas upon which it is exercised", nor have all that have the means "power of attention"'. 'Historical society is founded upon these difficulties' and Rousseau's views apparently overlooked this complexity.[117] He thus allowed 'the little to believe themselves great, to believe they understand, till they muddy all the fountains of truth'.[118] Rousseau did, in fact, distinguish between our universal capacity for reason and the unevenness of its actual development; it was on that very basis that he outlined the need for education and for a legislator who would tame public unreason.[119] But Yeats did not hesitate over these issues when criticizing the Rousseauvian vices of his times.

Rousseau had presented a sophisticated account of a social contract as a basis for legitimate rule, but Yeats appeared to believe that the entire contractarian tradition had culminated in moral and political disaster — most notably the French Revolution. Rousseau and the other Encyclopaedists were to blame, but the trouble had started, it seems, with Hobbes. 'After the individualist, demagogic movement founded by Hobbes and popularized by the Encyclopaedists and the French Revolution,' Yeats opined, 'we have a soil so exhausted that it cannot grow that crop again for centuries.'[120] The remark was so vague that it was virtually irrefutable, but it appeared to be broadly directed against an atomistic and voluntaristic outlook, the origins of which Yeats traced to Hobbes's social contract. Here the pre-political individual became the owner of natural rights, which dictated the necessary and sufficient conditions for political association. Yeats dismissed this method not simply for its individualistic starting-point, but also for its ethical voluntarism; political society, in other words, was not a product of the individual will.

---

116 M, 170.

117 E, 314.

118 M, 170. Yeats's references to fountains here and elsewhere in poems such as *Meditations in Time of Civil War* have a strong Burkean resonance. As Burke put it in the *Reflections*: 'France has always more or less influenced manners in England; and when your fountain is choked up and polluted, the stream will not run long, or not run clear with us, or perhaps with any nation.' W & S 8. 131.

119 'By itself the people always wills the good, but by itself it does not always see it. The general will is always upright but the judgment that guides it is not always enlightened. ... Hence arises the necessity of a Lawgiver.' *Social Contract*, 68.

120 VP, 828.

Yeats had always regarded the will with some trepidation.[121] He worried about a reification of the personality that resulted from an emphasis on will and criticized its anti-social features. He suggested that the 'will is by its very nature an antagonist of the social order'.[122] In their efforts to secure the autonomy of the will, individuals estranged themselves from their social environments; but, removed thus from its contexts, the will was simply a formal and negative principle. 'Will', he claimed, 'is always at crisis, or approaching crisis; everything else is made fantastic or violent that the will, without seeming to do so, may exceed nature'.[123] Characteristically, he tended to read the exercise of the will along class lines. In 1904, he contrasted a 'middle class literature that comes more out of will and reason' with a more genuine literature that is a product of 'imagination and sympathy'.[124] But he also associated an overassertive will with the doctrines of the French Revolution. The Rights of Man, he suggested, was an individualistic credo based upon a reductive 'logic' and a brutal 'will'.[125]

Yeats chose to promote family values against a wilful individualism. This was another restatement of Burkean wisdom.[126] Burke had insisted that political association must be understood on the basis of the family — an association with moral bonds that did not depend upon consent: 'the elements of the commonwealth in most cases begin, and always continue, independently of our will, so, without any stipulation on our own part, are we bound by that relation called our country'.[127] The French revolutionaries, he suggested, were dismissive of the institution of family and 'because the relation is not, of course, the result of *free election*; never so on the side of the children, not always on the part of the parents'.[128] Rousseau, 'a lover of his kind, but a hater of his kindred' was for Burke the concrete embodiment of this political disposition.[129]

Yeats insisted that 'the family is the unit of social life, and the origin of civilization which but exists to preserve it'.[130] His definition of family was an extremely broad one

121 Even though the will was one of the key dialectical motors of *A Vision*, he was careful to insist that 'when Will acts alone all is abstract utility, economics, a mechanism to prolong existence'. V, 195 [Yeats's emphasis]. Yeats's father was also a critic of the will. He told his son that 'will power is like the police in a city, and sometimes as you know, there are cities like Berlin where everything is in the hands of the police'. J. B. Yeats, *Letters to His Son and Others*, 124.

122 E, 271.

123 EI, 444.

124 PI, 135.

125 E, 270.

126 EI, 444.

127 Burke, *Works*, 6. 207.

128 W & S 8. 315–16 [Burke's emphasis].

129 W & S 8. 315. Yeats also made political capital out of Rousseau's children — 'When Rousseau dropped his babies in / The Foundling-basket it was sin' — and suggested that the Catholic Church replicated his disregard for the home by encouraging illegitimate children to be placed in public institutions. Quoted in Foster, *Arch-Poet*, 418.

130 E, 274. According to Marjorie Howes, Yeats 'casts sexuality and familial relations as the very origins and building blocks of civilization and simultaneously deprives them of the "natural" status which myths of origin usually enjoy'. *Yeats's Nations*, 110.

and could incorporate a range of political structures; he understood 'by family all institutions, classes, orders, nations, that arise out of the family and are held together, not by a logical process, but by historical association, and possess a personality for whose lack men are "sheep without a shepherd when the snow shuts out the sun"'.[131] In a set of reflections upon Balzac's politics, Yeats championed family 'against individual man armed with Liberty, Equality, Fraternity'.[132] The spirits with which Yeats was in communication in 1919 shared his love of family. 'What is the opposite,' he asked, 'of the abstraction which produces the rage to destroy?' The answer was simple but emphatic: 'family love'.[133] Yeats gave his own account of family affection in 'A Prayer for My Daughter' and hoped his child would perpetuate its attendant benefits — custom, ceremony and good manners.[134]

In 'A Prayer for My Daughter', Lady Gregory's wood is the one thing that offers protection from the 'roof-levelling wind'.[135] Here and elsewhere Yeats associated family values with aristocracy and contrasted both with the levelling forces of a democratic age. 'Privilege, pride, the rights of property', he suggested, were principles that protected the family from modern levellers armed with the 'Rights of Man'.[136] In A Vision, he juxtaposed 'kindred', 'aristocracy', and 'particularity' with 'democracy' and 'abstraction'.[137] It was a cliché of nineteenth-century political thought to associate aristocracy with concrete values — or what Yeats called 'particularity'. Aristocracies were the product of time and had stood its test; their very existence, therefore, were their own justification and they needed no external criterion or abstract ratification. Democracy had no such presumption in its favour and necessarily validated itself on an abstract basis. Democracies based their legitimacy on entities such as the general will, but aristocracies had no use for fictions of this kind. Democrats made much of equality, but their critics judged this to be a dangerous abstraction; aristocracy, according to its enthusiasts, was more aligned with the pattern of nature.

131 E, 273–74.
132 EI, 444. Yeats told Maud Gonne that Balzac had transformed his political outlook. The reading of Balzac between 1903 and 1904 had encouraged him to relinquish his 'republican' views. 'The great political service which Balzac did me was that he made authoritative government [...] interesting in my eyes.' See Yeats in Gonne MacBride, The Gonne–Yeats Letters, 434, 437.
133 George Mills Harper, The Making of Yeats's 'A Vision': A Study of the Automatic Script, 2 vols. (Houndmills, Basingstoke, Hampshire and London, 1987), 2. 362. Of course, the spirits had also the power to unnerve. Plagued for information about his own spiritual pedigree a harassed George declared that he was the reincarnation of the bastard son of the duchess of Orleans and Camille Desmoulins. This was not good news. Fortunately, the charge was later retracted. The Making of Yeats's 'A Vision', 2. 307.
134 Burke had maintained that manners were even more important than laws. An earmarked passage in Yeats's edition of Burke drew attention to the claim that when people of rank 'lose decorum they lose everything'. See the National Library of Ireland, 306. Yeats also suggests that politeness is a foundation of social life; this precept is, at least, implicit in Yeats's plans for Anne: 'In courtesy I'd have her chiefly learned.' VP, 404.
135 VP, 403.
136 EI, 444.
137 V, 52.

One of the most influential books in Victorian political thought, Tocqueville's *Democracy in America*, did much to bolster these views. Democracies, Tocqueville maintained, were 'passionately addicted to generic terms and abstract expressions', while aristocratic societies had 'an instinctive aversion' for such jargon.[138] In 1895 Dowden explicitly invoked Tocqueville to outline his concerns about democratic art. 'One of the chief intellectual infirmities of democracies', Dowden maintained, 'is the passion for abstractions'.[139] Yeats read this piece and while he rejected its critical account of art in Ireland, he ultimately endorsed its criticisms of democratic abstractions.[140] His distrust of democratic culture was also bolstered by his father's Tocquevillian account of American letters:

> The Democrat is proud of his reasoning power and rightly so, *and yet it is all he has got* — when he attempts poetry he only succeeds in being didactic and eloquent, and eloquent of what? Duty and morality and upliftment — matters which, however valuable, are not poetry — one cannot be eloquent of beauty — one can only pull away the curtain, and the less said about the vision the better.[141]

American culture, according to John Yeats, was proof of the thesis; the democratic Americans were 'the most idealistic people in the world and the least poetical'. 'Opinions such as theirs', he added, 'mean logic, oratory and didacticism'.[142] Here the Americans resembled the French, who also lived and wrote 'in the bondage of logic'.[143]

His son worried acutely that the Irish had also enslaved themselves to logic and he attributed this enslavement to the nation's enthusiasm for democracy.[144] In his *Memoirs*, his hatred of the literature of logic fuelled an explicit condemnation of democratic culture:

---

138 Tocqueville, *Democracy in America*, Book II, 15. In his study of the French Revolution, Tocqueville argued that the revolutionary penchant for abstract rhetoric had a catastrophic impact on the nation. The French language 'was cluttered up with abstract words, gaudy flowers of speech, sonorous clichés, and literary turns of phrase'. Alexis de Tocqueville, *The Old Regime and the French Revolution*, trans. Stuart Gilbert (New York, 1955), 147.

139 Dowden, *New Studies in Literature*, 9. Dowden, nevertheless, believed that anxieties about the cultural ramifications of democracy were exaggerated. Like Tocqueville, he continued to contrast democratic with aristocratic art, but he was convinced that the former was often superior. Walt Whitman, for Dowden, was the supreme democratic artist. See Edward Dowden, *Studies in Literature, 1789–1877* (London, 1906), 468–523.

140 For Yeats's criticisms of Dowden's remarks, see Yeats, UP 1. 346–49.

141 J. B. Yeats, *Letters to His Son and Others*, 170 [J. B. Yeats's emphasis].

142 *Letters to His Son and Others*, 135.

143 *Letters to his Son and Others*, 168. Yeats's father remained convinced that the 'intellectual awakening of the French Revolution has not yet really borne any poetical fruit'. *Letters to his Son and Others*, 206.

144 George Moore, for instance, was a democrat in spite of himself: 'He shares the mob's materialism and the mob's hatred of any privilege which is an incommunicable gift [...] he has the demagogic virtues which are all bound up with logic.' M, 270.

The literature of suggestion, richest to the richest, does not belong to a social order founded upon argument, but to an age when life conquered by being itself and the most living was the most powerful. What was leisure, wealth, privilege but a soil for the most living? The literature of logic, most powerful in the emptiest, subduing life, conquering all in the service of one metallic premise, is the art of democracy, of generations that have only just begun to read. They fill their minds with deductions just as they fill their empty houses, where there is nothing of the past, with machine-made furniture.[145]

Yeats also associated modern democracy with a disastrous addiction to abstract phrases. 'Democracy is dead', he announced in 1922. 'With democracy has died too the old political generalizations'.[146] The statement was somewhat premature, but the association of democracy with abstract generalities was firmly entrenched.

Against the dehistoricizing rhetoric of democracy, Yeats promoted the concrete virtues of aristocratic life. He was initially convinced that 'to belong to any aristocracy, is to be a little pool that will soon dry up'.[147] Doomed or not, he would soon choose for himself the little pool. Despite his own middle-class origins, he presented himself as a bold defender of noble values and an enemy of 'all Jacobin envy'.[148] He celebrated aristocracy as a time-bound institution in which great art thrives. 'Every day', he declared, 'I notice some new analogy between the long established life of the well-born and the artist's life'. The reasons for this were fairly predictable: 'We come from the permanent things and create them, and instead of old blood we have old emotions and we carry in our head that form of society which aristocracies create now and again for some brief moment at Urbino or Versailles. We too despise the mob and suffer at its hands.'[149] Synge suffered deeply and he would play the role of Marie Antoinette in Yeats's neo-Burkean critique of Irish fanaticism.

Yeats may have drawn on Burke's vocabularies to defend the rights of aristocracy, but this defence was often a violation of the statesman's values. Despite his reputation, Burke was not an uncritical apologist of aristocracy, and he was prepared to overrule its prescriptive rights in the name of a higher law. He did, however, defend traditional privileges and customs: their longevity and persistence was strong — albeit not sufficient — evidence of their utility and virtue. But once these traditional frameworks were undermined, it was no longer possible to invoke their existence as a presumption in their favour.[150] This

145 M, 209.
146 L, 695.
147 EI, 214.
148 Quoted in Foster, Arch-Poet, 251.
149 M, 156.
150 Burke had argued in a different context that 'when the reason of old establishments is gone, it is absurd to preserve nothing but the burthen of them. This is superstitiously to embalm a carcass not worth an ounce of the gums that are used to preserve it. It is to burn precious oils in the tomb; it is to offer meat and drink to the dead — not so much an honour to the deceased, as a disgrace to the survivors.' W & S. 3. 510.

was a problem Burke encountered in the wake of the French Revolution, but it proved an insurmountable difficulty for the belated Yeats. He often admitted that the political values he sponsored had virtually perished from the world. He continued to denounce nationalist abstractions, but the aristocratic ideals he championed were also abstract; they were counterfactual ideals in a depressingly democratic reality. Yeats professed himself to be content with the 'abstract joy' that his dreams and images afforded and left 'abstract hatred' to revolutionary malcontents. But this sanguine attitude was not sustained.[151]

His disgust for democracy produced its own rage and counter-revolutionary paradox.[152] He yearned for a moment of total rupture that would mark the end of a democratic age and the establishment of authoritarian rule across Europe. The exact profile of this new dispensation was unclear: it gestured back to a notional aristocratic past and towards a fascist future.[153] However vague the programme, it led him to reconsider the idea of a foundational violence, so tentatively addressed in 'Easter 1916'. Violence, for instance, was the dominant theme of 'Ancestral Houses'. The poem's key refrain — 'But take our greatness with our violence' — outlined the exorbitant costs of high ideals, but it also suggested that the price was worth paying.[154] The imperative 'take' is ambiguous and demands both the acceptance and removal of violence.[155] Either way, the poem advances a Nietzschean thesis that noble values are *necessarily* derived from great cruelty and brutal force.[156] Civilization depends on forceful and 'bitter' men — bold projectors whose potent violence makes everything else possible.[157] The 'planted hills' of aristocratic houses are the product of this force.[158]

In this reference to the plantations, Yeats looked back to the origins of Ascendancy rule in Ireland. The initial cause and animating spirit of this regime, he acknowledges, was the spirit of militant conquest. Burke's overarching ambition was to undo the spirit of conquest in the name of enlightened political deliberation.[159] He condemned the administration in Ireland for entrenching the spirit of bitter militancy when it should have concentrated on erasing its traces for good. Yeats, however, refuses to let the spirit of conquest rest

---

151 For his embrace of 'abstract joy', see VP, 427; for his condemnation of 'abstract hatred', see VP, 481.

152 According to Seamus Deane, Yeats 'was a revolutionary whose wars took place primarily within himself; and he knew that in the end, struggle as he might, it was a losing battle'. Seamus Deane, 'Yeats and the Idea of Revolution', in *Celtic Revivals: Essays in Modern Irish Literature, 1880–1980* (London, 1985), 38–50, 50.

153 Orwell's assessment of Yeats's politics was bald but perceptive: 'Throughout most of his life, and long before Fascism was ever heard of, he had had the outlook of those who reach Fascism by the aristocratic route.' George Orwell, *Essays* (London, 1968), 236.

154 VP, 418.

155 For a discussion of this feature of the poem, see Howes, *Yeats's Nations*, 124.

156 Nietzsche believed that a high price was paid for civilized values: 'how much blood and horror lies at the basis of all "good things"!' Nietzsche, *Genealogy of Morality*, 42. 'In much of Yeats's work,' according to Howes, 'civilisation is based on barbarism, beauty on violence and cruelty.' *Yeats's Nations*, 123.

157 VP, 418.

158 VP, 417.

159 For an account of Burke's attitude to conquest, see Bourke, 'Edmund Burke and the Politics of Conquest', 403–32.

and dwells upon its fertile violence. Burke had always argued that the rights of conquest were subordinate to the laws of nature, but 'Ancestral Houses' acknowledges few natural limits to human force. The almost surreal artifice of Yeats's 'planted hills' celebrates an aristocratic dominion over nature. He had invoked Burke's 'organic' metaphors — and would do so again — to check the voluntarist presumption of dangerous innovators, but his 'planted hills' and 'flowering lawns' are deliberate constructions that mark the triumph, not the subordination, of the will. Order, it seems, is not found in the world but is imposed upon it by forceful beings. The voluntarism that Yeats deplored in the name of aristocracy now becomes its source and sustaining ground.

This was a Nietzschean celebration of aristocratic power that had little in common with the political values of Edmund Burke. Nobility, for Nietzsche, was organized around the 'sovereignty of the will', but Burke maintained that the will should always remain subordinate to the dictates of reason and natural justice.[160] The sovereignty of untrammelled will was the politics of simple despotism. A pure aristocracy, for Burke, was the worst kind of despotic rule, precisely because it represented and sustained an ethos of conquest.[161] 'Ancestral Houses' did not offer a categorical endorsement either of despotism or of conquest. The poem expresses a pained uncertainty throughout: it ends with a question and its opening word — an embattled 'Surely' — stokes the very scepticism it sets out to extinguish. Noble mores, the poet admits, may not be a sufficient justification of their violent origins; this violence was arguably their indictment and refutation. But despite these doubts, Yeats would repeatedly turn to the notion of a salutary aggression.

In 'Blood and the Moon', for example, 'bloody, arrogant power' is the condition and even criterion of aristocratic greatness. 'Uttering' and 'mastering' its environment, Yeats's tower embodies a brutal but productive energy. The declaratory force of his assertions — 'I declare this tower is my symbol' — enact the constitutive power they exalt, and strive to invest utterance with the power of deeds.[162] Here the speaker dictates what shall stand as symbols through the raw force of will. Yeats had once commended symbols as a check to this kind of wilfulness; their meaning was not reducible to the intentions of individuals, but operated behind the backs of their specific users. Symbols, therefore, were a rebuff to a hubristic subject that posited itself as the origin and ground of meaning.[163] But the speaker of 'Blood and the Moon' refuses to be rebuffed. This symbol-maker is committed to a subjectivist outlook on language and value; all meaning derives, it seems, from the ego's will. Despite all the talk of blood, even ancestry is a

---

160 Nietzsche, Will to Power, 58. In Burke's eyes, the will of God was its own justification, because here will and reason were identical. See W & S 8. 145. But this fortuitous harmony was absent in human souls and individuals were required to subordinate their will to the laws of natural justice and right reason. Politics, Burke insisted, was 'not a matter of Will on any side'. In his eyes, 'Government and Legislation are matters of reason and judgement and not of inclination'. W & S 3. 69.

161 On this point, see Bourke, 'Edmund Burke and the Politics of Conquest', 430.

162 VP, 481.

163 See EI, 87.

choice. Yeats sires his forefathers and admits Berkeley, Swift, Goldsmith and Burke to his ancestral stair.

Yeats's account of aristocracy was thus replete with contradiction: the abstract individualism, overreaching voluntarism, radical innovation and consequent violence that he condemned in the name of aristocracy repeatedly served as the normative basis of this regime. For someone who professed to despise 'logic', these contradictions may have been a cause more for celebration than concern. The logical inconsistencies, however, reflected real and insurmountable difficulties in his world. They were sad evidence of the fact that the practices and values of aristocracy were in irreversible decline in Ireland. Some vestiges of 'inherited glory' remained in the country — most notably in Coole Park, the Gregory family estate — but Yeats was distrustful of legacies. Inheritance was often indistinguishable from an enfeebling indolence that culminated in physical degeneration. This led him back to the regenerative properties of violence and the form-giving power of will. 'I am a despotic man', he told Laura Riding, 'trying to impose my will upon the times'.[164] Yeats drew on a counter-revolutionary tradition to condemn the tyrannical features of nationalists armed with democratic principles; if these criticisms had a liberal foundation, this was exceeded and undermined by the poet's anti-democratic animus.

164 Quoted in Foster, Arch-Poet, 556. This remark described his attitude to his Oxford anthology of modern poetry, but it revealed something about his politics in general.

Part III
The Politics of Mass Communication

5 Newspapers and Nationalism in Ireland

1 The Press as a Political Idea

Young Ireland aimed to revive an ancient conception of an ethical community in a modern setting. Through the forum of the newspaper, the group believed, a vision of the good life could be collectively deliberated and shared. O'Connell's mass rallies had transformed public life in Ireland, but the newspaper, as Duffy pointed out, was a 'permanent monster-meeting' of minds.[1] With this in mind, Duffy, Dillon and Davis founded the *Nation* newspaper in October 1842. Over time the journal proved to be a considerable success, enjoying weekly sales of up to 15,000 and a readership of around 250,000. For Duffy and countless others after him, a 'new soul had come into Ireland with the *Nation*'.[2] This trope of spiritual revival and possession became standard in press discourse, with several subsequent journals claiming to have patented souls for the nation. 'Every nation has a soul', the journalist and editor D. P. Moran asserted, 'and its press ought to be the very face in which that soul shines and shows itself, the faithful index of its aspirations, its efforts, its passions and its fears'.[3] Yeats was always more inclined to present art as the

---

1   Duffy, *Four Years of Irish History*, 1. 6. See Stephen McKenna, *While I Remember* (London, 1921), 48. One of the most notable features of modern politics, McKenna declared, was the witnessing of 'the press rising victorious over the political mass-meeting'. But a century earlier, O'Connell had already recognized the power of newspapers; he claimed in the late 1820s to have spent £15,000 of the Catholic Association's money on the press. See Arthur Aspinall, *Politics and the Press 1780–1850* (Brighton, 1949), 320. For an account of O'Connell's frequent quarrels with the press see Inglis, *The Freedom of the Press in Ireland*, 220–24.

2   Duffy, *My Life in Two Hemispheres*, 2. 81.

3   *Leader*, 5 April 1902. While Moran commended the *Nation* for bringing 'a new soul into Ireland', he provided a variation on the theme when he declared that the *Leader* newspaper would procure for Ireland 'a new backbone'. *Leader*, 9 March 1901.

best indicator of the national spirit, but he also shared the general view that the *Nation* had 'brought a new soul into Ireland'.[4] Contemporary nationalist newspapers, he suggested, lacked the *Nation*'s unifying power and their vision of national life was a thoroughly enervated one.[5] 'National spirit,' he concluded in 1909, 'is, for the present, dying, because the influence of the *Nation* newspaper, which had this synthetic thought, has passed away.'[6] He initially entertained the hope that national spirit might be revived through the foundation of a 'new *Nation*' newspaper, but he quickly abandoned this scheme.[7] The newspaper industry had changed beyond recognition since the days of the *Nation*, and it was unlikely that a similar publication would enjoy the same popular success in the brave new world of twentieth-century journalism.

Yeats's jaundiced view of modern journalism was shared by many of his nationalist contemporaries. Criticisms of the press in Ireland often reflected a double disenchantment: not only had newspapers failed to instantiate or to guarantee certain political values, this failure also exposed the shortcomings of these ideals. I want to examine, therefore, on a general level some of the dominant modern political discourses — from democratic theory to classical liberalism — that were used both to explain and to legitimate the operation of the press. This language of legitimization exhausted itself over time; and the exhaustion was felt across Europe, not in Ireland alone.

During the French Revolution, the press consolidated its reputation as a truly formidable political force.[8] In his 'Thoughts on French Affairs', Burke was uncertain about the direction the 'French spirit of proselytism' would take, but he was convinced that the newspaper — an 'infinitely more important instrument than generally is imagined' — would dangerously extend its range.[9] He was scathing about the impact of journalists and intellectuals on the political fortunes of France. These ventriloquists of the national will, he believed, caused the ferment of opinion, which they then invoked as a popular judgement against established authority. The political journalists of France were often men of little talent and little renown, but they wielded a dangerous power:

---

4   UP 1. 223. In *PI*, 138, he celebrated the era of Young Ireland as 'an age of romance'. During this period, 'poetry slid into men's ears so smoothly that a man still living, though a very old man now, heard men singing at the railway stations he passed upon a journey into the country the verses he had published that morning in a Dublin newspaper'.

5   M, 185: 'Neither the grammars of the Gaelic League nor the industrialism of the *Leader*, nor the attacks upon the Irish Party in *Sinn Féin* give any sensible image for the affections.'

6   M, 180.

7   In M, 185–86, Yeats wrote that material derived from the work of Lady Gregory, J. M. Synge, Katharine Tynan, Lionel Johnson, and Standish O'Grady 'would enable a school of journalists with very simple moral ideas to build up an historical and literary nationalism as powerful as the old and nobler'.

8   Jeremy D. Popkin, *Revolutionary News: The Press in France, 1789–1799* (Durham and London, 1990), 180: 'It is impossible to imagine the French Revolution without the press: the events of 1789 to 1799 could not have occurred as they did and taken on the meaning that they assumed without it'. See also Hugh Gough, *The Newspaper Press in the French Revolution* (London, 1988); Harvey Chisick, ed., *The Press in the French Revolution* (Oxford, 1991).

9   W & S 8. 347–48.

The writers of these papers indeed, for the greater part, are either unknown or in contempt, but they are like a battery in which the stroke of any one ball produces no great effect, but the amount of continual repetition is decisive. Let us only suffer any person to tell us his story, morning and evening, but for one twelvemonth, and he will become our master.[10]

Others were less scathing but in general agreement. Lord Grenville, for instance, believed that the press was the most powerful cause of the French Revolution.[11] And in his life of Napoleon, Hazlitt judged the Revolution to be the 'remote but inevitable result of the invention of the art of printing'.[12] 'One Sansculottic bough that cannot fail to flourish is Journalism', Carlyle declared, and his History of the French Revolution repeatedly emphasized the profusion of newspapers in revolutionary France.[13]

The impact of print on the political fortunes of France was immediately recognized in Ireland. Radical Irish journalists drew their inspiration from Jacobin writers, and their opponents based their rebukes on a similar association. The Northern Star, founded by the United Irishmen in Belfast in 1792, reviewed events in France with considerable enthusiasm.[14] The Press — a Dublin venture begun by the United Irishmen in 1797 — also promoted the new gospel of the 'Rights of Man'. Arthur O'Connor, one of the main sponsors of the Press, championed the newspaper as the 'palladium of Liberty':

What overturned the Catholic despotism of France? The Press, by the writings of Montesquieu, Voltaire, Rousseau, Diderot, Seyes [sic], Raynal, and Condorcet. What has electrified England, and called down its curses on a Pitt? that Press he in vain attempted to silence. What illumined Belfast, the Athens of Ireland? — The Press and the Northern Star. Why did America triumph over tyranny? — a journeyman

---

10 W & S 8. 348.
11 See John Keane, The Media and Democracy (Cambridge, 1991), 34.
12 William Hazlitt, The Life of Napoleon Buonaparte, 2nd edn. (London, 1852), 58.
13 Thomas Carlyle, The French Revolution, 2. vols. ([1837] London, 1889), 1. 270. The growth of the press during the Revolution was indeed remarkable. Before 1789 there were roughly sixty newspapers in all of France, although foreign gazettes published in French were a significant supplement to this. By August 1792, however, there were close to 500 journals in Paris alone. See Simon Schama, Citizens: A Chronicle of the French Revolution (London, 1989), 525. Almost every political group seemed to start a paper and often enjoyed huge influence as a result. Circulation rates for Jean Louis Carra's Annales Patriotiques or the Abbé Cérutti's Feuille Villageoise were, by the standards of the time, enormous. The style and tone of these journals varied from the relatively dry and methodical manner of the Patriote Français to the vituperative tone of Elysée Loustalot's Révolutions de Paris or the blood-curdling cries of Jean-Paul Marat's L'Ami du Peuple. Unsurprisingly, political essayists such as Mirabeau, Desmoulins, Brissot and Royau won unprecedented fame and influence during the Revolution. Marat became the object of a quasi-religious cult after his death in 1793. Burke had not exaggerated when he complained that writers in France had become 'a sort of demagogues'. W & S 8. 162.
14 The circulation of the Northern Star reached an estimated and impressive 4,000. See Inglis, The Freedom of the Press in Ireland, 94. The circulation of the paper extended as far as Dublin, Edinburgh and London. See Oram, A History of Newspapers in Ireland, 41.

printer fulminated the decree of nature against the giants of England and the pen of a Franklin routed the armies of a King.[15]

The revolutionary potential of newspapers was also acknowledged by governmental efforts to suppress them. These involved direct legal restrictions on writers, publishers and printers, but taxes also provided a covert means of curtailing the growth of a radical press. Newspapers such as the *Volunteer's Journal* of the 1780s repeatedly incurred the government's wrath.[16] There were systematic attempts by the authorities — most notably through the Press and Stamp Acts of 1784 and 1785 — to check such dissidence. Legal and extra-legal measures — such as a military raid and the confiscation and destruction of equipment — were brought to bear on the *Northern Star*, which was compelled to close in 1797. The *Press* was also forced out of business after repeated prosecutions, the destruction of its printing equipment by the militia and the arrest of its owners and editors.

The government was often successful in quashing Irish radical newspapers and actively sponsored organs of its own.[17] Nevertheless, the newspaper would still be regarded as a revolutionary force across Europe. The French revolutions of 1830 and 1848 provided further illustration of the power of journalism.[18] According to Duffy, the Revolution of 1830 was 'the work of the press'.[19] Or, as he put it elsewhere, 'one branch of the Bourbons had been driven out of France at the point of the pen, and the branch in possession lived in constant fear of a handful of journalists and advocates, before whom they finally succumbed'.[20] Both a journalist and former advocate himself, Duffy delighted in the fact that among the 'new Decimviri' of France in 1848 there stood four journalists and four barristers.[21] Even before 1848, Duffy was convinced that 'the printing press has

15 Cited in Kevin Whelan, *The Tree of Liberty: Radicalism, Catholicism and the Construction of Irish Identity, 1760–1830* (Cork, 1996), 62. O'Connor may have regarded the newspaper as a bastion of liberty, but the tactics of the *Press* were sometimes underhand. According to Douglas Simes, it 'deliberately and calculatedly set out to arouse Catholic fears of genocide with elaborate fantasies of Orange plots'. See 'Ireland, 1760–1820', in Hannah Barker and Simon Burrows, eds., *Press, Politics and the Public Sphere in Europe and North America, 1760–1820* (Cambridge, 2002), 113–39, 122.

16 The paper boasted in 1784 that it had received two *informations ex-officio*, three rules to show cause, two indictments for misdemeanours and four indictments for high treason. This was hardly surprising. It had denounced the House of Commons as a 'den of thieves' and a 'Gomorrah of iniquity'; it had praised the American revolutionaries, and it issued instructions on the tarring and feathering of traitors. See Inglis, *The Freedom of the Press in Ireland*, 30, 23.

17 The government during Robert Peel's tenure spent approximately £20,000 per annum on newspapers. Inglis, *The Freedom of the Press in Ireland*, 149.

18 Theodore Zeldin, *France 1848–1945: Taste and Corruption* (Oxford, 1980), 146: 'The Revolution established the tradition by which, in 1830 and 1848, journalists played leading roles in overthrowing governments.'

19 *Nation*, 18 September 1847.

20 Duffy, *Young Ireland: A Fragment of Irish History*, i. 278. See James H. Billington, *Fires in the Minds of Men: The Origins of the Revolutionary Faith* (New York, 1980), 308: 'journalism was the most important single professional activity' for many of the leading German, French and Russian revolutionaries of the nineteenth and twentieth centuries. For a historical overview of the relationship between media and revolution, see Jeremy D. Popkin, ed., *Media and Revolution, Comparative Perspectives* (Lexington, 1995).

21 *Nation*, 4 March 1848.

shaken empires and dethroned kings'.[22] By no means an ardent revolutionary himself, he nevertheless glorified the newspaper's capacity to foment revolution:

> The cradle of modern revolutions has not been the *caserne* of military conspirators, or the *vente* of a secret society, so commonly as the cabinet of a journalist. In France, Belgium, Hungary, and Italy national movements, consummated by the sanction of legislatures and the solemn ceremonial of religion, began in a room strewn with newspapers and glaring with gas, among a few men, whose white hands were stained with ink.[23]

William Makepeace Thackeray only increased Young Ireland's pride when he judged Davis to be Marat's successor.[24] During the state trials of O'Connell in 1844, the attorney-general condemned the *Nation* and emphasized the revolutionary potential of an unbridled press. He insisted that it 'was by means mainly of the French press, and especially of the celebrated organ called *L'Ami du Peuple* that the French revolution was effected and the minds of the people were poisoned against their government'.[25] He believed that the *Press* had attempted to corrupt public opinion and to manufacture revolution in 1798 and insisted that Young Ireland pursued a similar objective with the *Nation*. The bishop of Elphin, Dr. Brown, also attacked the *Nation* as a revolutionary threat and assumed that the links between Jacobinism and journalism were general knowledge:

> How did the French revolution begin? What means were adopted to foster it? I will not name any particular journal; I don't wish to make anything like personal allusions; but we all know that by certain addresses in papers — certain infidel productions by persons who had not the manliness to come forward to proclaim their views, they insidiously proceeded in their attempts, and when they found they had the people's minds demoralised and prepared for wicked counsel, they unmasked their designs and subverted both the altar and throne ... Can we, for one instant, allow amongst us those principles that led to Jacobinism and other monstrous evils?[26]

The press may have been regarded as an agent of revolution, but it was also viewed by its critics and advocates alike as an intrinsically democratic force.[27] 'The press', Burke

---

22 *Nation*, 18 September 1847.
23 Duffy, *Four Years of Irish History*, 1. 57.
24 *Four Years of Irish History*, 1. 268.
25 *Nation*, 20 January 1844. I am indebted to Brendan Bradley for bringing my attention to this comment.
26 Quoted in *Four Years of Irish History*, 1. 327.
27 For a historical overview of the relationship between media and revolution, see Popkin, ed., *Media and Revolution*.

concluded, 'has made every Government, in its spirit, almost democratick'.[28] Carlyle also detected a strong complicity between democracy and print: 'Printing, which comes necessarily out of Writing, I say often, is equivalent to Democracy: invent Writing, Democracy is inevitable.'[29]

On one level, the relationship between modern democracy and print technology seems obvious enough. Modern systems of communication appeared to provide a technical solution to one of the standard objections made against democratic systems of government: that their sheer size made the idea of popular self-rule a dream. This was a common argument, not only against democracy, but against republican government in general. Print technology, however, removed some of these problems and offered new opportunities for popular discussion of political affairs. James Bryce, for instance, spelt out the significance of the press for modern democracies:

> It is the newspaper press that has made democracy possible in large countries. The political thinkers of antiquity assumed that a community of self-governing citizens could not be larger than one voice could reach, because only by the voice could discussion be carried on: and they might have added that only where the bulk of the citizens dwell near one another can they obtain by word of mouth the knowledge of political events that is needed to make discussion intelligent and profitable. Within the last hundred years the development of the press has enabled news to be diffused and public discussion to be conducted over wide areas; and still more recently the electric telegraph has enabled news and the opinions of men regarding it to be so quickly spread over a vast and populous country that all the citizens can receive both news and comments thereon at practically the same moment, so that arguments or appeals addressed to the people work simultaneously upon their minds almost as effectively as did the voice of the orator in the popular assembly.[30]

Perhaps the most persuasive account of the relationship between newspapers and democracy was provided by Tocqueville. Young Ireland liked to quote Tocqueville's opinion that 'nothing but a newspaper can drop the same thought into a thousand minds at the same moment' and the group's enormous confidence in the civilizing power of the press is best explained in relation to the Frenchman's more systematic views on the matter.[31]

A viable democracy, for Tocqueville, presupposed an informed public opinion and this demanded, in turn, a free press.[32] Newspapers, he suggested, not only sustained

---

28 W & S 9. 292.
29 Thomas Carlyle, *On Heroes and Hero-Worship* (London, 1872), 152.
30 James Bryce, *Modern Democracies*, 2 vols. (London, 1921), I. 104.
31 *Democracy in America*, Book 2, III.
32 *Democracy in America*, Book 1, 183: 'The sovereignty of the people and the liberty of the press may therefore be regarded as correlative, just as the censorship of the press and universal suffrage are two things which are irreconcilably opposed and which cannot long be retained among the institutions of the same people.'

democracy, but they also quelled some of its worst vices; they served as a check to bureaucratic despotism by creating a vigilant public opinion and also offset the atomizing effects of equality by providing a forum for public interaction. 'Equality', he concluded, 'deprives a man of the support of his connections, but the press enables him to summon all his fellow countrymen and all his fellow men to his assistance. Printing has accelerated the progress of equality, and it is also one of its best correctives'.[33] Tocqueville was not wholly blind to the dangers of newspapers, not least in his own country France, but he believed that the press was 'more necessary in proportion as men become more equal and individualism more to be feared'.[34] Newspapers, he suggested, not only protected freedom, they maintained civilization.

Newspapers had fostered modern democracy, but they also embodied for some commentators the worst vices of this system of rule. Tocqueville was too enamoured of the press to force home this judgement, but his general denunciation of democratic tyranny formed the basis for subsequent indictments of newspapers. Traditional authority, according to Tocqueville, had relied more on the coercion of bodies rather than of minds, but the power of a majority was both a physical and moral force that repressed 'not only all contest, but all controversy'.[35] The tyranny of the majority, for Tocqueville, was all the more dangerous because it was anonymous and indeterminate. The principle of equality allowed no individual to dominate over his peers, but this often meant that each person enjoyed merely an equality of insignificance before an omnipotent public. Individuals, according to J. S. Mill, were 'lost in the crowd'. It was clear to him that 'public opinion now rules the world'.[36] Both Mill and Tocqueville exaggerated the univocal nature of public opinion, but their concerns were real.[37]

Repeated criticisms of a bigoted but popular press showed that democratic values and liberal sensibilities were not necessarily harmonious. But the press also emphasized tensions within classical liberalism itself and seemed to challenge a prevailing assumption that free markets were a guarantor of more general freedoms. Both Mill and Tocqueville criticized the dominion of public opinion over private individuals, but they overlooked the ways in which powerful newspapers potentially produced the opposite result and allowed private interests to override the public good.[38] This oversight is

33 *Democracy in America*, Book 2, 324–25.

34 *Democracy in America*, Book 2, 111.

35 *Democracy in America*, Book 1, 263.

36 *Collected Works*, 18. 268–69. If Mill feared public opinion, this was partly because it was no longer drawn from established authorities: 'the mass do not now take their opinions from dignitaries in Church or State, from ostensible leaders, or from books. Their thinking is done for them by men much like themselves, addressing them or speaking in their name, on the spur of the moment, through the newspapers'.

37 As John Dewey argued, in *The Public and Its Problems* (Athens, 1927), 137, the problem of the public was not its unanimity or omnipotence; more often than not public opinion was 'too diffused and scattered and too intricate in composition'. Indeed, there were 'too many publics ... with little to hold these different publics together in an integrated whole'.

38 Tocqueville, *Democracy in America*, Book 1, 186. Tocqueville insisted that it was an 'axiom of political science ... that the only way to neutralize the effect of the public journals is to multiply their number'. He

understandable in the context of mid-nineteenth-century journalism, but the subsequent rise of powerful press barons and media monopolies provided ample illustration of the ways in which private interests could control the production and transmission of public opinion.[39] Market competition easily led to the concentration, not to the decentralization, of opinion. 'The tyranny of monopoly', as Bryce suggested, 'is even worse in opinion than in commerce', and he regarded the press syndicates of the twentieth century as a potential embodiment of this kind of concentration.[40]

By the start of the twentieth century, therefore, an unqualified endorsement of both the democratic character and the liberal function of the press was difficult to sustain. Mill had believed that newspapers had helped to establish a new agora, but the modern marketplace did not simply reconstitute the freedoms of democratic Athens.[41] Isonomia and isegoria — the equal right of all citizens to speak and to participate — were notably lacking in the virtual agora sustained by journalism. Precisely because moderns had relinquished the idea of direct democracy and had made their peace with a representative system, the press was a crucial institution: it allowed for some communication and transparency between the people and its representatives in modern polities.[42] But if a free press was a necessary means of rendering government accountable, what institution guaranteed the integrity of the press? Bryce regarded newspapers as a key constituent of modern democracy, but he was convinced that the 'power of the press is a practically irresponsible power'.[43] The problem of accountability under a representative system was not solved by the press. As with governmental representatives, so with journalists: were they delegates or trustees of the people? Neither government nor newspapers were simple embodiments of the people's will; at best, they were its representatives and reflected the practical difficulties of a system that allowed for the simultaneous delegation and retention of power.

These uncomfortable realities illustrated the inadequacies of traditional democratic theory — if not its actual practice — as well as the self-legitimizing discourses of the press. In the twentieth century, Joseph Schumpeter dismissed the idea that democracies reflected the will of the people. If it was possible to speak of such a thing at all in modern politics, it was 'largely not a genuine but a manufactured will'.[44] This was by no means to indict modern democratic practices, but to attack impossible doctrines such

placed his trust in market competition as a guarantor of this plurality and abundance, but overlooked the ways in which markets occasionally produced the opposite result.

39 For an account of these market forces see James Curran, 'Press History', in James Curran and Jean Seaton, eds., *Power without Responsibility: The Press and Broadcasting in Britain*, 5th edn. (London, 1997), 5–108.

40 Bryce, *Modern Democracies*, 1. 121.

41 Mill, *Collected Works*, 18. 165.

42 According to Mme de Staël, *Considérations sur les Principaux Evénéments de la Révolution Françoise*, 3 vols. (London, 1818), 1. 290, 'political newspapers began at the same time as representative government; and this government is inseparable from them'. 'Les journaux politiques ont commencé en même temps que les gouvernemens représentatifs; et ces gouvernemens en sont inséparables.'

43 Bryce, *Modern Democracies*, 1. 123.

44 Joseph A. Schumpeter, *Capitalism, Socialism & Democracy* (London, 1943; repr. 2000), 263.

as the *volonté générale* which had been traditionally used either to sanction or to explain their basic operation. The simple mechanics of mass media — where 'mere assertion, often repeated, counts more than rational argument and so does the attack upon the subconscious'—illustrated the dangers of romantic theories of public reason.[45] Arguably, this account of democracy was excessively cynical and relied for some of its fundamental assessments on a social psychology that had little empirical value.[46] But Schumpeter helped to emphasize the often distressing rupture between classical democratic theory and the basic functioning of modern politics. His attack on the language of democratic legitimization also called into question the media's traditional use of such a discourse when accounting for their own public role. His concerns about the modern media were not new, but they were evidence of a widespread belief that the newspaper's traditional language of self-legitimization was exhausted.

Young Ireland's faith in institutions like the press could seem in hindsight fundamentally misplaced. These young patriots may have praised the fourth estate as the agent and guarantor of liberty, but for many figures, journalism was simply a business concern. In September 1847, the *Nation* pointed to the ways in which commercial imperatives would dictate the future shape of newspapers. Here the *Nation* focused on the French press. No longer interested in the noble science of politics, French newspapers pursued money through salacious reports of crime:

> Through these organs, new ideas — ideas unconnected with government or policy, or with the defence of French honor, or with national liberty or greatness — were propagated. The current of men's thoughts was changed. The system of *feuilletons* — of romances continued from day to day in the columns of the newspaper press — was established. These romances were almost universally social — they dealt with the supposed crimes of society. In them scenes the most hideous were painted in a manner warm and attractive in the extreme, and the state of society therein depicted was continually held up before the eyes of Frenchmen as their own. Thus, by perpetually gazing upon abasement, the social system of France has really become base. And the men who devoted their pens to this corrupting office have been protected, honored, rewarded by the court.[47]

The displacement of politics by other issues — from breathless reports of romance to bloodcurdling accounts of crime — was a pattern repeatedly identified and condemned in Irish newspapers.

---

45 Schumpeter, *Capitalism, Socialism & Democracy*, 257–58. See also on this point Moisei Ostrogorski, *Democracy and the Organization of Political Parties*, trans. Frederick Clarke, 2 vols. (London, 1902), 1. 519, and Bryce, *Modern Democracies*, 1. 116.
46 See Gustave Le Bon, *The Crowd: A Study of the Popular Mind* (London, 1896), 171.
47 *Nation*, 18 September 1848.

Perhaps more alarming than the marginalization of politics by the imperatives of commerce was the newspaper's cultivation of political prejudices for the purposes of profit. For all its liberal pretensions, the press was an institution that often expressed and entrenched bigotry in Ireland.[48] John Sadleir's *Weekly Telegraph*, according to its critics, exemplified this vice. According to A. M. Sullivan, the *Telegraph* 'pandered to the fiercest bigotry'. While the *Nation* aimed at an inclusive nationalism united in civic friendship, the *Telegraph*'s 'catholicity', Sullivan maintained, 'was of that bellicose and extravagant character which was deemed best calculated at a time of such widespread religious animosities to delight and excite the masses'.[49] For Young Ireland, patriotism curbed the individualism intrinsic to the commercial spirit of the age, but the *Telegraph* showed that commerce could harness the rhetoric of patriotism for its own ends. The patriotic ardour of a commercial newspaper at the end of the nineteenth century — such as the *Daily Mail* in England or the *Independent* in Ireland — only seemed to confirm the effectiveness of this menacing conflation of political virtue and commerce. [50]

Davis declared the press to be one of the great 'schoolmasters' of Ireland, but for many later commentators the commercial interests of newspapers superseded, if they did not wholly supplant, their educative function.[51] The problems of the press were symptomatic of broader difficulties. It may have been an agent of democracy, but it also appeared to embody some of the worst aspects of majoritarian rule. Young Ireland had set out 'to foster and to create public opinion' and hoped to check arbitrary government in Ireland through the force of reasoned debate. But public opinion, as Tocqueville and Mill had maintained, was not necessarily enlightened or indeed liberal. Opinion, according to Moisei Ostrogorski's influential survey of modern politics, was 'at once a capricious despot and a docile slave'.[52] In 'Nineteen Hundred and Nineteen', Yeats dismissed the dream of a self-perfecting public reason — 'Public opinion ripening so long / We thought it would outlive all future days' — as an idle dream.[53] He increasingly regarded the press as a corrupt and illiberal force in public life and criticized the peculiar 'destructiveness

---

48 According to K. Theodore Hoppen, *Elections, Politics and Society in Ireland, 1832–1885* (Oxford, 1994), 458, the newspaper was the 'creator of tribal political loyalties and identities'. Simes, 'Ireland, 1760–20', 128, arrives at a more moderate conclusion, but still insists that the 'press reinforced and exacerbated old animosities'.

49 Sullivan, *New Ireland*, I. 343.

50 By the twentieth century, Bryce's thoroughly disenchanted view of the press was a common perspective among European political commentators; *Modern Democracies*, I. 111: 'Though it still claims to stand as the purveyor of truth and the disinterested counsellor of the people, it is now primarily a business concern, an undertaking conducted for profit like any other.'

51 Davis, *Essays Literary and Historical*, 202. Ostrogorski, *Democracy and the Organization of Political Parties*, I. 409: 'it is only as a channel of political information that the newspapers contribute to the enlightenment of the public, and even this statement requires qualification. But, as for improving the political judgment of their readers, the great majority of the newspapers utterly fails to do so'.

52 Ostrogorski, *Democracy and the Organization of Political Parties*, I. 514.

53 VP, 428. In M, 181, he complained that 'the cultivated remnant has no power on public opinion' both in Ireland and the world at large. In V, 27, his attitude was more ambivalent: 'we writers are public opinion's children though we defy our mother'.

of journalism here in Ireland'.[54] He was a particularly scathing critic of newspapers and his distrust was shared by many of his nationalist contemporaries. The newspaper may have brought a soul to Ireland in the 1840s, but by the end of the nineteenth century it was widely perceived to have corrupted the national spirit.

2 Newspapers and Nationhood

The rapid growth of nationalism in nineteenth-century Ireland and the major expansion of its press appeared to be causally related.[55] The repeal of the taxes on newspapers in the 1850s paved the way for the transformation of the industry.[56] Up to then, the average price of newspapers was roughly fourpence halfpenny. In 1853 the tax on advertisements — one shilling and sixpence for each, irrespective of length — was abolished; the removal of the 'penny stamp' duty followed two years later. These reforms, as well as the later abolition of paper duty, greatly accelerated the rise of a cheap press. Further, the transfer of the entire telegraphic system to government control in 1868 had an enormous impact on journalism in Ireland. While a government monopoly was a matter of concern for those pledged to an independent press, anxieties were much assuaged by the Post Office's decision to reduce charges considerably.[57] By 1870, over 400 towns and villages had a telegraph office, and newspaper circulation had increased by 50 per cent since 1850.[58] Both the distribution of newspapers and the mobility of journalists were greatly extended by massive developments in the railway network. Between 1845 and 1853, the main arteries of the railway system were laid when Dublin was connected to Cork, Galway and Belfast. By the end of the century, Ireland possessed one of the densest railway systems in the world.[59]

---

54 M, 178.
55 The complicity of newspapers and nationalism in Ireland appears to endorse some celebrated theories of nationalist politics. According to Benedict Anderson's influential study of the phenomenon, for instance, 'print-capitalism' is constitutive of modern nationalism. Anderson extended Ernest Gellner's functionalist account of nationalism by suggesting that print-systems provide the technological foundations for a national structure of feeling. By producing a sense of shared simultaneity across space, print-systems reconstituted the frameworks in which political agents operated, allowing them to become citizens of an imagined community. See Benedict Anderson, *Imagined Communities*, rev. edn. (London, 1991).
56 These reforms, according to one contemporary journalist, were 'the chief element in bringing about the great revolution in the newspaper world which then took place'. See Andrew Dunlop, *Fifty Years of Irish Journalism* (Dublin, 1911), 280.
57 Dunlop, *Fifty Years of Irish Journalism*, 42. Until then, telegraph charges were prohibitively expensive in Ireland: 'There was for about three years practically no telegraphing; only the most important news was telegraphed and that in a very condensed form, the cost being something like a dozen times what it became when the transfer to the Government took place ...'
58 Legg, *Newspapers and Nationalism*, 44.
59 Joseph Lee, *The Modernisation of Irish Society 1848–1918* (Dublin, 1973), 13.

Although it became routine to relate the growth of newspapers to educational reforms and to underplay the importance of price reductions in boosting demand for newspapers, their growth in circulation was undoubtedly helped by a sharp rise in literacy levels in Ireland. In 1841, 53 per cent of the population was totally illiterate, while a further 19 per cent could only read but not write. Subsequent educational reforms had such an effect that by 1891, the year of Parnell's death, the totally illiterate comprised only 18 per cent of the population. In 1877, Sullivan celebrated the apparently reciprocal growth of newspapers and literacy rates. According to him, 'the school and the newspaper have proved the powerful literacy agencies of moral and political regeneration'.[60] Indeed, Sullivan was convinced that these agencies had produced a social revolution in Ireland:

> ... socially and politically considered, nothing short of a revolution has been effected. There is now scarcely a farmhouse or working man's home in all the land in which the boy or girl of fifteen, or the young man or woman of twenty-five, cannot read the newspaper for 'the old people,' and transact their correspondence ... For public news the peasant no longer relies on the Sunday gossip after mass. For political views he is no longer absolutely dependent on the advice and guidance of Father Tom. He may never find counsellor more devoted and faithful; the political course he may now follow may be more rash or more profitable, more wise or more wrong; but for good or ill it will be his own. He will still, indeed, trust largely to those whom he judges worthy of his confidence, and largely follow their lead; but not in the same way as of yore.[61]

'Political leadership in the sense in which it prevailed in our fathers' time,' Sullivan concluded, 'is gone for ever.'[62] 'Father Tom' did not always appreciate this erosion of authority, and the journalist was often castigated as a destructive, radical element in the community. The novels of the writer and journalist William Ryan offer valuable insights into this struggle for authority. In *Starlight through the Roof* (1895), a young journalist, Gerald O'Hara, is denounced by Father Curran as 'an enemy, an upstart, and a plotter', a disseminator of 'hate, disaffection, and new-fangled and irreligious notions'.[63] It was a strangely prescient work that anticipated Ryan's own rift with the clergy, described in his autobiographical novel, *The Plough and the Cross* (1910) — a work based upon the suppression of Ryan's newspaper, the *Irish Peasant*, by the Irish clergy and by Cardinal Logue in particular.[64] As Ryan put it in *The Pope's Green Island* (1912), 'the time had come to let the bishops know, not violently but squarely and unmistakably, that the days when they held the Irish nation in the hollow of their hands, or could knock independent-

60 Sullivan, *New Ireland*, 1. 94.
61 *New Ireland*, 1. 35–36.
62 *New Ireland*, 1. 36.
63 Kevin Kennedy [pseud. for William P. Ryan], *Starlight through the Roof* (London, 1895), 92.
64 William P. Ryan, *The Plough and the Cross* (Point Loma, 1910).

minded men on the head with impunity, were as dead as the Middle Ages'.[65] George Moore had similar ambitions. In a short story entitled 'The Wild Goose' (1903), he outlined the efforts of a young journalist to create an anti-clerical newspaper entitled the *Heretic*. The paper's formidable task is 'To rid Ireland of her priests'.[66] The priests, of course, would attempt to rid Ireland of its heretics by sponsoring their own organs of opinion. Publications such as the *Catholic Bulletin* worked hard to defend orthodox religious values in early twentieth-century Ireland.

Whatever the effects of the clergy's ambivalent attitudes to the press, newspapers continued to flourish. The growth of mass communications reflected and fostered the growth of mass politics. The key electoral reforms of 1867 and 1884 introduced a mass electorate, thus altering the face of British politics.[67] Both the increase of the electorate and its protection under the Secret Ballot Act contributed to a general shift of politics beyond relatively autonomous or local interests or, at the very least, it forced those interests to become articulate on a national level. The success of the Land League, for instance, was based on this ability to harness rural radicalism on a national scale. Newspapers played a crucial role in this process by publishing announcements of meetings and providing detailed reports of their contents. Advances in telegraphy allowed speeches in diverse parts of the country to be published within a day of their delivery. The newspaper had refashioned the time-space in which politics was conducted in Ireland. One journalist, Michael McCarthy, summed up its significance for Irish citizens: 'it enabled them to hear their friends at a distance, talking to them in accents of power about the wondrous works of the Land League in regaining for them the independence filched from their ancestors'.[68]

The effectiveness of newspapers in co-ordinating agrarian struggle in Ireland was acknowledged by the coercion measures of 1887, which banned the reporting of League meetings considered dangerous by the government. The Parnellite organ, *United Ireland*, was judged to be particularly dangerous and was condemned by Chief Secretary Forster 'as truly a part of the instruments of assassination as the dagger and the mask'.[69] The paper had been founded by Parnell in 1881 under the editorship of William O'Brien as a means of organizing the agrarian movement nationally, while also contributing a support base to the Home Rule party. With the support of *United Ireland* as well as other major journals such as the *Freeman's Journal*, Parnell soon became a national icon. The chief secretary's wife, Florence Arnold-Forster, outlined in despairing tones the role of newspapers in Irish public life:

65 William P. Ryan, *The Pope's Green Island* (London, 1912), 164.

66 George Moore, 'The Wild Goose', in *The Untilled Field* (Gerrards Cross, 1976), 217–80, 265.

67 Indeed, the franchise reform of 1884 alone trebled the number of voters in Ireland.

68 Michael J. F. McCarthy, *The Irish Revolution. Volume 1: The Murdering Time, from the Land League to the First Home Rule Bill* (Edinburgh and London, 1912), 129.

69 William O'Brien, *Recollections* (London, 1905), 505. See Michael MacDonagh, *William O'Brien* (London, 1928), 14: '*United Ireland* was the most militant newspaper ever published in Ireland ...'

For a year and a half past the Chief Secretary has been longing for an opportunity to come face to face with the Irish people, to be able to speak his mind to them, to let them hear for once something besides the violent one-sided statements, the deliberate or unintentional falsehoods and misrepresentations, the open or veiled incitements to dishonesty, sedition and murder which have been dinned into their ears from the 'national' platform or through the 'national' press without cessation since the opening of Mr Parnell's constitutional agitation …

The newspaper and the speakers who week after week and day after day, edified the people by enlarging on the gratuitous wickedness of the English Govt., on the tyranny, the cruelty, the injustice of the Ch. Secretary and all those responsible for the administration of the law and the suppression of crime and outrage in Ireland, have been for two years past the only leaders whose words have reached the people.[70]

According to one unionist pamphlet, the part played by the 'so called "National" journals in educating "the people of Ireland" up to their present standard of irreconcilable hatred towards England' had 'scarcely received the attention it deserves'.[71]

If the press was deemed to constitute a 'public opinion' that remained independent and often critical of the state, then this served the interests of an irredentist nationalism well.[72] Nationalist newspapers often marketed themselves as a more legitimate and representative authority than government institutions at Westminster. 'In our day', Lecky suggested, 'the press is becoming far more than the House of Commons the representative of the real public opinion of the nation'.[73] He had mixed feelings about this transformation, but for many defenders of the Union in Ireland it had distressing implications.

Commentators right across the political spectrum worried about the growing power of journalism. In an account of the Parnell movement, a journalist for the *Freeman's Journal* claimed that 'the younger generation educated in the national schools were very impressionable and ready to accept all printed matter which chimed in with their own ideals as more or less inspired, the daily or weekly newspaper leaped into the place occupied by the Bible in Great Britain'. 'Every statement of the Land League leaders',

---

70 T. W. Moody and Richard Hawkins, eds., *Florence Arnold-Forster's Irish Journal* (Oxford, 1988), 392–93.

71 Anon., *Ireland: Union or Separation?* (Dublin, 1886), 14.

72 The emergence and erosion of an independent and critical form of public opinion is the well-known theme of Jürgen Habermas's early work, *The Structural Transformation of the Public Sphere*, trans. Thomas Burger with the assistance of Frederick Lawrence (Cambridge, 1989).

73 Lecky, *Democracy and Liberty*, 1. 215–16. In 'The Soul of Man under Socialism' (1891), Oscar Wilde argued that the press could no longer be called the fourth estate: 'at the present moment it really is the only estate. It has eaten up the other three. The Lords Temporal say nothing, the Lords Spiritual have nothing to say, and the House of Commons has nothing to say and says it. We are dominated by Journalism'. See *Collins Complete Works of Oscar Wilde* (Glasgow, 1999), 1188.

the same reporter maintained, 'was accepted as Gospel truth by the people'.[74] Lecky also feared the influence of newspapers on an undereducated public: 'An immense proportion of those who have learnt to read never read anything but a party newspaper — very probably a newspaper specially intended to inflame or to mislead them and the half-educated mind is peculiarly open to political utopias and fanaticisms'.[75] These dark judgements cast suspicion on Sullivan's optimistic belief that newspapers facilitated the exercise of personal autonomy and critical independence in the public sphere. In 1903, R. J. Smith rallied individuals against the tyranny of newspapers. 'Irish voters', he proclaimed, 'liberate yourselves from newspaper dictation, deception and trickery! Emancipate yourselves!'[76] James Joyce more subtly criticized the authoritarian nature of newspapers. A character in *Dubliners* (Eliza in 'The Sisters') mistakenly refers to the '*Freeman's General*' instead of the *Freeman's Journal*; it was a telling, if accidental, criticism of the newspaper's self-presentation as a great emancipator.[77] Yeats also criticized the tyrannical features of 'newspaper government'.[78]

He directed much of his ire at nationalist journals, but they were themselves often the most virulent critics of the influence of newspapers on Irish public life. Predictably, Irish nationalists had traditionally regarded the British press with considerable distrust. Repeated assaults on Parnell in the London *Times* and the latter's notorious circulation of the Pigott forgeries — in which Parnell seemingly endorsed the murders of Ireland's Chief Secretary, Lord Frederick Cavendish, and his permanent Under-Secretary, Thomas Burke — only served to entrench beliefs that the British press was an apologist for empire and a promoter of anti-Irish prejudice.[79] Joyce argued that English journalists 'act as interpreters between Ireland and the English electorate' and insisted that the interpretation was often unfair.[80] He presented the unfortunate Myles Joyce — an Irish-speaking farmer convicted for murder in a court proceeding he could not understand

---

74 McCarthy, *The Irish Revolution*, 129.

75 Lecky, *Democracy and Liberty*, 1. 270. Earlier in his career, Lecky was considerably more upbeat about the 'intellectual revolution' journalism seemed to have effected. See W. E. H. Lecky, *History of European Morals from Augustus to Charlemagne*, 2 vols. (London, 1869), 1. 136.

76 R. J. Smith, *Ireland's Renaissance* (Dublin, 1903), 8.

77 James Joyce, *Dubliners*, ed. Terence Brown (London, 1992), 8. His later description of the *Freeman's Journal* as the *Freeman's Urinal* in *Ulysses* was, more disparaging. *Ulysses*, ed. Jeri Johnson (Oxford, 1993), 434.

78 E, 149.

79 'Pigottism', as E. T. A. Cook remarked, struck a blow against 'journalistic credit' in general and 'anonymous journalism' in particular. Quoted in Stephen Koss, *The Rise and Fall of the Political Press in Britain* (London, 1990), 298. Mark Hampton suggests that the paper was quickly 'forgiven' and the Pigott scandal was 'merely a fleeting episode with which opponents could embarrass *The Times*'. See Mark Hampton, *Visions of the Press in Britain 1850–1950* (Urbana and Chicago, 2004), 90. However, memories of the Pigott scandal died hard in Ireland. In 1900 the *Freeman's Journal* invoked the affair as a notable precedent to the jingo-journalism of the Boer War. 'Jingo patriotism flies to Pigottry,' the paper declared, 'with a natural instinct as its first weapon.' *Freeman's Journal*, 14 October 1900.

80 James Joyce, *Occasional, Critical and Political Writing*, ed. Kevin Barry (Oxford, 2000), 146. Marx had also observed that British prejudices against Ireland were 'artificially kept alive and intensified by the press'. See Karl Marx, *Selected Writings*, ed. David McLellan, 2nd edn. (Oxford, 2000), 640.

due to his ignorance of the English tongue — as a symbol of Ireland at the bar of English public opinion. The jingoistic fervour of British newspapers during the Boer War, in particular, strengthened the conviction in Ireland (and sometimes in England) that the British press was no more than the mouthpiece of imperialism.[81] But, increasingly, nationalist opprobrium was directed against Irish national newspapers; they were accused of subverting the very foundations of patriotism.

Nationalist contempt — or the rhetoric of contempt — for newspapers reached a certain high-point during the rancorous years of the Parnell split. Here newspapers were accused, particularly in Parnellite circles, of base betrayal and ruthless opportunism. In October 1891, the *Freeman's Journal*, Ireland's leading nationalist daily, staged its famous *volte-face*, throwing its lot behind the anti-Parnellite majority in the face of plummeting sales. The paper never lived down this betrayal. Nine years later Arthur Griffith would recall how the '*Freeman's Journal*, as a result of a clerical intrigue, ratted from his cause'.[82] George Moore's *Bending of the Bough* restaged the narrative of journalistic betrayal, although it is uncertain whether the play's editor-Judas resembles young Gray of the *Freeman*, or William O'Brien, the editor of *United Ireland*. Just as Parnell came to represent an integrity lost to modern politics, the Parnell split was also seen — by journalists in particular — to herald the end of respectable standards in Irish journalism. Leopold Bloom still ruminates in 1904 on the 'scurrilous effusions from the facile pens of the O'Brienite scribes at the usual mudslinging occupation, reflecting on the erstwhile tribune's private morals'.[83] According to Bloom's assessment, 'the weeklies, addicted to the lubric a little, simply coined shoals of money' out of the gratuitous reporting of Parnell's amatory escapades with Katherine O'Shea.[84] Bloom's unsentimental assessment of the venal interests of newspapers was an attitude widely shared in Ireland after the Parnell affair.

Critical attitudinizing about the political and moral shortcomings of large scale, commercial newspapers became the hallmark of nationalist authenticity in some circles. The Citizen's denunciation of Irish newspapers in *Ulysses* is a perfect expression of this kind of polemic:

> For the old woman of Prince's street [the *Freeman's Journal*], says the citizen, the subsidised organ. The pledgebound party on the floor of the house. And look at this blasted rag, says he. Look at this, says he. *The Irish Independent*, if you please, founded by Parnell to be the workingman's friend. Listen to the births and deaths in the *Irish all for Ireland Independent* and I'll thank you and the marriages ... How's

81 See J. A. Hobson, *The Psychology of Jingoism* (London, 1901). According to Griffith's *United Irishman*, British jingoism was a form of human degeneration; it spawned individuals who lived on 'gutter newspapers and such-like putrifying vegetable matter'. *United Irishman*, 28 July 1900.
82 *United Irishman*, 25 August 1900.
83 *Ulysses*, 761.
84 *Ulysses*, 756.

that eh? ... How's that for a national press, eh, my brown son? How's that for Martin Murphy, the Bantry jobber?[85]

As the Citizen's invective suggests, nationalist criticisms of newspapers were related to their increasing commercialization.

The Irish Independent was perhaps the most striking example of this process. Founded by Parnell after the split, the newspaper was bought by the anti-Parnellite MP and successful businessman William Martin Murphy — 'old foul mouth' in the Yeatsian lexicon — in 1900.[86] After incurring heavy losses, Murphy overhauled the Independent in 1904 on the advice of his friend, Lord Northcliffe, the hugely successful founder of the English Daily Mail.[87] He acquired two new printers from the Goss Company in Chicago, moved the offices of the Independent from Trinity Street to larger rooms in Middle Abbey Street, expanded his staff, and — crucially — cut the price so that it became the first halfpenny daily in Ireland. The results were extraordinarily successful and the Independent soon became the largest selling daily in Ireland, commanding a circulation three times greater than its nearest rival. Figures like Moran, who worked for a time on the London press, recognized the journalistic techniques — sensational tales of crime, of suicide and of divorce, introduced by provocative headlines and accompanied by pictures — which the Irish Independent seemed to adopt from British papers such as the Daily Mail. Moran's Leader and Griffith's United Irishman functioned, in turn, as nationalist meta-journals and condemned the inconsistency and unprincipled profiteering of large scale nationalist newspapers. 'Metropolitan newspapers conducted on strictly commercial lines', the Leader announced, 'are at this moment the greatest evil from which this land is suffering'.[88]

Anxieties about the social and moral consequences of commerce have often seized upon a particular mediating image. Adam Smith, for instance, projected his concerns about social mobility, the decline of civic virtue and the ultimate transformation of politics under capitalism onto the figure of the merchant. Dedicated to profit not the patria, the merchant in Smith's view was 'not necessarily the citizen of any particular country'.[89] In turn-of-the-century Ireland, however, it was the journalist who was the supreme embodiment of this rootlessness. The journalist was as mobile as the capital from which

85 Ulysses, 384–85. See Patrick Maume, 'The Irish Independent and Empire, 1891–1919', in Potter, ed., Newspapers and Empire in Ireland and Britain, 124–42; 141. William Martin Murphy's newspaper 'aimed at a market composed of those who enjoyed or aspired to a middle-class consumerist lifestyle. In this context, for the Independent as for British Liberal commentators, membership of an empire reformed around liberal principles of self-government could be justified as a legitimate commercial proposition bringing mutual benefits. This acceptance, however, was modified by suspicion that the imperial government was too short-sighted and narrow-minded to develop Irish resources and treat Irish nationalists as equals'.

86 VP, 292.

87 For an account of Murphy and the Independent, see Thomas Morrissey, William Martin Murphy (Dundalk, 1997), 31–40; Donal McCartney, 'William Martin Murphy: an Irish Press Baron and the Rise of the Popular Press', in Farrell, ed., Communications and Community in Ireland, 30–39.

88 Leader, 23 March 1901.

89 Smith, Wealth of Nations, 1. 426.

he derived his living. In his influential history of Ireland, published in 1907, Paul-Dubois reformulated Smith's aversion and asked, 'Who was it that said that journalism has no fatherland?'[90] Journalism, like capitalism itself, had no respect for national borders and was regarded by many nationalists as the epitome of modern rootlessness.

This view received sociological backing in 1889 when Ferdinand de Tönnies made his famous distinction between *Gemeinschaft* and *Gesellschaft*.[91] Here Tönnies outlined the rationalization of social life by economic systems organized in the forms of markets and by political systems, such as the state, characterized by its legal apparatus and administrative practices. These mechanisms produced a form of social interaction that was largely context-independent and stood removed from the concrete traditions of *Gemeinschaft*. Public opinion, in other words, was not racy of the soil, but was increasingly isolated from the traditional frameworks in which things like norms, values, and personality were formerly forged. The communicative infrastructure of *Gesellschaft* was produced and maintained by the modern press — a 'universal power', according to Tönnies, that was 'comparable with and in some respects superior to the material power which states can wield through their armies, exchequers and official bureaucracies'.[92] He suggested that the state might even find itself ultimately overwhelmed by the development of modern media:

> ... it [the press] is not restricted to national boundaries, but is totally international in its propensities and possibilities, and thus comparable in power with permanent or temporary alliances between states. It can be claimed that its ultimate aim is to do away with the many different states and to replace them with a single *world republic*, equal in extent to the world market, which would be ruled by intellectuals, scholars and writers and could dispense with all means of coercion other than those of a psychological kind.[93]

The press threatened to overthrow the social formations it had earlier helped to install. Tönnies dismissed a world republic as an unlikely outcome, but the recognition of its possibility, he suggested, allowed us 'to grasp the important fact that the development of nation states is only a temporary barrier to an international market society without national boundaries'.[94]

---

90 L. Paul-Dubois, *Contemporary Ireland* (Dublin, 1908), 167.
91 Ferdinand de Tönnies, *Community and Civil Society*, ed. Jose Harris, trans. Jose Harris and Margaret Hollis (Cambridge, 2001), 17–91.
92 *Community and Civil Society*, 242. See also Ostrogorski, *Democracy and the Organization of Political Parties*, 1. 519.
93 *Community and Civil Society*, 242–43 [Tönnies's emphasis].
94 *Community and Civil Society*, 243.

Irish nationalists also regarded newspapers as a cosmopolitan force that undermined national differences.[95] Moran, for instance, deplored the denationalizing tendency of a metropolitan press. 'They draft to the remotest districts of the country,' he declared, 'the defiling alluvia of Cockney rubbish.'[96] Moran's defence of cultural particularity was arbitrary; the national identity he defended, moreover, potentially overruled small scale forms of solidarity and traditional forms of social interaction. Nor was nationalism necessarily opposed to the levelling impact of market forces; indeed, according to some interpreters, it was their inevitable by-product.[97] Thus, when Moran attacked the homogenizing tendency of newspapers on nationalist lines, he condemned something that was arguably internal to nationalism itself. These contradictions were not unique to Moran. Indeed, Irish writers of the Literary Revival repeatedly invoked the idioms of nationalism to attack the corrupting effects of the press.

3 The Irish Literary Revival and the Demonization of Newspapers

In an arresting moment in *The Celtic Twilight*, Yeats described how the devil accosted a young Mayo woman in the form of a newspaper flapping across the road. 'She knew by the size of it that it was the *Irish Times*', and presumably by the latter's unionist affiliations, that it was the devil disguised.[98] Although Yeats identified a specific newspaper for largely political reasons, the tale also functioned as an indictment of the press in general. He had frequently presented the destruction of tradition in Ireland as a process of anglicization and the unionist *Irish Times* was a fitting metonym for the encroachment of modern communicational systems on older cultural practices.[99] 'It is not Shakespeare and Milton,' he noted, 'that have been superseding the Gaelic poets in Ireland, but the half-penny comics; in fact, Anglicisation has meant vulgarisation.'[100] In this light, Yeats's folktale presented itself as an act of resistance, waged in defence of traditional speech-communities against the polluting effects of modern mass media. The *Irish Times*, in the form of litter, invades a natural landscape which is henceforth unrecognizable. But in this instance, folklore recycles litter, assimilating it into a mythic

---

95 For an earlier application of Tönnies's *Gemeinschaft/Gesellschaft* distinction to Irish nationalism, see Terry Eagleton, *Heathcliff and the Great Hunger: Studies in Irish Culture* (London and New York, 1995), 230.

96 *Leader*, 23 March 1901.

97 Gellner, *Nations and Nationalism*, 46: 'it is the objective need for homogeneity which is reflected in nationalism'. In other words, modern market economies dictate the need for a homogeneous language and culture that is sponsored by the state and ideologically championed by nationalism.

98 W. B. Yeats, *The Celtic Twilight* (London and Stratford-upon-Avon, 1902), 62. Hereafter cited as CT.

99 CL 2. 537. In a letter to Lady Gregory: 'To transmute the anti English passion into a passion of hatred against the vulgarity of a materialism whereon England founds her worst life & the whole life that she sends us has always been a dream of mine.'

100 UP 2. 288.

order under the sign of the devil. Thus, folklore protracts its own existence and secures traditional ways of seeing from the corrupt intelligence of journalism.

Yeats's story may be read in light of the crude, but influential, dichotomies that distinguish a modern from a traditional world-view, in terms of what Hans-Georg Gadamer once called Enlightenment's 'abstract contrast between myth and reason'.[101] Among nineteenth-century liberals, at least, newspapers were frequently taken to represent the triumph of reason over superstition and myth. This dichotomous logic, for instance, was basic to Bentham's striking account of the newspaper: 'before this talisman, not only devils but ghosts, vampires, witches and all their kindred tribes are driven out of the land, never to return again, for the touch of holy water is not as intolerable to them as the bare smell of printer's ink'.[102] But for Yeats, the journalist was the embodiment of a rationalizing intelligence that bled the world of all mystery and imagination.[103] He was prepared to concede that journalists were not entirely irredeemable: 'even a newspaper man, if you entice him into a cemetery at midnight, will believe in phantoms, for every one is a visionary, if you scratch him deep enough'. But 'the Celt is a visionary without scratching'.[104] The oppositions, however qualified, were firmly in place: the journalist was the antithesis of the authentic Celt, just as a demystifying rationality was opposed to the enchantment of vision. God, perhaps, was dead, but the devil was alive and well.

Throughout all the shifts in Yeats's career, he remained remarkably consistent on one point: newspapers were a source and symbol of modern degradation. He repeatedly derided the 'base idioms of the newspapers', 'the-rough-and-ready conscience' of the press, and mocked the 'pomp and gallantry of journalism'.[105] Predictably, he distinguished genuine art from the verbiage of newspapers and dismissed inferior literary forms — such as realism — as glorified journalism.[106] In these attitudes, he was very much his father's son. In his *Autobiographies*, Yeats described his initial disappointment with his suburban home in Bedford Park, for his new abode failed to tally with his father's initial account of it: 'I had thought he said, "There is to be a wall round and no newspapers to be allowed in". And when I had told him how put out I was at finding neither wall nor gate,

---

101 Gadamer, *Truth and Method*, 273.

102 Jeremy Bentham, *The Handbook of Political Fallacies* (New York, 1962), 49.

103 This seemed to overlook the fact that many leading journalists — the most famous being W. T. Stead — were practitioners of spiritualism and enthusiasts of the occult. See Aled Jones, *Powers of the Press: Newspapers, Power and the Public in Nineteenth-Century England* (Aldershot, 1996), 80–81.

104 PI, 4.

105 E, 95, 311; EI, 312.

106 E, 140: 'Literature is not journalism because it can turn the imagination to whatever is essential and unchanging in life'. L, 549: 'This is the first generation in which the spirit of literature has been conquered by the spirit of the press, of hurry, of immediate interests.' See also EI, 227: Realism, is 'the delight to-day of all those whose minds, educated alone by schoolmasters and newspapers, are without the memory of beauty and emotional subtlety', and 274: Ibsen, the arch-realist, produced a mere 'leading-article sort of poetry' and was 'the chosen author of very clever young journalists, who, condemned to their treadmill of abstraction, hated music and style'.

he explained that he had merely described what ought to be.'[107] True to his father's spirit, he declared to Ernest Rhys: 'I use all my great will power to keep me from reading the newspapers and spoiling my vocabulary.'[108] Yet these reading restrictions did not prevent him from writing for newspapers. Yeats, in fact, produced a large body of journalism; it was a major source of his income for a considerable period of his writing life.

Some of Yeats's best-known poems made their first appearance in newspapers. 'The Lake Isle of Innisfree', published in the *National Observer* in December 1890, was one of the most famous. Throughout the 1890s, he produced articles for both the ultra-Tory *National Observer* and the nationalist *United Ireland*. He published in élite organs such as the *Yellow Book*, in more middle-brow journals like the *Irish Fireside* and in popular magazines such as the *Girls' Own Paper*.[109] He operated as a gregarious 'Celt in London' for the *Boston Pilot* and contributed also to the *Providence Sunday Journal*. In his private correspondence — where he meted out advice to would-be reviewers about the distinctive requirements of different journals — he displayed a shrewd awareness of the journalistic field both in Ireland and England. He was, moreover, an adept and enthusiastic 'log-roller'. He recognized the diversity and range of journalism; yet he continued to deride in broad terms 'a style rancid, coarse and vague, like that of the daily papers'.[110] His own journalism was cast in different styles and was addressed to different readerships, yet it did little to refine his broad criticisms of 'newspaper English'.[111]

Yeats was not the only figure to wage war on journalism in the name of an authentic Irish culture. Douglas Hyde, one of the founding fathers of the Irish Cultural Revival, also distrusted newspapers. In his Preface to *Beside the Fire*, he blamed O'Connell and the Catholic clergy for dismantling an authentic Irish identity: 'their more than indifference to things Gaelic put an end to all that was really Irish, and taught the people to speak English, to look to London, and to read newspapers'.[112] Hyde went on to insist that folklore and poetry offered a richer form of discourse than anything a newspaper, however avowedly Irish, might muster. As he put it, 'the man who reads Irish MMS., and repeats Ossianic poetry, is a higher and more interesting type than the man whose mental training is confined to spelling through an article in *United Ireland*'.[113] Yeats adopted this opposition between newspapers and native culture in his appraisal of Hyde's own works: 'His imagination is indeed at its best only when he writes in Irish or

---

107 A, 43.
108 IR 1. 36.
109 See Foster, *Apprentice Mage*, 97.
110 UP 2. 438.
111 UP 1. 143.
112 Douglas Hyde, *Beside the Fire: A Collection of Irish Gaelic Folk Songs* (London, 1890), xxiii. See also Hyde's complaint in *A Literary History of Ireland from the Earliest Times to the Present Day* (London, 1899), x–xi, that 'poetry is an unknown term' among the people of Ireland. Moreover, 'there exists little or no trace of traditional Irish feelings, or indeed seldom of any feelings save those prompted by (when they read it) a weekly newspaper'.
113 Hyde, *Beside the Fire*, xlv.

in that beautiful English of the country people who remember too much Irish to talk like a newspaper.'[114] Lady Gregory also used the newspaper as a litmus test of authenticity in her assessment of Hyde:

> It was only a few years ago, when Douglas Hyde published his literal translations on Connacht Love Songs, that I realized that, while I have thought poetry was all but dead in Ireland, the people about me had been keeping up the lyrical tradition that existed in Ireland before Chaucer lived. While I had been looking at the columns of Nationalist newspapers for some word of poetic promise, they had been singing songs of love and sorrow in the language that has been pushed nearer and nearer to the western seaboard — the edge of the world.[115]

Synge employed the same rhetorical tactics. 'In writing *The Playboy of the Western World*, as in my other plays,' he declared, 'I have used one or two words only, that I have not heard among the country people of Ireland, or spoken in my own nursery before I could read the newspaper.'[116] Yeats distinguished Synge's writing from the inferior works of Padraic Colum and William Boyle: 'Mr Colum and Mr. Boyle ... write of the countryman or villager of the East or centre of Ireland, who thinks in English, and the speech of their people shows the influence of the newspaper and the National Schools.'[117] The linguistic vitality of Elizabethan England could only be found, Yeats suggested, in modern Gaelic or in those areas 'where the schoolmaster or the newspaper has not corrupted it'.[118] Although George Russell was later to become a successful editor of the *Irish Homestead* and *Irish Statesman*, he was quick to associate newspapers with the decline of an authentic Gaelic culture. 'Today', he opined, 'it is not the bard or story-teller who comes to our doors, but the daily press with its arid statistics of the crime of the world, and the bitter speeches of public men. Yes, let us go back to Gaelic Ireland'.[119]

Moore argued that the entire English language had been corrupted by journalism. He predicted its imminent demise — although slow enough to allow the non-Irish-speaking Moore to equip himself with English translations of 'remote idioms':

> The English language in fifty years will be as corrupt as the Latin in the 8th century, quite as unfit for usage, except in the counting-house and the newspaper office. English will become, in my opinion, a sort of volapuk, strictly limited to commercial letters and to journalism; what happened before will happen again, and nothing written in the universal language will survive. The future literature

114 PI, 135.
115 Augusta Gregory, *Poets and Dreamers: Studies and Translations from the Irish* (Gerrards Cross, 1974), 43.
116 J. M. Synge, *Collected Works. Volume 4: Plays*, ed. Ann Saddlemyer (London, 1968), 53.
117 E, 183.
118 E, 167.
119 Quoted in Grattan Freyer, *W. B. Yeats and the Anti-Democratic Tradition* (Dublin, 1981), 47.

of the world, I am convinced, will be written in Irish, in Flemish, in Hungarian, in Welsh, perhaps in Basque — languages which have not been written thread-bare or polluted by journalism, and for still another century perhaps enough of the English language will remain to enable the translators of the future to give adequate rendering of the original works which will be written in remote idioms.[120]

Yeats also insisted that the English language and English manners had been thoroughly corrupted by journalism. 'The English mind', as he put it, 'excited by its newspaper proprietors and its schoolmasters, had turned into a bed-hot harlot'.[121] In *Hail and Farewell*, Moore suggested — somewhat disingenuously — that his own anti-journalistic polemic was largely a ventriloquization of Yeats's more committed views on the matter. Yeats had helped him to recognize 'the beauty of living speech when living speech is fast being driven out by journalists'.[122] When Moore initially dismissed the 'brogue' of Sligo peasants as 'the ugliest dialect in the world', Yeats curtly responded: 'No dialect is ugly, ... the bypaths are all beautiful. It is the broad road of the journalist that is ugly'.[123] 'Folk', according to Yeats, 'is our refuge from vulgarity'.[124]

In William P. Ryan's quasi-autobiographical novel *Daisy Darley; or, The Fairy Gold of Fleet Street* (1913), which depicts his work for the *Star*, the opposition between folklore and vulgar journalism presents itself in even starker terms, because the novel aspires towards their ultimate reconciliation. In a spirit of wild optimism, the novel's protagonist, Arthur Clandillon, hopes to spiritualize England through his unique blend of Celtic and Oriental philosophy. On the desk before him at the portentous opening of the novel is 'a copy of a London evening paper and a small volume of Celtic folk-tales'.[125] Arthur's is an ambitious project:

> incidentally and deftly, in reviews and studies and notes, they were to bring before the ken of the British democrat the philosophy of the Oriental and the Celt, the immemorial gnostic and mystical conceptions of life and soul and destiny, to show him that progress is a concern of the psychic and the mental as well as the physical and social plane, and so to hearten him with a subtle and cosmic vision.[126]

According to a colleague's earlier assessment, this is yet another futile attempt of the 'Celt to spiritualise the British Empire'.[127] Unsurprisingly, Arthur's project fails and we

---

120 *United Irishman*, 3 March 1900. This speech was published in a somewhat modified form as 'Literature and the Irish Language', in Gregory, ed., *Ideals in Ireland*, 43–51.
121 E, 443.
122 Moore, *Hail and Farewell*, 329.
123 Quoted in *Hail and Farewell*, 84.
124 Quoted in *Hail and Farewell*, 331.
125 William P. Ryan, *Daisy Darley; or, The Fairy Gold of Fleet Street* (London and Toronto, 1913), 1.
126 *Daisy Darley*, 160–61.
127 *Daisy Darley*, 14.

are left with a damning account of contemporary journalistic practice, sustained by 'a feverish interest in murder' and committed to 'mere sensations, fancy-flourishes and futility'.[128] Like his author, William P. Ryan, Arthur returns to Ireland disgusted with British journalistic practice.

The newspaper, for some commentators, was simply the most virulent expression of the vices of print-culture in general. Yeats frequently confessed to a natural dislike 'of print and paper' and celebrated 'the spoken word that knits us to normal man'.[129] His objections to the printed word were multiple and diverse, but one of his main difficulties with print — in his early career at least — was that it seemed to encourage the privatization of human experience. The printed word could be consumed in solitude and allowed individuals to abstract themselves from their immediate speech-communities. The press may have provided access to other forms of collective life — and this was one reason why it was applauded by nationalists throughout the nineteenth century — but it also threatened to undermine face-to-face interaction in local environments. Yeats believed that this was an unnatural development:

> It is a much more natural thing to listen than to read. For a man who has to work all day, it is hardly possible for him to get culture in any other way. It is natural for him to sit among his friends and listen to a tale told or a song sung, but not natural for him to mope in a corner with a book.[130]

The juxtaposition of the natural and gregarious features of speech with the artifice and isolation of print became a recurrent motif. 'When a man takes a book into the corner', Yeats explained, 'he surrenders so much life for his knowledge, so much, I mean, of that normal activity that gives him life and strength; he lays away his own handiwork and turns from his friend'.[131]

It is not surprising that Yeats's attacks on print-culture diminished over time; these polemics may have emphasized the remedial value of theatre — which depended on the spoken word and face-to-face interaction — but they also rebounded on his own career as a writer. But he never surrendered the conviction that newspapers presided over a destructive form of abstraction. The rhetoric of the press, he believed, was necessarily abstract; in order to maximize audiences, newspapers needed to be accessible and transparent to all. A condition of that accessibility was the removal of all historical texture and local idiom from language. Newspapers struggled to produce — in so far as

128 *Daisy Darley*, 42, 44.
129 EI, 266.
130 Yeats, 'Four Lectures by W. B. Yeats', 84. A famous and more recent example of the ontological dimensions of this question is to be found in the discussion of Rousseau in Jacques Derrida, *Of Grammatology*, trans. Gayatri Chakravorty Spivak (Baltimore and London, 1976), 165–71.
131 E, 207.

it was possible — a form of communication that could remain context-independent.[132] The rhetoric of the press, Yeats believed, resembled the language of science in its efforts to rid its descriptions of the troublesome contingencies of time and space. He often suggested that there was a spiritual cousinship between 'science and good journalism' and insisted that the press had substituted the concrete speech-practices of a historical community with a bloodless logic.[133] Logic had unpleasant democratic implications for the later Yeats, but his early objections to the abstractions of the press had a more communitarian emphasis. He recoiled from the 'obvious logic' or the 'confident logic' of the press, and believed that the rhetoric of newspapers deprived language of its historical substance. In Yeats's estimate the 'formulas and generalisations in which a hidden sergeant has drilled the ideas of journalists and through them the ideas of all but all the modern world, have created in their turn a forgetfulness like that of soldiers of battle'.[134] His aim was to reverse this terrible forgetfulness by resuscitating traditional forms of communication.

Folklore was one kind of discursive practice that Yeats championed as a counterforce to the reification of language. His introduction to a folktale published in the *Scot's Observer* provides a clear indication of his ambition:

> Most men know the prophecy of Thomas of Erceldoune: 'The time is coming when all the wisdom of the world shall centre in the grey goose quill.' So much of the prophecy has been fulfilled. Tradition seems half gone. Thomas of Erceldoune and his like go with it. The newspaper editors and other men of the quill, this long while have been elbowing fairy and fairy seer from hearth and board. Maybe yet the creatures have more vitality than they think.[135]

He was not always so optimistic: 'Surely the hum of wheel and clatter of printing presses have driven away the goblin kingdom and made silent the feet of the little dancers.'[136] Ironically, both of these opinions were published in newspapers. But Yeats largely ignored the obvious performative contradiction in his anti-journalistic journalism. He continued to contrast folklore with journalism and grew 'indignant with those who would substitute for the ideas of the folk-life the rhetoric of the newspapers', even though his own published tales did much to undermine the terms of this antithesis.[137] The blurring of boundaries was embarrassingly apparent when he published a prose account of the Countess Cathleen in *Fairy and Folk Tales*. Yeats claimed that he had discovered the tale

---

132 For Derrida, abstraction from a context was a general feature of all language and was a basic condition of meaning. See Jacques Derrida, *Margins of Philosophy*, trans. Alan Bass (Brighton, 1982), 318.
133 EI, 284. Elsewhere (EI, 272), he grouped together 'the thoughts of the newspapers' with those of 'the market-place' and those of 'men of science'.
134 EI, 154.
135 *Scot's Observer*, 2 March 1889.
136 PI, 58.
137 E, 151.

in some unspecified locale in the west of Ireland, but this was roundly rejected by John Augustus O'Shea in a letter to the *Star* newspaper:

> Mr. Yeats told me he heard it in the west of Ireland. This would be a surprising coincidence were it not ... that I had it printed in the *Shamrock* of Dublin [6 October 1867] which largely circulates among Irish people ... Singularly enough, it was reprinted in the same periodical at a comparatively recent date.[138]

Yeats acknowledged his error, but he refused to address the broader difficulties of a folk revival sustained by modern systems of communication.

Joyce duly mocked Revivalist prejudices against journalism in his story 'A Little Cloud'. The tale revolves around Little Chandler's encounter with an old friend, Gallaher, who has become 'a brilliant figure on the London Press'.[139] After meeting Gallaher in a Dublin pub, Little Chandler begins to resent the journalist's confident swagger and patronizing tone: 'Gallaher's accent and way of expressing himself did not please him. There was something vulgar in his friend which he had not observed before.' He attributes this new vulgarity to Gallaher's immersion in journalism — 'the bustle and competition of the Press'.[140] Despite the solace this snobbery affords, there is not much to distinguish Little Chandler's mind from the world of 'tawdry journalism' he condemns.[141] Earlier in the evening he fantasises about writing a successful poem and wonders if Gallaher 'might be able to get it into some London paper for him'. The complicity between Celticism and journalism is further exposed by Chandler's fantasies of success. He is incapable of producing a single line of poetry; instead, he begins 'to invent sentences and phrases from the notices which his book would get. *Mr Chandler has the gift of easy and graceful verse ... A wistful sadness pervades these poems ... The Celtic note*'. He also considers it 'a pity his name was not more Irish-looking'.[142] Joyce's story points to a fundamental contradiction in the Revivalist hostility to newspapers: if the projects of the Revival were to succeed on a national level, they remained paradoxically dependent on the newspaper as their supporter and mouthpiece.[143]

Hyde's popularity, for instance, owed much to his use of the press he apparently despised. He was critical of the influence of newspapers on traditional speech-

---

138 CL 2. 539.
139 Dubliners, 65.
140 Dubliners, 71–72.
141 Dubliners, 75.
142 Dubliners, 69.
143 George Russell made this point in no uncertain terms to Yeats in 1905: See Richard J. Finneran, George Mills Harper, William M. Murphy, eds., *Letters to W. B. Yeats*, 2 vols. (London and Basingstoke, 1977), I. 154: 'The fact is the position you wish to hold of general autocrat in literary, dramatic and artistic matters in Dublin or Ireland is a position accorded through love and cannot be assumed and without a press to back you up or a band of energetic propagandists to carry your opinions about, you may be as right as God Almighty in his secrecy but with as little influence in the lives of men.'

communities, but the alternatives he promoted — folklore and poetry gleaned largely from Irish-speaking communities in the west of Ireland — were published widely in newspapers. According to Lady Gregory, many of Hyde's poems achieved a mass audience through their circulation in the weekly press: 'The poems had already been published, one by one, in a weekly paper; and a friend of mine tells me he has heard them sung and repeated by country people in many parts of Ireland — in Connemara, in Donegal, in Galway, in Kerry, in the Islands of Aran.'[144] Yeats also claimed that Hyde's influence was felt throughout the nation. A poem that appeared during the Boer War was, he suggested, evidence of such influence. Significantly, the poem was published anonymously in a newspaper and was celebrated throughout Ireland:

> I don't think Ireland's anger against her destiny has ever been expressed with so powerful a passion. It appeared anonymously in some Nationalist newspaper during the Boer War, and it has gone through the whole country. Its authorship has never been acknowledged, but it shows the influence of that direct and simple style which Dr. Hyde has rediscovered from his study of old songs and from his passionate, direct nature. I remember a priest saying when he first heard that poem: 'With the help of God, every child in my parish will know that by heart before Christmas Day.' And he was right.[145]

Although Yeats dismissed journalism in 1909 as 'a most un-Celtic thing', newspapers played a crucial role in the Celtic Revival.[146] In particular, the Parnellite *United Ireland* popularized interest in Irish cultural matters after the fall of Parnell. Both the *Leader* and the *United Irishman* did much to garner nationalist support for Yeats and other cultural figures at the turn of the century, although they probably did as much to withdraw it later.[147] The unionist *Daily Express*, under the editorship of T. P. Gill, actively promoted the Irish National Literary Theatre in its formative years. George Moore was of the opinion that the *Daily Express* was the 'first paper that had attempted to realise that Ireland had an aesthetic spirit of her own', while Yeats enthused that the newspaper had taken 'upon Irish & Celtic things with great vigour'.[148] When Gill resigned from his editorship of the *Express*, Yeats described it as 'a great blow' to the revival of culture in Ireland.[149] 'You cannot have a national theatre', he eventually conceded, 'without creating a national

---

144 Gregory, *Poets and Dreamers*, 62.
145 Yeats, 'Four Lectures by W. B. Yeats', 109.
146 M, 178.
147 In 1900, Lady Gregory was convinced that D. P. Moran had made 'a great change in Ireland by the "Leader", & helps in the building up of the nation better than anyone else had done'. Gregory, *Poets and Dreamers*, 294.
148 Moore, *Hail and Farewell*, 123. CL 2. 285.
149 CL 2. 455.

audience, and that cannot be done by the theatre alone, for it needs the help of schools and newspapers, and of all the teachers of the people.'[150]

Wyndham Lewis dismissed the 'romantic persons who go picking about in the Arran [sic] Islands ... or elsewhere for genuine human "antiques"'. These romantics, according to Lewis, 'are today on a wild-goose chase, because the sphinx of the Past, in the person of some elder dug out of such remote neighbourhoods, will at length, when he has found his tongue, probably commence addressing them in the vernacular of the *Daily Mail*'.[151] Traditional speech-practices, he suggested, were no longer recoverable in a media-saturated age. In 1900, the successful journalist, Michael MacDonagh, described 'the almost universal reading of newspapers and periodicals' in Ireland. Moreover, he expressed his amazement at the popularity of 'London penny weekly publications such as *Tit Bits, Answers, Home Chat, Pearson's Weekly, Woman's Life* ... in even the remote towns of Ireland'. 'Week after week enormous bundles of these journals are sent to all the chief towns and villages throughout the country.' In MacDonagh's estimation, 'there is not a cabin in any part of Ireland ... in which copies of these journals will not be found'.[152] Moran berated Irish men and women for reading these foreign journals. Each week 'low imported entertainment', from foreign newspapers to 'nigger minstrelsy', to 'Cockney music-hall singers', was subjected to a rhetorical lynching in the *Leader*.[153] Moran criticized foreign journals and Irish metropolitan newspapers on nationalist lines, but nationalism was an expression of the problem of 'print-capitalism' and not its solution.

In his later years, Yeats managed to combine robust attacks on nationalism with scathing attacks on newspapers. These criticisms also marked the abandonment of the broad communitarian values that informed his early indictments of the press. His anxieties about the privatizing features of print now gave way to an almost opposite concern: mass media had made genuine privacy increasingly difficult to sustain.

---

150 UP 2. 469.
151 Wyndham Lewis, *Time and Western Man*, ed. Paul Edwards (Santa Rosa, 1993), 80–81.
152 Michael MacDonagh, 'In the Bye-Ways of Rural Ireland', *Nineteenth Century*, 48 (July 1900), 75–88.
153 *Leader*, 13 July 1901.

6   Journalism and Authenticity

1   Journalists and the Great Refusal

In William P. Ryan's novel, *Daisy Darley; or, The Fairy Gold of Fleet Street*, a Celtic poet —
obviously Yeats — warns the journalist-hero, Arthur Clandillon, against the destructive
effects of journalism. The poet is lost and begs directions from Clandillon who points
to Fleet Street behind him:

> 'I am glad,' said the poet, 'that my back is turned to Fleet Street. Fleet Street is an
> enemy of the Immortal Moods. I seem to have heard, though maybe it was a dream,
> that you have something to do with a newspaper. I hope it is not true. You would
> lose all cohesion of personality. Your soul would be scattered like rags on bushes in
> a 'wildering wind. It could never become a little golden phial of intense and radiant
> emotion which the high gods could hold between their fingers in the starlight.'[1]

Yeats had regularly condemned newspapers and print-culture more generally for their
'individualising' tendencies, but he ultimately yielded to a fear that journalism eroded
genuine personality altogether. Even at the beginning of his career — when he was
himself as much a journalist as a poet — he condemned journalists for their existential
poverty. 'I hate journalists,' he declared to his close friend Katherine Tynan in 1888.
'There is nothing in them but tittering jeering emptiness. They have all made what Dante
calls the Great Refusal. [sic] that is, they have ceased to be self centred [and] have given
up their individuality.'[2] Against the corruption of journalism, he produced a complex

1   Ryan, *Daisy Darley*, 166–67.
2   CL 1. 91.

model of authenticity — an ethics of the self in which he delivered strong and often rival judgements about the individual's duties to itself and to its world.[3] This language was not entirely Yeats's own creation; he relied heavily on others such as Nietzsche for some of its basic terms.[4] Nor was he unusual in presenting the journalist as the antithesis of the authentic soul, for this prejudice was shared by cultural mandarins across Europe.

'Just look at these superfluous people', Nietzsche declared, 'they vomit their bile and call it a newspaper. They devour one another and cannot digest themselves'.[5] In Henry James's *The Reverberator*, the journalist, George Flack, was 'not a specific person, but had … the quality of the sample or advertisement, the air of representing a "line of goods" for which there is a steady popular demand'.[6] Flack, according to James, would be better identified by a number than by a name. The journalist's forfeiture of self was directly related to his apparently dependent position in the marketplace of ideas. No artist could transcend the dictates of the market, but the journalist was judged to be wholly in thrall to its capricious will. He was a 'paper slave' and relied entirely on the directives of editors and the tastes of readers for both the source and content of his work.[7] 'What the devil do I need with an opinion of my own' a journalist declares in Patrick MacGill's *Children of the Dead End*; the object of journalism, after all, was simply to amplify the ideas of others.[8] The dependent status of journalists also made them inconstant and unreliable. For Leopold Bloom, they were 'Weathercocks': 'Hot and cold in the same breath. Wouldn't know which to believe. One story good till you hear the next.'[9]

The guardians of genuine culture exaggerated their own independence in the market of ideas, but even journalists conceded that their trade was bad for the soul. In a guidebook to the profession, John Oldcastle declared that writing for newspapers led to a gradual erosion of the self. The journalist, he declared, breaks 'up his individuality into a thousand separate fragments, not one of which bears the stamp of his name. The man is scattered and lost, the character of his work is dissipated by dissemination.'[10] Ryan parodied Yeats's views on journalism, but he also believed that the profession destroyed the mind. In *The*

---

3   For general discussions of authenticity, see Lionel Trilling, *Sincerity and Authenticity* (London, 1974); Charles Taylor, *The Ethics of Authenticity* (Cambridge and London, 1991); Bernard Williams, *Truth and Truthfulness: An Essay in Genealogy* (Princeton and Oxford, 2002), 172–205.

4   For an account of Nietzsche's general influence on Yeats, see Otto Bohlmann, *Yeats and Nietzsche: An Exploration of Major Nietzschean Echoes in the Writings of William Butler Yeats* (London, 1982).

5   Friedrich Nietzsche, *Thus Spoke Zarathustra*, trans. R. J. Hollingdale (London, 1961), 77.

6   Henry James, *A London Life and The Reverberator* (Oxford, 1989), 159. In James's story, 'The Papers', the unpromisingly named Maud Blandy seems to have surrendered a stable self to journalism: 'She was fairly a product of the day — so fairly that she might have been born afresh each morning, to serve, after the fashion of certain agitated ephemeral insects, only till the morrow.' Henry James, 'The Papers', in *Complete Stories, 1898–1910*, ed. Denis Donoghue (New York, 1996), 542–638, 543.

7   Friedrich Nietzsche, *The Birth of Tragedy and Other Writings*, trans. Ronald Speirs (Cambridge, 1999), 96.

8   Patrick MacGill, *Children of the Dead End: The Autobiography of a Navvy* (Ascot, 1980), 277.

9   *Ulysses*, 121. Oscar Wilde also derided a school of journalism invented by 'Janus Weathercock'. Wilde, *Complete Works*, 1101 [Wilde's emphasis].

10 John Oldcastle [pseud. for Wilfrid Meynell], *Journals and Journalism: With a Guide for Literary Beginners* (London, 1880), 72.

Plough and the Cross, journalism is described as having 'a harassing and dissipating effect upon the mind', which 'broke intellectual coherence and spoiled artistic expression'.[11] Journalists, it seems, were neither owners of their rhetoric nor guardians of their soul. Forced to express themselves for a living, they lacked the rhetorical continence that was basic to the formation of character. In Ryan's fiction, the existential costs of journalism are exorbitant: 'the mind made pieces of, day in day out, for ephemeral enthusiasms and transient ends'.[12] Lost to the contingencies of their own profession, journalists were forced to relinquish the hope of a unified personality. Staring at the great printing machines of the *Freeman's Journal*, Leopold Bloom believes that they could '[s]mash a man to atoms'.[13] 'The newspaper', Yeats declared, 'is the roar of the machine', and it consumed the personalities of both its producers and consumers alike.[14]

One of the more obvious grounds for the popular distrust of journalists lay in the indeterminate social status of their profession as a whole. According to Weber, the journalist lacked 'a fixed social classification', and belonged, as a result, 'to a sort of pariah caste, which is always estimated by "society" in terms of its ethically lowest representative'.[15] Even journalists engaged in this persecution. Griffith, for instance, dismissed his fellow journalists as 'a worthless, unprincipled class, too low almost for an honest man's contempt'. Although he did concede that there were 'some honest and honourable men amongst these journalists', he maintained that they were few in number and occupied 'mostly subordinate posts'.[16] The massive expansion of the newspaper industry at the end of the nineteenth century in Britain reduced the entry requirements to the journalistic field, while reforms like the Education Act of 1870 also meant that more people had the educational capital to meet them. According to one practitioner, it was precisely 'the openness of the profession of Journalism' which made it so attractive: 'Anyone who readily puts pen to paper, and who has some perception of what manner of things his fellows will be interested to hear of and read, commands at once, as it seems, a facile avenue up which he may amble or even dart to fame and fortune.'[17] The relative accessibility of the profession attracted many a soldier of fortune, but this feature of the trade also appalled others; 'any untrained scribbler calls himself a journalist'.[18]

The journalist often appeared as a curiously disconnected creature, whose untrustworthiness reflected his untraceable origins. His homelessness in the world had a geographical, social and even an ontological character. In George Moore's novel, *The Lake* (1905), it was precisely the mobility and rootlessness of journalism that appealed to its protagonist, Father Oliver:

11 Ryan, *The Plough and the Cross*, 296.
12 *The Plough and the Cross*, 17.
13 *Ulysses*, 114.
14 A, 463.
15 Weber, *From Max Weber*, 96.
16 *United Irishman*, 22 June 1901.
17 Walter Besant, *The Pen and the Book* (London, 1899), 231.
18 *New Age*, 25 February 1915.

Journalists flutter like bats about newspaper offices. The bats haunt the same eaves, but the journalist drifts from city to city, from country to country, busying himself with ideas that were not his yesterday, and will not be his tomorrow. An interview with a statesman is followed by a review of a book, and the day after he may be thousands of miles away, describing a great flood or a railway accident. The journalist has no time to make friends, and he lives in no place long enough to know it intimately; passing acquaintance and exterior aspects of things are his share of the world. And it was in quest of such vagrancy of ideas and affections that he was going.[19]

In Joyce's story, 'A Little Cloud', the journalist Gallaher is a wandering spirit with ostentatiously cosmopolitan tastes. 'Gallaher's vagrant and triumphant life', inspires both envy and disgust in those he encounters.[20] The life of the 'vagabond journalist' had its attractions for MacGill, but it was also a degrading existence.[21] It was the very vagrancy — real and metaphorical — of journalism that led many figures to present it as a fundamentally corrupt profession.

It was double jeopardy for the significant number of Irish journalists working in England. In the 1870s Hugh Heinrick observed how the 'London press, daily and weekly, is notably recruited from Ireland'.[22] Over thirty years later, Paul-Dubois noted that 'Ireland furnishes a good part of the *personnel* of the British press, even of the anti-Irish section of it'.[23] Anti-Irish stereotypes often combined with received opinions about journalists to provide damning accounts of the modern press. If the Irish, as Carlyle believed, were 'a people that knows not to speak the truth, and to act the truth', then this mendacity lent them some success in journalism.[24] Thackeray's *Pendennis* did little to dislodge this kind of prejudice. Hoolan and Doolan — lovable idiots full of drink and blather — emphasized the incurable incontinence of the Celt and the journalist. Thackeray drew a more sympathetic portrait of the journalist, Captain Shandon, probably based on the brilliant figure William Maginn, editor of *Fraser's Magazine*. But Shandon, like Maginn, is an alcoholic; he is also unprincipled and opportunistic. Irish character — mendacious, loquacious, and invariably boozed — lent itself to the trade of journalism. Even sympathetic commentators were consumers of the myth. In a survey of modern Ireland, Paul-Dubois declared that the Irishman 'is, above all, a born journalist'. With a long tradition of oratory and a national preoccupation with the rhetorical arts behind him, he 'has all the qualities of the profession, ease, spirit, and verve'. Dubois disapproved of this facility, which had, he believed, condemned Ireland to 'wordy

19 George Moore, *The Lake* (Gerrards Cross, 1980), 170–71.
20 *Dubliners*, 75.
21 MacGill, *Children of the Dead End*, 280.
22 Hugh Heinrick, *The Irish in England* (Liverpool, 1874), 8.
23 Paul-Dubois, *Contemporary Ireland*, 167 [Paul-Dubois's emphasis].
24 Carlyle, *Critical and Miscellaneous Essays*, 6. 126.

agitation and ... destructive rhetoric'.[25] Yeats also emphasized the journalistic facility and glibness of his compatriots; the Irish, he suggested, were 'essentially a nation of public speakers and journalists'.[26]

By the end of the nineteenth century, the figure of the drunken, reckless, nomadic journalist was on the wane and was replaced by a more professional, stalwart model. The foundation of regional press clubs and organizations such as the National Association of Journalists in 1886 helped to consolidate a professional code for journalists that enhanced the respectability of their trade.[27] But if stereotypes of the Irish journalist survived the general change, their content altered: an increasingly lucrative form of blarney, for instance, displaced traditional drunkenness and squalor as a dominant characteristic. The prolific success of Irish journalists such as T. P. O'Connor and Justin McCarthy helped this change in perspective.[28] The journalist in Joyce's 'A Little Cloud' embodies the successful Mick on the make in English journalism.[29] Gallaher is both a social and geographical vagabond who has little respect for class boundaries; in his lurid stories of London and Paris he spares 'neither rank nor caste'.[30] He intends, of course, to marry money.

Jim Fay, the Irish journalist in Charles Montague's A Hind Let Loose (1910), is also a success. Fay has all the character traits of the sympathetic Celt: 'he had eyes like a nice beast's, ... a mouth all atwitch with responsiveness to anyone's mood; mobile colour; and, just where in English faces the firmly blank chins are, a waiting alphabet of meaning dimples, to be marshalled by each moment's emotion into copious scriptures of expression'.[31] Fay is a lovable but unprincipled figure; he passionately supports opposing positions for different political publications, he plagiarizes his own articles and he writes pious editorials that can be tweaked to fit almost any situation. But this want of principle is simply a function of Fay's infinite sympathy — 'the Celt's ... shy ardour of longing to understand you, please you, concur with you'.[32] A concept of integrity — or an honour owed to oneself — cannot apply here, because the Celt lacks the basic existential prerequisites for that. This had its dividends in journalism. As one

25 Paul-Dubois, Contemporary Ireland, 167.
26 UP 1. 326; see also, 250: 'We produce good correspondents, good journalists, and good talkers and few profound and solitary students.'
27 On the shift in public perceptions of journalism, see Jones, Powers of the Press, 113–39.
28 In novels such as Warde Lyneworth and Percy Russell's Fate's Grim Sport (London, 1895) and C. F. Keary, The Journalist (London, 1898) Irish journalists are also relatively successful social climbers, even though they meet considerable resistance on the way. For a study of this social mobility, see Stephen Donovan, 'Literary Modernism and the Press, 1870–1922', doctoral dissertation, Göteburg University, 2001, 52–59.
29 According to R. F. Foster, Paddy and Mr. Punch: Connections in Irish and English History (London, 1995), 290, 'the history of the middle-class Irish on the make can be traced through one profession in particular: the press'.
30 Dubliners, 73.
31 C. E. Montague, A Hind Let Loose (London, 1910), 32.
32 Montague, A Hind Let Loose, 33.

editor suggested, the journalist was 'a moral and intellectual Proteus' who 'must be prepared to assume every mood that the occasion requires'.[33] The Celt was a master of these Protean arts.

A cross-pollination of prejudices produced the image of the pressman Paddy. If this creature epitomized at times the treachery of journalism, he also reflected more general anxieties about the profession's uncertain social status. Deprived of a definite public profile, the journalist was a kind of non-person. But the same social facts also led to an almost opposite account of the journalist: instead of being radically self-effacing, he was disconcertingly assertive, a tremendous egotist who had little respect for the world in which he moved. For Virginia Woolf, the journalist embodied both these extremes. On the one hand, he was not a real human being, but was a parasitical insect that lived on 'anybodies blood' but his own. On the other hand, she derided the 'egotist's journalist's pobbing and boobling ... in the stew of his greasy complacency'.[34] The journalist's egotism was another sign of his social deprivation: he lacked the guidance of an established social code or system of manners and found his only co-ordinates within himself. 'Self-confidence unalloyed by arrogance or egotism', Lecky once remarked, were the virtues of a gentleman, one who had intuitive access to shared norms of good conduct.[35] Yeats expressed a similar outlook and believed that the well-bred soul embodied a virtuous mean; it was self-possessed but not self-promoting: 'A gentleman is a man whose principle ideas are not connected with his personal needs and his personal success.'[36] The lower-bred or the socially mobile, he believed, lacked this magnanimity and self-restraint. He despised an 'ill-breeding of the mind', which was characterized by crass confidence and vulgar self-assertion.[37] Yeats wanted to develop a well-bred poetical style, 'where there is nothing ostentatious, nothing crude, no breath of parvenu or journalist'.[38] At the end of his life, it was for him a point of pride that he was 'hated by journalists and groundlings'.[39]

If the journalist was a 'parvenu', this made him appear to the aristocrats of 'Art' both self-effacing and self-aggrandizing. Indeed, the very style of journalism embodied this ambivalence. The anonymity of an article could be taken as an abdication of personality by the journalist. But it could also be viewed as an irresponsible form of self-elevation, giving private judgements an aura of impersonal authority. In the final quarter of the nineteenth century, the personal tone of the 'new journalism' replaced an earlier formality. For some this marked a considerable advance in the 'humane' reporting of public affairs; for others, it brought the vanity and crassness of journalism to new and

---

33 Matthias Bodkin, *Recollections of an Irish Judge: Press, Bar and Parliament* (London, 1914), 28.
34 See 'Appendix B' in Quentin Bell, *Virginia Woolf: A Biography* (New York, 1972), 253–54.
35 Lecky, *Democracy and Liberty*, 1. 322.
36 A, 489.
37 M, 139; 140.
38 E, 228. In his diaries, he dismissed a group of journalists as 'essentially parvenus in intellectual things'. M, 141.
39 EI, 523.

dangerous levels. The novelty of new journalism was in some senses more illusory than real — to Wilde, it was but 'the old vulgarity "writ large"'.[40] Many of the supposedly defining characteristics of new journalism — striking headlines, short paragraphs, a personal or chatty style, and an investment in sensation — were all well in place before Arnold first used the term in 1887.[41] Arnold attributed the invention of new journalism to W. T. Stead, the famous editor of the *Pall Mall Gazette*, but it was often Irish journalists who were particularly associated with it. T. P. O'Connor, was one of the most famous of the 'new' journalists and was a strong advocate of the 'more personal tone of the more modern methods'.[42] Ryan was employed by O'Connor on the *Star* and offered a thinly disguised portrait of his former boss in *Daisy Darley*: 'He used the first person singular as naturally as if it had been waiting for him all the ages; there seemed an epic fitness in his egoism; he had made the sorrows of men and women his own; his momentous, world-weary yet prophetic "I" spoke for all mankind.'[43] O'Connor's egotism is so immense that it resembles a kind of world-spirit and is virtually indistinguishable from a vast altruism. Moral distinctions of a most basic kind seem to collapse under the 'personal' touch.

Above all, journalism eroded a dividing line between public and private values that was basic to conventional notions of personality. Lecky complained bitterly of that obscene habit 'which has so long existed in America, and which is rapidly growing in England, of treating the private lives of eminent men as if they were public property; of forcing their opinions on all subjects into constant publicity by newspaper interviews'.[44] This degraded private values and undermined public life. Figures like Charles Dilke and Charles Stewart Parnell were famous victims of this kind of publicity. In the year of Parnell's death, Oscar Wilde denounced the way newspapers 'drag before the eyes of the public some incident in the private life of a great statesman'. Journalists once had their ears nailed to the pump; nowadays, however, 'journalists have nailed their own ears to the keyhole'. He deplored this kind of intrusiveness and the 'tyranny that it proposes to exercise over people's private lives'.[45] He was himself to be one of the most celebrated victims of this tyranny. Joyce bitterly recalled Wilde's public humiliation during his imprisonment: 'The newspaper journalists were admitted into the prison and, through the window of his cell, were able to feed on the spectacle of his shame'.[46] As Wilde himself acknowledged: 'In the old days men had the rack. Now they have the Press'.[47]

Many deplored the curiosity and vulgarity of the press, but others defended this as the 'humanising of politics' and of letters.[48] In Ryan's *Daisy Darley* a young journalist devises

---

40 Wilde, *Complete Works*, 1145.
41 Matthew Arnold, 'Up to Easter', *Nineteenth Century*, 21 (May 1887), 629–43, 639.
42 T. P. O'Connor, 'The New Journalism', *New Review*, 1 (October 1889), 423–34, 423.
43 Ryan, *Daisy Darley*, 57.
44 Lecky, *Democracy and Liberty*, 1. 112.
45 Wilde, *Complete Works*, 1189.
46 *Occasional, Critical and Political Writing*, 149.
47 *Complete Works*, 1188.
48 *Daisy Darley*, 98.

a means of 'humanising ... the whole literary and quasi-literary fraternity'.[49] Human, all too human, his plan is to produce a literary gossip column that provides 'sketches of popular authors; peeps into the souls of poets; what young writers saw in their pipe-bowls, and authors in the sunset ... and delicate hints of literary courtships of the season'.[50] Yeats reflected upon this journalistic climate in his *Autobiographies*: 'We were not allowed to forget that in our own day there was a popular Press, and its opinions began to affect our casual acquaintance, and even our comfort in public places'.[51] Despite this frosty dismissal, Yeats had himself written a literary gossip column for the *Manchester Courier* from 1889 to 1890. Here he seemed to flout Wilde's explicit advice: 'literary gossip was no job for a gentleman'.[52]

Journalists may have shown an obsessive interest in the intimate lives of others, but Yeats rarely wavered in his belief that journalism was an impersonal discursive machine. He duly condemned those 'who wrote for the newspapers to discourage capricious, personal writing'.[53] In his *Memoirs*, he listed newspapers among the 'thousand impersonalities' that have consumed the world.[54] Towards the end of his career he insisted that his 'private thoughts' were not suitable reading for journalists or for politicians — figures who clearly failed to understand the rudiments of intimate life.[55] But since journalism also made a fetish of private experience, it was difficult to secure the sanctity of the personal realm or to promote a concept of personal integrity against the rhetoric of newspapers. As Wilde observed, a 'publicist, nowadays, is a man who bores the community with the details of the illegalities of his private life'.[56] Yeats also disparaged these public confessions and their related cult of personality. He spoke in derision of that 'exaltation of the individual life that had little importance before modern journalism'; this kind of individuality, he believed, was largely fraudulent.[57] He was forced, therefore, to distinguish between the authentic personality and its false incarnations. But this was not an easy task.

His own endorsement of 'sincerity' embodied the problem. Yeats had hoped to foster in Ireland a 'more precise thought, of a more perfect sincerity' and attacked the 'shopkeeping timidity and insincerity' that seemed to characterize so much of modern life.[58] The man of genius, he suggested, distinguished himself from his pale imitators through his 'greater sincerity'.[59] 'The half-educated mind' was 'never sincere in the arts'.[60] Genuine style

---

49 *Daisy Darley*, 158.
50 *Daisy Darley*, 160.
51 A, 324.
52 A, 136.
53 A, 204.
54 M, 169; and 139, where he described newspapers as the greatest embodiment of 'impersonal mechanism'.
55 E, 429.
56 Wilde, *Complete Works*, 1101.
57 E, 417.
58 E, 122, 225.
59 A, 109.
60 E, 193.

required a 'purification from insincerity'.[61] He condemned didactic art for being 'oratorical and insincere', and although he had once applauded demotic art for its 'simplicity and sincerity', he later suggested that 'popular poetry' and 'sincere poetry' were largely antithetical.[62] Some forms of utterance were simply 'too sincere, too personal, too original for general acceptance'.[63] Sincerity was a necessary condition of artistic excellence, but it was by no means a sufficient one. Ibsen was sincere, but he was also banal, and Ferguson's 'eighteenth-century sincerity' hampered his work from the start.[64] But it was journalism, above all, which exposed the limits of sincerity as a criterion for good writing: 'Do not our newspapers with their daily tide of written oratory, make us cry out, "O God, if this be sincerity, give us a little insincerity, a little of the self-possession, of the self-mastery that go to a conscious lie."'[65] However, when Yeats noted that 'the journalist makes up his lies / And takes you by the throat', he was none too happy.[66]

Yeats's problems with sincerity were perhaps internal to the concept itself; it demanded the simultaneous cultivation of both a truthful and of a distinctly 'personal' attitude, but these demands could sometimes pull in opposite directions. The problem was apparent in his account of his two great heroes, Synge and Parnell. Both were sincere men. Yeats praised Parnell for driving 'into dust & vacuum no end of insincerities'; Synge he admired for his 'courage and sincerity'.[67] But these figures also engaged in projects of radical self-creation. Arguably, their self-authorship made sincerity possible; it produced the very self that was the condition and ground of a sincere attitude. But this self-fashioning also strained against a model of sincerity grounded upon spontaneous and transparent utterance. For Yeats, self-becoming — involving at times the deliberate deceit of others — ultimately took priority over truthful self-disclosure; a particular form of authenticity, in other words, supplanted the paler virtues of sincerity in his moral universe. If Parnell and Synge were emblems of the authentic life, it was also a measure of their greatness that they were despised by journalists.

61 EI, 319.
62 EI, 199; PI, 73; EI, 164.
63 CL 3. 51
64 E, 166; A, 396, and see A, 166: 'Ibsen has sincerity and logic', but he lacked 'beautiful and vivid language'. See also UP 2. 155, for his dislike of the 'heroic and unadorned sincerity of a play like "Ghosts" or the "Wild Duck"'.
65 UP 1. 309. In 'The Decay of Lying', Complete Works, 1072, Wilde decried the fact that newspapers 'may now be absolutely relied upon'.
66 VP, 598.
67 CL 1. 237; A, 570.

2 The Übermensch of the Western World

Synge was a crucial figure in Yeats's assaults on journalism in Ireland.[68] In his *Memoirs*, he even suggested that newspapers had killed Synge. After fulminating against the 'half-men of letters or rather half-journalists, that coterie of patriots who have never been bought because no one ever thought them worth a price', he turned to Synge, 'dying at this moment of their bitterness and ignorance'.[69] He persuaded his young friend, Ezra Pound, that Synge was the tragic victim of a calumnious newspaper campaign. In an article entitled 'The Non-Existence of Ireland', Pound combined a vigorous defence of Synge with a violent denunciation of Irish newspapers:

> Careful study of modern print leaves me convinced of two things, first, that there are a few dozen worthy and entertaining writers of fiction who call themselves Irish, and secondly, that there is an incredible bog or slum or inferno of blackness somewhere in swamps off Liverpool which produces the 'Irish Papers'.[70]

Synge first courted controversy with *In the Shadow of the Glen*. Even before this famous 'insult to Irish womanhood' was performed in October 1903, the *Independent*, a major nationalist daily, had denounced it for 'failing to derive its inspiration from the Western Isles'.[71] With characteristic energy, Yeats defended Synge in three pieces of polemic published in the *United Irishman*. The second piece, entitled 'The Theatre, the Pulpit and the Newspapers', attacked the *Independent*, whose peculiar fusion of fervour and piety made it the leader of 'those enemies of life, the chimeras of the Pulpit and the Press'.[72] In a third article, Yeats again condemned the 'influence of a violent contemporary paper' on Irish public life.[73] The attack was ostensibly aimed at the *Independent*, but it also incorporated its host journal, the *United Irishman*. His vigorous defence of the Irish origins of Synge's work rebutted the insinuations of Griffith, editor of the *United Irishman*, that Synge had lifted his play from the old story of the Widow of Ephesus.[74] Griffith had argued that the play combined plagiarism with insult to reflect badly on

---

68 For Yeats's other uses of Synge, see R. F. Foster, 'Yeats, Synge, and Anglo-Irish Etiquette', in *Paddy and Mr. Punch*, 195–211; Nicholas Grene, 'Yeats and the Remaking of Synge', in Terence Brown and Nicholas Grene, eds., *Tradition and Influence in Anglo-Irish Poetry* (London and Basingstoke, 1989), 47–62.

69 M, 161.

70 *New Age*, 25 February 1915.

71 *Independent*, 10 October 1903.

72 E, 119.

73 UP 2. 306–07.

74 Griffith had been an enthusiastic supporter of Yeats, insisting wildly at one point that 'Yeats is Irish literature and Irish belief and Irish faith, hope and aspiration'. *United Irishman*, 27 April 1901. By October 1903, however, his attitude had notably cooled. Yeats's increasingly authoritarian handling of affairs in the Irish National Theatre Society, reflected in his attempts to substitute his own selection criteria for plays above that of the Reading Committee, incurred the wrath of Griffith as well as Douglas Hyde and Maud Gonne.

Irish women. In January 1905, Griffith repeated the charge, insisting that 'Mr. Synge's adaptation of the old Greek libel on womankind — "The Widow of Ephesus" — has no more title to be called Irish than a Chinaman would have if he printed "Patrick O'Brien" on his visiting card'.[75]

When *The Playboy of the Western World* was first performed in 1907, Griffith and others were predictably outraged. Reflecting on the riots a few years later, Yeats presented the conflict as evidence of the incantatory power of modern journalism:

> A patriotic journalism which had seen in Synge's capricious imagination the enemy of all it would have young men believe, had for years prepared for this hour, by that which is at once the greatest and most ignoble power of journalism, the art of repeating a name again and again with some ridiculous or evil association. The preparation had begun after the first performance of *The Shadow of the Glen*, Synge's first play, with an assertion made in ignorance, but repeated in dishonesty, that he had taken his fable and his characters, not from his own mind nor that profound knowledge of cot and curragh he was admitted to possess, but 'from a writer of the Roman decadence.' Some spontaneous dislike had been but natural, for genius like his can but slowly, amid what it has of harsh and strange, set forth the nobility of its beauty, and the depth of its compassion; but the frenzy that would have silenced his master-work was, like most violent things, artificial, that defence of virtue by those who have but little, which is the pomp and gallantry of journalism and its right to govern the world.[76]

Synge was the tragic victim of a mean-spirited journalism, but he was also its heroic antithesis. The genuine artist, was 'an ascetic not of women and wine, but of the newspapers'.[77] Yeats liked to present himself as such a figure, despite his frequent descents from the mountaintop into the world of journalism; Synge, however, was Yeats's true ascetic.

In the Preface to *The Playboy*, Synge announced that his work deployed a language that antedated all contact with the modern press.[78] But newspapers are mentioned twice in the play and the speech-community it depicts is arguably a parodic incarnation of a contemporary newspaper public defined by its lurid and hypocritical fascination with violence. Synge's journals suggest that his own imagination was stimulated by spicy newspaper reports of crime; an account of parricide in a French journal, for instance, provided the basis for unsettling dreams in 1900.[79] If these details strained against Yeats's subsequent myth of Synge, even more compromising were Synge's articles on

---

75 *United Irishman*, 7 January 1905.
76 *EI*, 311–12.
77 *EI*, 286.
78 Synge, *Collected Works*, 4. 53.
79 J. M. Synge, *Collected Works. Volume 2: Prose*, ed. Alan Price (London, 1966), 29.

the Congested Districts Board for the *Manchester Guardian*. Yeats quarrelled with the Synge family and the publisher George Roberts of Maunsel & Company for their inclusion of these articles in a posthumous edition of Synge's works. As he declared in a letter to the playwright, John Drinkwater, in 1911: 'I rejected the Congested District Essays after hesitating over them as I considered that they were really little more than journalism and took away from the value of his more deliberate work.'[80] Roberts, however, insisted on publishing the essays and Yeats was left brooding on the injury done to Synge's reputation.[81] Despite the evidence, he insisted upon presenting Synge as a literary purist — a man 'all folded up in brooding intellect, knowing nothing of new books and newspapers, reading the great masters alone'.[82] Synge had exhibited a relatively sophisticated political intelligence in his articles on the Congested Districts Board, but, according to Yeats, he 'seemed by nature unfitted to think a political thought'.[83] Lady Gregory colluded in this depiction of Synge as a political idiot: 'While staying with us,' she noted, 'he hardly looked at a newspaper. He seemed to look on politics and reforms with a sort of tolerant indifference'.[84]

But Yeats was capable of thinking political thoughts, and Synge served as a useful epitome for the aristocratic values he increasingly revered. Synge's claim to Ascendancy status was considerably more assured than Yeats's own; and, if Yeats is to be believed, Synge was 'almost as proud of his old blood as of his genius'.[85] Journalists like Griffith may have been gripped by 'hysterical pride', but Synge was 'too confident for self-assertion'.[86] This was a measure of Synge's noble origins; he 'belonged to a very old Irish family and, though a simple courteous man, remembered it and was haughty and lonely'.[87] Synge's proud loneliness became a key motif in an extravagant vision of 'aristocratic' autonomy. The true gentleman traditionally enjoyed an independence that was grounded on property and wealth; but Yeats supplemented this with motifs drawn from Nietzsche's descriptions of the noble soul. Synge, in all his haughtiness and his loneliness, was a practitioner of what Nietzsche called the '*good* solitude' — a glorious self-sufficiency unknown to the herd.[88]

By the end of the first decade of the twentieth century, Nietzsche had become for Yeats a useful 'counteractive to the spread of democratic vulgarity'.[89] Nietzsche had also

80   Yeats, 6 March 1911 (Berg Collection).
81   M, 263.
82   EI, 310.
83   EI, 319.
84   Augusta Gregory, *Our Irish Theatre* (Gerrards Cross, 1972), 74.
85   M, 201. On the subtle differences in the class backgrounds of Yeats and Synge, see Foster, *Paddy and Mr. Punch*, 198–99.
86   VP, 601; M, 206.
87   A, 567.
88   Friedrich Nietzsche, *Beyond Good and Evil*, trans. R. J. Hollingdale, intro. Michael Tanner (London, 1990), 56 [Nietzsche's emphasis].
89   Quoted in Patrick Keane, *Yeats's Interactions with Tradition* (Columbia, 1987), 97. Yeats would undoubtedly have been aware of Nietzsche's work by 1896. In April of that year the *Savoy* published the first essay

declared his contempt for 'every kind of culture that is compatible with reading, not to speak of writing for, newspapers'.[90] Those who consumed the 'vomit' of the press were incapable of genuine selfhood; they hungrily devoured others but failed to 'digest themselves'.[91] Yeats too believed that journalism represented a turn from the self; he condemned 'the threadbare, second-hand imaginations that flow in upon a man out of the newspapers'.[92] In 1903 he created his own superman, Paul Ruttledge, to wage war on 'newspapers' in the name of life.[93] In the same year Yeats defended Synge from the calumny of the press and promoted in response an ethos of muscular individualism:

> Instead of individual men and women and living virtues differing as one star differeth from another in glory, the public imagination is full of personified averages, partisan fictions, rules of life that would drill everybody into the one posture, habits that are like the pinafores of charity-school children. The priest, trained to keep his mind on the strength of his Church and the weakness of his congregation, would have all mankind painted with a halo or with horns. ... The newspaper he reads of a morning has not only the haloes and horns of the vestry, but it has crowns and fools' caps of its own. Life, which in its essence is always surprising, always taking some new shape, always individualising, is nothing to it, it has to move men in squads, to keep them in uniform, with their faces to the right enemy, and enough hate in their hearts to make the muskets go off. It may know its business well, but its business is building and ours is shattering. We cannot linger very long in this great dim temple where the wooden images sit all round upon thrones, and where the worshippers kneel, not knowing whether they tremble because their gods are dead or because they fear they may be alive. In the idol-house every god, every demon, every virtue, every vice, has been given its permanent form, its hundred hands, its elephant trunk, its monkey head. The man of letters looks at those kneeling worshippers who have given up life for a posture, whose nerves have dried up in the contemplation of lifeless wood. He swings his silver hammer and the keepers of the temple cry out, prophesying evil, but he must not mind their cries and their prophecies, but break the wooden necks in two and throw down the wooden bodies. Life will put living bodies in their place till new image-brokers have set up their benches.[94]

of Havelock Ellis's 'Friedrich Nietzsche' series alongside Yeats's 'Rosa Alchemica' and 'Two Poems Concerning Peasant Visionaries'. However, it was only after reading Nietzsche in 1902 that he fully succumbed to the 'strong enchanter'. See CL 3. 284.

90 Nietzsche, The Will to Power, 80.

91 Nietzsche, Thus Spoke Zarathustra, 77.

92 E, 134.

93 W. B. Yeats, The Variorum Edition of the Plays of W. B. Yeats, ed. Russell K. Alspach, assisted by Catherine C. Alspach (London, Melbourne, Toronto, 1966), 1070.

94 E, 119–21.

The tone and much of the content of this polemic — its hints of God's death; its sketch of religion as a bid for power through the institutionalization of weakness; its contempt for the craven herd and its love of the genuine individual; as well as its celebration of a vague set of values called 'life' — was decisively Nietzschean. The defining feature of herd-morality, according to Nietzsche, was its absolutism: it attempted to construct a moral unanimity that was fundamentally at odds with the temporal nature and plural character of life itself.[95] Yeats was Zarathustra's disciple: 'he who has to be a creator in good and evil, truly, has first to be a destroyer and break values'.[96] The artist was the supreme iconoclast, who embraced life's contingency and abandoned the false solace of static forms. But this iconoclasm had also a clear theological resonance that added salt to existing wounds in Ireland — it was waged by a Protestant in defence of a fellow Protestant against his largely Catholic persecutors.

Yeats promoted a gospel of radical individualism in his defence of his friend. He cast Synge as its presiding Christ. 'Nothing interested him,' according to Yeats, 'but the individual man.'[97] Synge was 'that rare, that distinguished, that most noble thing, which of all things still of the world is nearest to being sufficient to itself, the pure artist'.[98] The same 'astringent joy' that Yeats first experienced in Nietzsche was also a quality he praised in his friend.[99] He explicitly compared Synge's heroic independence to Nietzsche's account of the artist's autonomy: 'He had that egotism of the man of genius which Nietzsche compares to the egotism of a woman with child.'[100] In a copy of Nietzsche's work, Yeats underlined an account of noble self-sufficiency drawn from *Beyond Good and Evil* that would repeatedly re-emerge in his portrait of Synge:

> The noble type of man regards *himself* as the determiner of worth, it is not necessary for him to be approved of, he passes the judgment: 'What is injurious to me is injurious in itself'; he recognises that it is he himself only that confers honour on things — he is *a creator of worth* ... his morality is self-glorification.[101]

Similarly, Synge was his own justification and 'did not speak to men and women, asking judgment, as lesser writers do'. As Yeats put it, 'he had no need of our sympathies'.[102] Synge's works were a testament to his superb self-sufficiency; they owed 'nothing to observation, and all to some overflowing of himself'.[103] Here Yeats reverted to his

---

95 Nietzsche, *Beyond Good and Evil*, 75: 'The slave wants the unconditional and understands only what is tyrannical, in morals too.'
96 Nietzsche, *Thus Spoke Zarathustra*, 138.
97 UP 2. 484.
98 EI, 323.
99 See CL 3. 284.
100 A, 511.
101 Cited in Bohlmann, *Yeats and Nietzsche*, 115 [Nietzsche's emphasis].
102 A, 511.
103 EI, 326.

favourite image of the fountain, a symbol used by Burke and Shelley, but also championed by Nietzsche.[104] Life in general, for Nietzsche, was a 'fountain of delight', but he also believed that it was spoiled by the herd, for 'where the rabble also drinks all wells are poisoned'.[105] Yeats also condemned those 'who would muddy what had begun to seem a fountain of life with the feet of the mob'.[106] Synge was a glorious self-sustaining force that inevitably attracted the mob's resentment.[107] 'How could they that dreaded solitude', Yeats observed, 'love that which solitude had made?'[108]

The mob's rancour was the opposite of Synge's self-affirming temperament: it was wholly dependent upon what it must negate. As Nietzsche explained, 'this *inevitable* orientation to the outside instead of back onto itself — is a feature of *ressentiment*: in order to come about, slave morality first has to have an opposing, external world, it needs, physiologically speaking, external stimuli in order to act at all, — its action is basically a reaction'.[109] Synge required no stimulation from the outside; indeed, Yeats explicitly contrasted his internal motivation with the inferior character of George Moore, for whom every thought is 'a reaction not a creation'.[110] The mob's hatred of Synge was similarly reactive. In the year of his friend's death, Yeats outlined the sterile nature of Irish hatred:

> The root of it all is that the political class in Ireland — the lower middle-class from whom the patriotic associations have drawn their journalists and their leaders for the last ten years — have suffered through the cultivation of hatred as the one energy of their movement, a deprivation which is the intellectual equivalent to the removal of the genitals. Hence the shrillness of their voices. They contemplate all creative power as the eunuchs contemplate Don Juan as he passes through Hell on the white horse.[111]

He wrote these lines with Griffith in mind. As he acknowledged to Lady Gregory in 1909: 'I wrote a note a couple of days ago in which I compared Griffith and his like to the Eunuchs in Ricketts's picture watching Don Juan riding through Hell'.[112] Gregory had circulated the view that the trigger for the *Playboy* riots was the mentioning of a woman's underclothes; Yeats mocked this prurience, but his sexual taunts had also deeper implications; they pointed to a kind of visceral knowledge that Synge had apparently possessed.

---

104 In EI, 83–84, 'The Philosophy of Shelley's Poetry', Yeats studied his predecessor's symbolic use of fountains and traced its origins to Porphyry.

105 Nietzsche, *Thus Spoke Zarathustra*, 120. Zarathustra had described his soul (129) as 'a leaping fountain'.

106 E, 151.

107 In poems such as 'Ancestral Houses', Yeats compared 'life's own self-delight' to a fountain — an autonomous energy-source which he related to an aristocratic ethos.

108 E, 253. He also insisted elsewhere that it was Synge's 'solitude that got him into trouble'. See PI, 173–74.

109 Nietzsche, *Genealogy of Morality*, 21–22 [Nietzsche's emphasis].

110 A, 473.

111 M, 176.

112 L, 525.

Synge enjoyed an integrated self that transcended traditional dichotomies of body and soul. Nietzsche had traced this opposition to Plato, whose fundamental distinction between sensible and super-sensible realities led to an ascetic denial of the flesh.[113] Zarathustra condemned the 'despisers of the body' and Synge was one of his school — one of those rare artists who had 'thoughts that tighten the muscles, or quiver and tingle in the flesh, and so stand like Saint Michael with the trumpet that calls the body to resurrection'.[114] His art was a hymn to the senses; it celebrated 'all that has edge, all that is salt in the mouth, all that is rough to the hand'.[115] His speech was health itself; the 'thoughts of journalists', on the other hand, are 'neither healthy nor unhealthy, not having risen to that state where either is possible'.[116] The rude health of Synge's art was a form of self-overcoming. His reverence for life derived from his own ill-health. He was acutely aware of his own mortality, but he regarded life's finitude as the source rather than the negation of all good things.[117] Through his active acknowledgement of death, he made the most of his freedom. His life was 'a perpetual "Last Day", a perpetual trumpeting and coming up for judgment'.[118]

In these portraits, Yeats liked to suggest that Synge's magnificent independence and love of life went hand in hand. At times, however, Synge's commitment to an ideal of autonomy seemed to demand a thorough rejection of the world.[119] This asceticism is evident in Synge's own works. In *The Well of the Saints*, for instance, Maire and Michael Dall prefer to remain blind than to witness directly the cruelties of their social world, and a similar rejection of a corrupt community is also a feature of *The Playboy*. But Yeats often amplified Synge's repudiation of society until he became a hermetic artist sealed in his own dream; for Synge, 'nothing existed but his thought'.[120] This may have been the independence of the superman, but Nietzsche had worried that his account of individual autonomy would be misinterpreted for a simple rejection of the world, that the great man's 'solitude will be misunderstood by the people as though it were flight *from* reality, whereas it is just his way of being absorbed, buried and immersed in reality'.[121] But the solipsistic and anti-social features of radical independence were manifest in Yeats's sketches of Synge. In his efforts to become a radically self-determining, self-legitimizing

---

113 *Beyond Good and Evil*, 37.

114 *Thus Spoke Zarathustra*, 61; EI, 316.

115 EI, 326–27.

116 EI, 323. See EI, 318, 'all art which appeals to individual man and awaits confirmation of his senses and his reveries, seems, when arrayed against the moral zeal, the confident logic, the ordered proof of journalism, a trifling, impertinent, vexatious thing, a tumbler who has unrolled his carpet in the way of a marching army'.

117 EI, 321: 'I am certain that my friend's noble art, so full of passion and heroic beauty, is the victory of a man who in poverty and sickness created from the delight of expression, and in the contemplation that is born of the minute and delicate arrangement of images, happiness and health of mind.'

118 A, 511.

119 A, 509. According to Yeats, Synge recommended the unification of 'stoicism, ascetism and ecstasy'.

120 A, 512.

121 *Genealogy of Morality*, 71 [Nietzsche's emphasis].

being, Synge had to rid himself of all 'those thoughts which unite us to others'.[122] Authenticity, it seemed, demanded a thoroughgoing rejection of a shared world.

The reasons for this hermetic turn can be traced to a conception of personal autonomy advocated by Nietzsche and reiterated by Yeats. Nietzsche's views on the individual were by no means stable. He initially suggested that individuation in general was an illusion that was grafted onto a primordial unity.[123] Later he maintained that the truly autonomous subject had yet to appear in human history, while on other occasions he declared that the 'sovereign individual' had lately come into being.[124] Subjectivity, for Nietzsche, was sometimes indistinguishable from subjugation, but elsewhere it was the apotheosis of freedom defined as the perfect autonomy of the will. But this autonomy was difficult to conceptualize. In order for the will to instantiate itself as 'mine', it presumably required an object over which it remained sovereign. But this was also a condition of dependency: the will's need for an empirical ratification of itself ultimately rendered it heteronymous. Nietzsche may have endorsed a noble yea-saying and condemned the slave's negativity and reactive temperament, but he failed to explain how any subject can say 'yes' to itself without also saying 'no' to all that is non-self. If, on the other hand, the subject lacked a fixed determination, it became difficult to imagine how a substantive model of autonomy could be produced. Nietzsche conceded at one point that 'nothing is self-sufficient', but he often seemed to demand that human beings should strive to become so.[125] His overrigorous conception of personal independence occasionally led him to repudiate collective life as such. Only the most austere notion of autonomy could present the 'common good' as a contradiction in terms.[126] Yeats's conception of heroic solitude often made similarly exorbitant demands.

Problems surfaced in Yeats's vision of things when he set out to fuse a radical model of personal autonomy with traditional aristocratic virtues. Aristocratic independence — or what Yeats called the 'freedom of the well bred' — was economic and social in its foundations, but the autonomy championed by Nietzsche is different.[127] The object here is to be radically free or wholly self-determining; there can be no prior or independent foundations for this freedom, for a conditioned freedom in this schema is a contradiction in terms. Such autonomy departs from the independence normally accredited to aristocracies in that it cannot be seen to have a social origin. In traditional aristocratic societies — at least as they were subsequently understood — duty was

---

122 EI, 321.

123 In *The Birth of Tragedy*, 52–53, he partially endorsed 'the fundamental recognition that everything which exists is a unity; the view that individuation is the primal source of all evil; and art as the joyous hope that the spell of individuation can be broken, a premonition of unity restored'.

124 In *Twilight of the Idols*, he suggested that the individual would have to be 'made possible'. See *The Anti-Christ, Ecce Homo, Twilight of the Idols and Other Writings*, 216. In *Genealogy of Morality*, 40, he presented 'the *sovereign individual* as the ripest fruit' on the tree of history [Nietzsche's emphasis].

125 *Will to Power*, 532.

126 *Beyond Good and Evil*, 71 and 214: 'All community makes somehow, somewhere, sometime "common".'

127 EI, 253.

not simply self-prescribed but derived from one's social station. Hegel's 'noble soul', for instance, conjoined 'obedience' to an established code of honour with a sense of inner reverence for these values.[128] Nietzsche also admitted that 'honour' had a social foundation: it 'insists unconditionally on good manners on the part of every one'.[129] But the independence he sponsored was often bad-mannered, rejecting, as it did, any social basis for one's values. According to Yeats's father, this was not aristocratic honour, but the values of the 'Yahoo'.[130] Nietzsche insisted late in life that his philosophy was not a form of individualism, but was strongly aristocratic; however, his noble spirit had little in common with the traditional aristocrat who identified intuitively with his given social role.[131] Hegel's 'noble soul' lived in this way; he may have lacked a full sense of autonomy, but he existed in harmony with his world. The noble soul confirmed this bond through the 'heroism of service'.[132]

Yeats often praised this kind of service. He admired *noblesse oblige* or the virtuous embrace of duties prescribed by one's social role. Lady Gregory embodied this ethos for Yeats; he commended 'her sense of feudal responsibility, not of duty as the word is generally understood, but of burdens laid upon her by her station and her character'.[133] Moreover, he worried that Nietzsche had made no provision for this noble service.[134] Lady Gregory had also emphasized the need for a code of honour that one obeyed almost as a matter of instinct. Our social station, she informed Yeats, gave us a pre-reflective understanding of good conduct and our moral competence was not necessarily improved upon by self-conscious deliberation.[135] Yeats's immediate response to this suggestion was that the automatic obedience of a code made moral life a rather dull affair, but he was clearly struck by the force of Gregory's views. He provided a sympathetic account of this aristocratic ethos in *A Vision*. In phase twenty-four of the lunar cycle the 'code must rule, and because that code cannot be an intellectual choice, it is always a tradition bound up with family, or office, or trade, always a part of history'.[136] Lady Gregory had intuitive access to an established code of manners; in 'Coole Park, 1929', she appears

128 Hegel, *Phenomenology of Spirit*, 305. On this point, see Trilling, *Sincerity and Authenticity*, 35.

129 *Will to Power*, 499.

130 J. B. Yeats, *Letters to His Son and Others*, 97.

131 *Will to Power*, 162: 'My philosophy aims at an ordering of rank not at an individualistic morality.'

132 *Phenomenology of Spirit*, 306.

133 A, 395. Even here, however, he insists that this duty is a 'choice constantly renewed in solitude'. He remains reluctant, in other words, to forgo entirely a voluntarist and individualistic basis to *noblesse oblige*.

134 Yeats wrote in the margins of his edition of Nietzsche's works: 'Yes, but the necessity of giving remains. When the old heroes praise one another they say "he never refused any man."' Cited in Bohlmann, *Yeats and Nietzsche*, 7. Nietzsche did, in fact, acknowledge the virtues of generous service. See *The Anti-Christ, Ecce Homo, Twilight of the Idols and Other Writings*, 59–60.

135 Burke had made a similar point about prejudice in the *Reflections*, W & S 8. 138: '[it] is of ready application in the emergency; it previously engages the mind in a steady course of wisdom and virtue and does not leave the man hesitating in the moment of decision, sceptical, puzzled and unresolved'.

136 V, 170.

as a locus of instinctive honour lending orientation to the lives of others; her 'powerful character' can 'keep a swallow to its first intent'.[137]

Yeats may have been one of those lucky swallows, but he often felt he lacked an intuitive sense of direction in the world. His reflective disposition, or his poetic vocation or, perhaps, his distressingly non-aristocratic social pedigree conspired to deny him immediate access to a code of honour. A rare and painful quarrel with the Gregorys led to anxious self-questioning. 'Do I lack', he asked himself, 'the instinct of honour and conduct?'[138] In a letter of apology to Robert Gregory, Yeats argued that he had destroyed through analysis an intuitive sense of right and wrong. 'My dear Robert', he began, 'I want you to understand that I have no instincts in personal life. I have reasoned them all away'.[139] Here Yeats presented himself as the archetypal, 'unhappy consciousness'; he had destroyed through reflective deliberation an intuitive understanding of right action. Yeats, therefore, often felt he had to construct his own framework of values, 'to create in [him]self ... that thing which is to life what style is to letters'.[140] He compared the subjection of oneself to a rule of one's own deliberate making to the adoption of a mask, and he explicitly contrasted this with the satisfaction of a pre-existing and external moral standard. 'Active virtue as distinguished from the passive acceptance of a current code', he concluded, 'is therefore theatrical, consciously dramatic, the wearing of a mask'.[141] This self-conscious moral artistry, however, was wholly at odds with the instinctive virtues of the 'noble soul' defended by Lady Gregory. Equally anomalous was the 'tradition of [him]self' that Yeats set out to create in the absence of any credible alternatives.[142]

There was, therefore, a basic ambivalence in Yeats's rhetoric of authenticity; it celebrated, on the one hand, a noble soul that identified with its own social basis in an instinctive pursuit of an established code of honour; on the other hand, it championed an individual who had no need for social incorporation and was entirely self-creating. These contrasting accounts of character came together in Yeats's portrait of Synge. On the one hand, Synge stood aloof from all social environments and abandoned himself to a world of his own making; his great loneliness, on the other hand, derived from the proud recognition of his aristocratic descent. Here Yeats suggested that alienation attends upon privilege; 'the Anglo-Irish hate to surrender the solitude we have inherited'.[143] But this loneliness was the property of a class and only belonged to the individual through his affiliation with that class. A basic tension remained between the socially incorporated subject and the radically autonomous self. Synge may have 'inherited' his loneliness, but existential legacies of any kind undermined an absolute claim to independence and

137 VP, 489.
138 M, 256.
139 M, 252.
140 M, 258.
141 M, 151.
142 A, 463.
143 PI, 173. In E, 325, he also spoke of Berkeley and 'of others born into the Anglo-Irish solitude' in ways that equated authenticity with breeding.

implied that the origins of oneself were not entirely of one's own making. An autonomy that was another's bequest was not — in the Nietzschean schema so admired by Yeats — proper autonomy at all. When it came to describing his own solitude, Yeats suggested that it was his own creation, but he also problematically extended the same achievement to his entire class. He enjoyed, as he put it, an 'Anglo-Irish solitude, a solitude I have made for myself, an outlawed solitude'.[144] This many-headed solitude pointed to a fundamental ambiguity in Yeats's account of authentic life: that is, its simultaneous endorsement of an individuality that was both conditioned and self-conditioning. In the solitude of Yeats's other great hero, Charles Stewart Parnell, lay a similar ambiguity.

3 The Masks of Parnell

Like Synge, Parnell embodied, for Yeats, a heroic integrity lost to modern Ireland.[145] He was 'that lonely and haughty person below whose tragic shadow we of modern Ireland began to write'.[146] Initially, Yeats had trouble noticing this shadow. Parnell made a rare and undistinguished appearance in his early journalism as a 'famous agitator'.[147] His subsequent work for United Ireland — a strongly Parnellite newspaper — sharpened his political wits and gradually schooled him in the language of Parnellism. After Parnell's death in 1891, he produced the banal poetic commemoration, 'Mourn — and then Onward!', for United Ireland.[148] But as Yeats's quarrels with Irish public opinion intensified, his interest in Parnell deepened. In moments of particular duress — in his disputes with the Dublin Corporation over Hugh Lane's proposed art gallery, for instance — he summoned Parnell's ghost to mediate his criticisms of Irish vices.[149] Here and elsewhere, Parnell stood as the noble antithesis — or anti-self — of Irish baseness. 'Parnell was a proud man,' Yeats maintained, but his self-esteem was no upstart insolence.[150] Pride and privilege were happily conjoined in this 'landowner and haughty man'.[151] Like Synge, Parnell acknowledged only one authority: 'his master solitude'.[152] His loneliness too was a paradoxical condition: it was both a decision and a fate, a tradition bequeathed by his ancestors and a credo of his own making. Parnell's independence was his defining

---

144 M, 213. He merely restated the problem when he insisted that 'the power of self-conquest, of elevation has been Protestant, and more or less a thing of class'.
145 For other accounts of Yeats's views on Parnell, see Michael Steinman, Yeats's Heroic Figures: Wilde, Parnell, Swift, Casement (London, 1983), 54–102; John Kelly, 'Parnell in Irish Literature', in D. George Boyce and Alan O'Day, eds., Parnell in Perspective (London, 1991), 242–83.
146 PI, 139.
147 UP 1. 146.
148 United Ireland, 10 October 1891; See VP, 737.
149 'To a Shade', VP, 292–93.
150 VP, 587.
151 A, 358.
152 VP, 543.

feature; it was the core motif in a general language of authenticity that the poet assembled around the politician.

Yeats was not the first to laud the heroic autonomy of Parnell. A man of 'unconquerable self-command', 'self-controlled', 'self-restrained', 'self-possessed', 'self-contained', 'so self-centred as to be unconscious of anybody's existence but his own', Parnell was configured and reconfigured as someone who enjoyed an unparalleled independence.[153] 'The light of his mild, proud, silent and disconsolate sovereignty', according to James Joyce, made 'Disraeli look like an upstart diplomat dining wherever he can in rich people's houses, and Gladstone like a portly butler who has gone to night school'.[154] Yeats outlined — and exaggerated — his youthful fascination with the figure of Parnell, focusing on his magnificent autonomy:

> ... whenever we did not speak of art and letters, we spoke of Parnell. We told each other that he had admitted no man to his counsel; that when some member of his party found himself in the same hotel by chance, that member would think to stay there a presumption, and move to some other lodging; and, above all, we spoke of his pride, that made him hide all emotion while before his enemy.[155]

Admitting few to his counsel, Parnell stood aloof from the gossip of journalists. As Parnell himself explained to William O'Brien, a 'newspaper man would rather sell his immortal soul than keep a secret worth blabbing'.[156] Parnell was a man who could keep secrets, and his extreme reserve was a measure of his total self-possession. He was also, therefore, the polar opposite of the incontinent Celt.

The rhetoric of Parnellism derived its vocabulary from established descriptions of national character. Parnell reputedly embodied an autonomy that was often regarded as distinctly English. The Irish lacked this self-command. 'The Celt, undisciplinable, anarchical, and turbulent by nature', according to Arnold, was not endowed with 'a promising political temperament'.[157] Celts were by nature, it seemed, incapable of self-government; they were the racial embodiment of pure sensibility, which Kant described at one point as 'a kind of rabble without law or rule'.[158] Incapable of legislating for himself, the Celt needed to receive his rules from others — luckily, rational Saxons were often near at hand and willing to oblige. And so on. But a figure like Parnell disturbed these preconceptions. He was the living antithesis of unbridled sensibility. Michael McCarthy

153 M. M. O'Hara, *Chief and Tribune: Parnell and Davitt* (Dublin and London, 1919), 317; *Freeman's Journal*, 8 December 1890; William O'Brien, *The Parnell of Real Life* (London, 1926), 20; O'Brien, *Recollections*, 339; *Daily News*, 17 December 1890; *Spectator*, 26 November 1898; McCarthy, *The Irish Revolution*, 368.

154 *Occasional, Critical and Political Writings*, 194.

155 A, 232.

156 When O'Brien pointed out that he was himself a newspaper man, Parnell insisted that he was a Don Quixote rather than a journalist. See O'Brien, *The Parnell of Real Life*, 62.

157 Matthew Arnold, *The Study of Celtic Literature* (London, 1910), 92–93.

158 Immanuel Kant, *Lectures on Ethics*, trans. Louis Infield (London, 1930), 140.

suggested that 'never was there an Irish leader more completely devoid of sentiment'.[159] Parnell's poor oratorical skills, lent mystique through taciturn silence, reversed old orthodoxies about gifted gabs and a country of talkers. As O'Connor put it, 'the world had not yet been taught that a nation of orators could be governed by an inarticulate leader'.[160] Yeats was also drawn to Parnell largely because he was no 'loose-lipped demagogue'.[161]

Parnell, in many respects, was simply the exception that proved the rule of racial type. 'I think he was very English', Lord Cowper averred, and 'had neither the virtues nor the vices of an Irishman. His very passion was English, his coolness was English, his reserve was English'.[162] Parnell allowed commentators to reassert the laws of national character in the very act of acknowledging their transgression. 'Unlike the mass of his countrymen, Mr. Parnell', one commentator suggested, 'is never witty, never impassioned, never pathetic, never excited, never ridiculous'.[163] When Parnell appeared to lose his self-control under the strain of the divorce scandal and its political fallout, it was celebrated in some quarters as the emergence of his true Irish essence: 'He is clearly an Irishman at bottom, though an Irishman of peculiar temper; and his original assumption of what we may call the English character, the note of which is chilling reserve ... must have been quite deliberate.'[164] Yeats applauded Parnell precisely because he remained an Irishman at heart. An Englishman, 'is reserved because of his want of sensibility — Parnell was reserved in spite of it'.[165] Parnell did not abandon, but rather mastered his Celtic temperament. Yeats, nevertheless, extended a tradition of interpretation that cast Parnell as a noble exception to the general rule of Irish public life. The Irish public was drawn 'to the solitary and proud Parnell as to her anti-self'.[166] This dialectic seemed to imply that Parnell's virtues were also his supporters' deficiencies; his self-command was at odds with their abandon; his solitude was distinct from their dependency; his pride was the opposite of their craven natures. In Yeats's estimate, Parnell had come 'face to face with Irish futility' and served both as its measure and its counterforce.[167]

Here and elsewhere, Yeats exploited a basic paradox of Parnellism: it was a highly popular form of anti-populism. Reflecting on Parnell's fate, he extended Goethe's views on Catholics to the Irish in general: they were 'like a pack of hounds, always dragging down some noble stag'.[168] Yeats was again reminded of Goethe when he discussed the

159 McCarthy, The Irish Revolution, 100.
160 T. P. O'Connor, Charles Stewart Parnell; A Memory (London, New York, and Melbourne, 1891), 74.
161 VP, 542.
162 Quoted in McCarthy, The Irish Revolution, 138.
163 Anon., 'Studies in Character: Mr. Charles Stewart Parnell, M. P.', New Review, 9 (February 1890), 172–84, 181.
164 Spectator, 20 and 27 December 1890. Cited in Frank Callanan, The Parnell Split (Cork, 1992), 72.
165 Reported in Augusta Gregory, Lady Gregory's Diaries, 1892–1902, ed. James Pethica (Gerrards Cross, 1996), 169.
166 A, 195.
167 UP 2. 362.
168 A, 316. Johann Eckermann, Goethe's Conversations with Eckermann, rev. edn., trans. J. Oxenford (London, 1892), 391. The Parnellite press, in particular, repeatedly invoked images of a hunt in which a noble

fate of Synge and he repeated his indictment of Irish blood sports in 'To a Shade' and 'Parnell's Funeral'.[169] He remained convinced that 'popular rage' had 'dragged this quarry down'.[170] Yeats did not attend Parnell's funeral, but just as he did in the case of John O'Leary's funeral, he converted this failure into an expression of loyalty to Parnell's heroic spirit: 'I did not go to the funeral, because being in my sensitive and timid youth, I hated crowds, and what crowds implied.'[171] 'Parnell's Funeral' recasts this contempt for the crowd in poetic form: 'All that was said in Ireland is a lie / Bred out of the contagion of the throng'.[172] Parnell's killers lacked the courage of their cannibalistic convictions; too timid to eat the great man's heart, they failed to benefit from its energizing properties. Even Yeats's more forgiving poems embodied the antinomies that structured the myth of Parnell. In 'Come Gather Round Me, Parnellites', the politician's famous pride becomes the basis for a celebratory tipple: 'a proud man's a lovely man, / So pass the bottle round'.[173] The poem's tone of folk camaraderie and boozy solidarity is oriented towards a man who famously despised such fellowship; it embodies a form of populist élitism that was a staple feature of Parnellite rhetoric in general.

Parnell himself participated in the construction of this rhetoric. He attributed his unexplained absences from public meetings to the 'ethics of kingship', appropriate enough for a man remembered as Ireland's 'uncrowned king'.[174] He named his most famous horse 'Dictator' and invited the same label for himself.[175] He was said by many to enjoy a nearly demagogic power.[176] His immense authority owed something to structural changes in British politics which had been created by the electoral reforms of 1867 and 1884. The enormous increase of the franchise and its protection under the Secret Ballot Act contributed to a general shift of politics beyond local concerns; at the very least, it forced those local interests to become vocal on national topics. Parnell's own focus wavered intriguingly between the two; he converted a range of agrarian grievances into a national campaign for land reform and he transmuted a broad nationalist sentiment into a concerted bid for Home Rule. He also put together a highly disciplined party machine. Gone were the days of that gentlemanly independence in politics, so respected by Isaac Butt; all were now subordinate to the dictates of the great leader. 'The soldier who goes

---

animal was dragged down by curs. For an unusual statistical analysis of this trope, see William Michael Murphy, *The Parnell Myth and Irish Politics, 1891–1956* (New York, 1986), 61–63.

169 A, 483. *VP*, 292–93, 541–43.

170 *VP*, 542.

171 *VP*, 834.

172 *VP*, 542.

173 *VP*, 587.

174 For this ethics of kingship, see Katherine O'Shea, *Charles Stewart Parnell: His Love Story and Political Life*, 2 vols. (London, 1914), 2. 160.

175 Tim Healy defended Parnell from these charges: 'Mr. Parnell has been accused of being a dictator, but he was sorry to say that Mr. Parnell was not being sufficiently dictatorial. There was no party in which there was so much individual liberty.' *Freeman's Journal*, 15 April 1884. Cited in Frank Callanan, *T. M. Healy* (Cork, 1996), 100.

176 Michael J. F. McCarthy, *Mr. Balfour's Rule in Ireland* (Dublin, 1891), 67.

into the field of battle', Tim Healy explained to the electorate, 'must be prepared to surrender his own independence'.[177] Parnell represented a new kind of political animal; 'a Caesarist plebiscitarian element in politics — the dictator of the battlefield of elections — had appeared in the plain'.[178] Weber associated this democratic Caesarism with Gladstone, but Parnell was also both its abettor and emblem. Significantly, Weber also identified the journalist as 'the most important representative of the demagogic species' and he certainly played a key role in Parnell's empire.[179] Newspapers provided the vital communicative infrastructure that allowed Parnell to convert his political ambitions into a national campaign.[180]

Admittedly, since Parnell was a famous victim of newspapers, he could also be cast — by Yeats and by others — as their greatest opponent. In his reflections on Parnell, Joyce noted bitterly that the 'Irish press poured the phials of their spitefulness over him and the woman he loved'.[181] Tim Healy's articles for the *National Press* — 'underbred and untruthful', according to Yeats — were just the most famous examples of the high-minded invective and sexual innuendo that dominated the journals of the time.[182] Yeats poured scorn on this frenzy: 'The leading articles, the speeches, the resolutions of the shocked Irish and English politicians, the sudden reversal of all the barrel-organs, the alphabets running back from Z to A, sycophantic fiction become libel, eulogy vituperation, what could be more amusing?'[183] Yeats was not always so amused. In 'To a Shade' he angrily turned upon Parnell's former persecutor, William Martin Murphy, who had sponsored attacks on Parnell through the foundation of the *National Press* and exacerbated the betrayal by taking over Parnell's own paper, the *Independent*. But

---

177 *United Ireland*, 31 October 1885. Cited in Callanan, *T. M. Healy*, 100.

178 Weber, *From Max Weber*, 106. Weber clearly based his views on Ostrogorski's famous analysis of modern democratic practices; see Ostrogorski, *Democracy and the Organization of Political Parties*, 1. 586. Ostrogorski attributed the practice of 'plebiscitary Caesarism' to Disraeli's form of Toryism. But Disraeli, along with Gladstone in whom the temperament of the demagogue found its 'fullest expression', was indicative of a new kind of 'Caucus' politics involving highly regulated party machines constituted by disciplined professional politicians. According to Ostrogorski, the 'freedom and independence of political thought was now repressed; for every difference of opinion was a blow struck at the unity of the party of which the Caucus had constituted itself the permanent guardian'.

179 Weber, *From Max Weber*, 96. Ostrogorski also emphasized this point in *Democracy and the Organization of Political Parties*, 1. 608.

180 For an account of Parnell's uses of the press, see James Loughlin, 'Constructing the Political Spectacle: Parnell, the Press and National Leadership, 1879–86', in Boyce and O'Day, eds., *Parnell in Perspective*, 221–41.

181 Joyce, *Occasional, Critical, and Political Writings*, 196.

182 UP 1, 309. For Healy's anti-Parnellite journalism, see Callanan, *T. M. Healy*, 257–435. According to William O'Brien, Healy 'affected a brutality of speech at which Rabelais or even Swift in his least dainty moment might have hesitated'. See O'Brien, *Recollections*, 250; *National Press*, 6 July 1891. Healy's attacks were, in O'Connor's eyes, 'fierce and vindictive and, part of the time, indecent'. T. P. O'Connor, *Memoirs of an Old Parliamentarian*, 2 vols. (London, 1929), 1. 105.

183 EI, 487.

the awkward fact remained that Parnell had in fact founded a paper and called upon a network of journalists in Britain and Ireland to service his political ambitions.

Writing after Parnell's death, Justin McCarthy observed how 'Mr. Parnell seems to have made up his mind from a very early period of his political life that the first thing to do was to get a strong force of public opinion … behind him'.[184] He was helped in this by the remarkable number of journalists within his own party. Edmund Dwyer Gray, A. M. Sullivan, William O'Brien, James Carew, James Leahy, Edward and Timothy Harrington, Luke P. Hayden, Frank Hugh O'Donnell, Tim Healy, Thomas Sexton and Justin McCarthy were all journalists and MPs and all helped to construct the myth of Parnell in the press. While initially critical of Parnell and the obstructionists, in general, Gray eventually threw the enormous resources of his *Freeman's Journal* behind Parnellism. Sullivan, who owned the *Nation* newspaper, supported Parnell from the start. He continued this advocacy despite some understandable bitterness over Parnell's decision to start a rival weekly, *United Ireland*, under the editorship of William O'Brien. This new journal did much to promote Parnell among agrarian radicals in Ireland.[185] Meanwhile, O'Donnell, Healy, McCarthy and O'Connor sold Parnellism to the English public. As O'Connor admitted: 'I used every power and influence I possessed as a writer in newspapers to exalt him'.[186] Healy was more inclined to see authorship as a collective process: 'We created Parnell and Parnell created us. We seized very early in the movement the idea of this man with his superb silences, his historic name, his determination, his self-control, his aloofness — we seized that as the canvas of a great national hero.'[187] According to O'Donnell, Parnell's publicists 'were Parnell'.[188]

This fact complicated Yeats's attempts to present Parnell as the spiritual antithesis of the press. His status in the media was based around a cult of personality, nourished by the journalistic search for the 'real' Parnell. The press sought Parnell 'at home'; it looked for the passionate Parnell behind the cold exterior of his public self. Behind the hater of John Bull, newspapers rummaged for the lover of Kitty O'Shea. Healy's article 'The Secret of Mr. Parnell's Power' typified the self-proliferating quality of the Parnell myth.[189] The politician was depicted as a sphinx-like creature and the riddle he posed was often the after-effect of the rival solutions provided. Parnell, according to O'Connor, was the 'mystery man' of British politics:

> Never seen in the drawing-room, rarely seen in Parliament, speaking to no man outside his own party, and very rarely to any of them, and surrounded by the nimbus of a romantic love affair, guessed at, speculated upon, but entirely unknown with

184 Justin McCarthy, 'Charles Stewart Parnell', *Contemporary Review*, 60 (November 1891), 625–36, 634.
185 O'Connor, *Memoirs*, I. 143.
186 *Memoirs*, I. 127.
187 Cited in Conor Cruise O'Brien, *Parnell and his Party* (Oxford, 1957), 10.
188 O'Donnell, *A History of the Irish Parliamentary Party*, 289 [O'Donnell's emphasis].
189 *Pall Mall Gazette*, 28 December 1883.

certainty in any of its details, he grew to the dim, and misty, and awful proportions of a veiled prophet.[190]

The enigma of Parnell was such that in 1891 the 'certified and registered' phrenologist G. H. J. Dutton enlisted the services of modern science to provide a definitive description of the man. Dutton arrived at the unsurprising conclusion that 'the popular conception as to one faculty, secretiveness, is undoubtedly correct', for the 'head is most prominent where that organ is located'.[191]

Reflecting on Parnell's career, John Morley declared that '[n]o public man of his time was more free of the evil art of Pose, nobody more disdainful of playing to the gallery'.[192] Parnell, however, clearly colluded in the myth of himself. Although he may have despised the glare of the public, O'Connor maintained that he 'conducted his programme in the spirit of a showman and with an ability that might have made Barnum envious'. Parnell, he suggested, recognized that many attended his meetings out of sheer curiosity and in America, in particular, he avoided the streets before meetings, suspecting 'it would satisfy sufficient curiosity to keep a certain number of people away'. [193] 'The Wink of the Sphinx', a story told by Parnell's brother, John, is a well-known example of the politician's studied self-construction. According to John Parnell, he had once arranged to meet his famous brother, but happened to encounter him by chance in a Dublin street in advance of the planned meeting. Charles, however, merely winked at his brother and strolled on undisturbed. According to John: 'Charley simply wished to show that he had seen and recognized me, but did not wish to disturb his demeanour of perfect composure and aloofness.'[194] In his memoirs, Tim Healy outlined a similar tale of Parnellite self-fashioning. He described Parnell's petulant hurt when, on his return to Ireland with Healy from the American tour, he mistakenly believed that his parliamentary colleagues had not turned out to greet him at Queenstown. Discovering his mistake, Parnell recovered magnificently, banishing 'all traces of emotion and became the superman once more'. According to Healy, Parnell's 'acting was superb'.[195] Most famously, the O'Shea divorce proceedings led to the circulation of sensational reports of Parnell's use of pseudonyms and disguises. The resourceful Dutton drew on the science of phrenology to account for Parnell's capacity to 'throw a veil over countenance, expression and conduct'.[196] Punch —

---

190 O'Connor, Memoirs, I. 143. William O'Brien, in The Parnell of Real Life, 118–19, insisted that Parnell had an 'inborn simplicity of character'. 'The legend of Parnell as a mystery-man', he dismissed as 'the concoction of journalists who knew nothing of him except the caution with which he surrounded his personal movements'.

191 G. H. J. Dutton, A Delineation of the Character and Talents of the Late C. S. Parnell, M.P. and the Right Hon. W. H. Smith, M.P. (Skegness, 1891), 3.

192 John Morley, Recollections, 2 vols. (New York, 1907), I. 241. Quoted in Steinman, Yeats's Heroic Figures, 54.

193 O'Connor, Charles Stewart Parnell, 74.

194 John Howard Parnell, Charles Stewart Parnell: A Memoir (London, 1916), 127.

195 T. M. Healy, Letters and Leaders of My Day, 2 vols. (London, 1928), I. 89.

196 Dutton, A Delineation of the Character and Talents of the Late C. S. Parnell, 3.

deeply critical of Parnell while he lived — referred to his magnificent self-construction in a tone bordering on awe; however, 'the task / Of coldly keeping up the Stoic mask / O'er taxed him at the last.'[197]

These accounts of a political *poseur* might seem to undermine Yeats's faith in Parnell's heroic integrity, but they did the opposite. He revered Parnell's 'stony *Mask*': it was a sign of his authenticity.[198] Healy clearly missed the point when he insisted that Parnell's 'ordinary reserve was merely a mask'.[199] Masks were highly fashionable in the last two decades of the nineteenth century.[200] 'In so vulgar an age as this', Wilde declared, 'all need masks'.[201] Nietzsche had also recommended the mask as a refuge from vulgarity. 'Every profound spirit needs a mask', he declared in *Beyond Good and Evil*. Disguises, he suggested, preserved our freedom by shielding us from the intrusion of others.[202] 'One must know how *to conserve oneself*', he insisted, because so much of modern life intrigued against autonomy.[203] Yeats also hoped to bolster his own 'self-possession' by improving his 'capacity for disguise'.[204] He regarded the mask as a form of protection; it offered 'the only escape from the hot-faced bargainers and the money-changers'.[205] Parnell was the greatest exemplar of this doctrine of the mask. He knew how to conserve himself and could 'hide all emotion while before his enemy'.[206] Parnell's studied aloofness, as his brother suggested, was a defensive shield: it 'was not only an armour against the English; it was a robe that attracted the loyalty, and even the wild enthusiasm, of his own countrymen, while at the time repelling their intimacy'.[207] The mask of Parnell was both a public shrine and a private refuge.

The mask, as Nietzsche and Yeats suggested, was a protective cover for an existing self, but it was also an incitement to different forms of self-creation. One thing was needful, Nietzsche declared in *The Gay Science*: 'To "give style" to one's character — a great and rare art!'[208] Yeats also believed that style and self-fashioning went hand in hand. He defined style as 'personality — deliberately adopted and therefore a mask'.[209] Parnell had succeeded, it seems, in moulding himself to a style and thus distinguished himself from

197 *Punch*, 17 October 1891. Quoted in Foster, *Paddy and Mr. Punch*, 191.

198 V, 123 [Yeats's emphasis].

199 Healy, *Letters and Leaders*, I. 89.

200 Even Parnell's unfortunate betrayer, Richard Pigott, is equipped with a mask. According to one commentator, Pigott was 'as inscrutable a personage as "The Man in the Iron Mask"'. See James O'Connor, *Recollections of Richard Pigott* (Dublin, 1889), 7, 26. Another biographer, Dick Donovan [pseud. for Joyce Emmerson Muddock], *The Crime of the Century; Being the Life Story of Richard Pigott* (London, 1904), 16, recounted Pigott's ability to mask 'the true bent of his thoughts and the drift of his intentions by a singularly calm exterior'.

201 Oscar Wilde, *The Letters of Oscar Wilde*, ed. Rupert Hart-Davis (London, 1962), 353.

202 *Beyond Good and Evil*, 161.

203 *Beyond Good and Evil*, 70 [Nietzsche's emphasis].

204 A, 356.

205 A, 461.

206 A, 232.

207 John Howard Parnell, *Charles Stewart Parnell*, 127.

208 Friedrich Nietzsche, *The Gay Science*, trans. Walter Kaufmann (New York, 1974), 232.

209 A, 461.

inauthentic spirits who could not discipline themselves to a rule. 'Domination through emotional construction' was the defining feature of those who lived authentically under phase ten of the moon and Parnell was one such figure.[210] The assumption of a mask implied a form of active virtue that distinguished itself from the simple acceptance of a pre-existing code like that so valued by Lady Gregory. Parnell did not passively receive his values from elsewhere but managed to 'create some code of personal conduct, which implies always "divine right"'.[211] Parnell's privileges, however, were radically different to those traditional entitlements that monarchs derived from God. Parnell was his own divinity and the forger of his own values.

His self-conquest was all the more impressive precisely because he remained, for Yeats, a passionate Celt. O'Connor repeatedly insisted, that behind his 'apparent imperturbability there were very tempestuous depths in his strange soul'.[212] Parnell's speech at the Rotunda in December 1890 was a famous instance of these antinomies of self. Katherine Tynan reported that 'despite his calm, pale face, the hand inside the breast of his frock coat clenched till the nails bit in the flesh and made it bleed'.[213] This account reappeared in Barry O'Brien's biography of Parnell and in O'Connor's memoirs. It also won a place in Yeats's political hagiography; the poet recalled Parnell's 'apparent impassivity when his hands were full of blood because he had torn them with his nails'.[214] Parnell's reserve was heroic precisely because he was a passionate man. Self-conquest, Nietzsche had suggested, was a real achievement only when there was a tumultuous self to be conquered: where '"man" shows himself strongest one finds instincts that conflict powerfully (e.g., in Shakespeare), but are controlled'.[215] Yeats also celebrated the self-control of Shakespeare's characters. They were masters of their own *hysterico passio* and although the world might collapse around them, neither Hamlet nor Lear, nor Ophelia, nor Cordelia 'break up their lines to weep'.[216] Parnell too was an actor who refused to break the laws of his own craft. He managed to approach 'life as a stage play where there is only one good acting part' and to respect the discipline of his assumed role.[217] Parnell never revoked the responsibilities of his mask, in Yeats's eyes; his accusers, however, capitulated to their own hysterical passion.

Through the metaphor of the mask, then, Yeats projected different and even rival conceptions of selfhood. On one level, it was a protective shield for a pre-existent self; alternatively, the metaphor pointed to a process of self-discipline in which a higher-order accord was imposed on lower-level passions. To adopt a terminology that Yeats sometimes used, one constructed genuine 'personality' from the muddled contingencies

210 V, 121.
211 V, 122.
212 O'Connor, Memoirs, 1. 119.
213 Irish Weekly Independent, 6 October 1894.
214 VP, 835.
215 Nietzsche, Will to Power, 507.
216 VP, 565.
217 V, 123.

of 'character' through the use of a mask. In both of these scenarios, there remained a distinction between the surface of the self and its inner core, between the mask assumed and the reality it disguised or transfigured. As Yeats put it, 'what I have called "the Mask" is an emotional antithesis to all that comes out of … internal nature'.[218] Here Yeats implicitly conceded to the notion of a real or given self even as he promoted the idea of total self-construction. But there was another existential possibility latent in the mask, which undermined any opposition between pre-existing selves and their assumed disguise. Here nothing existed behind the mask and the self had no essential core or established foundation in nature. The mask did not merely impose an appearance on a given reality, but it resisted entanglement in these kinds of dualism. To become one's mask, in this scenario, was to abandon all metaphysical ballast for the self. 'What is "appearance" for me now?' Nietzsche asked. 'Certainly not the opposite of some essence: what could I say about any essence except to name the attributes of its appearance! Certainly not a dead mask that one could place on an unknown x or remove from it!'[219]

Yeats may have insisted that there 'is always a living face behind the mask', but his portraits of Parnell appear to suggest otherwise.[220] In his reflections on Parnell's funeral, he pointed to the void behind the politician's mask, an absence so intense as to cast doubt on his very humanity:

> Leave nothing but the nothings that belong
> To this bare soul, let all men judge that can
> Whether it be an animal or a man.[221]

This 'bare soul' is not simply naked, but is fundamentally empty — a collection of 'nothings'. Parnell could acknowledge his essential non-being — something that was the very basis of authenticity for Nietzsche and for Heidegger as well as for the late Yeats. In this respect O'Connor missed the high seriousness of the joke 'that to Mr. Parnell the being Parnell does not exist'.[222]

As someone who was resigned to his own lack of substance, Parnell easily made his peace with death. Yeats was drawn to Mrs O'Shea's famous report of her experiences on Brighton pier when Parnell held her in a raging storm and suggested they drown themselves together. 'Perhaps unmotivated self-immolation,' Yeats mused, 'were as great evidence as such a man could give of power over self, and so of the expression of the self.'[223] On one level, he suggests that Parnell mastered all his desires by overcoming his

---

218 A, 189.
219 The Gay Science, 116.
220 A, 505.
221 VP, 542.
222 T. P. O'Connor, The Parnell Movement (London, 1886), 239. O'Donnell also made mocking reference to 'the ubiquitous, untiring, inexhaustible, ever-ready, non-existent Parnell'. See History of the Irish Parliamentary Party, 289.
223 A, 233.

own desire to live. On another level, this self-conquest was based upon the recognition that the self has no objective reality as such. In this context, suicide was a paradoxical form of self-expression, and permitted human beings to return to their essential nothingness. But in other settings, a sense of one's own non-being allowed one to make something of oneself; constrained by no existing foundations, one could become one's own mask.

There was, perhaps, something consoling for Yeats in the idea of Parnell's self-authorship. Parnell affirmed the possibility of meaningful agency in a complex world by becoming the creator of his own myth. In other words, he became the subject of the rhetoric that described him rather than remaining its passive by-product. At the end of his life he could survey the story of himself and say 'I willed it thus'.[224] Moreover, through a radical theory of the mask, Yeats strove to escape the frivolous humanism of the modern world. A problem he faced in his battles with journalism was that the entire practice seemed to be organized around an all-too-human preoccupation with the personal. One of Yeats's responses was to deny that there was a real core of personality as such. Here it became a measure of the self's authenticity that it relinquished any faith in its own substance. Parnell was a figure who embraced his 'proper dark' and realized that his person had no fundamental core. By acknowledging the groundlessness of his being, he successfully created himself and enjoyed an independence that was denied to the herd: 'Their school a crowd, his master solitude'.[225] But rather than dwelling on the ways in which public recognition gave reality and meaning to one's mask, Yeats tended to equate authenticity with isolation. The mask was a means of deceiving others, but it was arguably a way of deceiving oneself with illusions of independence.

This exclusive model of authenticity had also unpromising social and political implications. In his reflections on the Parnell affair in the 1930s, Yeats contrasted the honour of Parnell with the hypocrisy of both his antagonists and defenders. As he put it, 'all were caught in that public insincerity which was to bring such discredit to democracy'. His disgust for democratic hypocrisy fuelled his admiration for dictatorship. 'All over the world,' he enthused, 'men are turning to Dictators, Communist, or Fascist.'[226] He treated Parnell's death as the start of a new revolution of the gyre, where a heroic, antithetical, era would replace the objectivism and democratic quality of nineteenth-century life. Here Yeats expressed his admiration for the 'personal autocracy of Parnell'.[227] Autocracy, literally self-rule, was a basis of legitimacy for the rule of others. 'Insincerity', by contrast, was an ethical shorthand for the herd morality of modern democratic politics, and was measured against the integrity of the self-grounding, self-legitimizing dictator. For all

---

224 'All "It was" is a fragment, a riddle, a dreadful chance — until the creative will says to it: "But I willed it thus!"'. See Nietzsche, *Thus Spoke Zarathustra*, 163.
225 VP, 543.
226 EI, 488.
227 V, 172.

their failings, dictators had, at least, autonomy and conviction.[228] In this account, we find a powerful illustration of the fact that an investment in authenticity — propelled by a one-sided account of personal autonomy — can be ethically and politically disastrous.

228 If Mussolini for Yeats, 'represented the rise of the individual man as against what he considered the anti-human party machine', it reflected his misunderstanding of the structural realities of modern politics. See IR 2. 409.

Bibliography

Primary Sources

Manuscript Material

Berg Collection, New York Public Library
Yeats Collection, National Library of Ireland

Contemporary Newspapers and Journals

Blast (London)
Freeman's Journal (Dublin)
Independent (Dublin)
Irish Weekly Independent (Dublin)
Leader (Dublin)
Nation (Dublin)
New Age (London)
Scot's Observer (Edinburgh)
Spectator (London)
United Irishman (Dublin)

Contemporary Books and Articles

Anon. *Ireland: Union or Separation?* (Dublin, 1886).
Anon. 'Studies in Character: Mr. Charles Stewart Parnell, M. P.', *New Review*, 9 (1890),
        172–84.
Aristotle. *The Politics*, trans. T. A. Sinclair, ed. Trevor J. Saunders (London, 1981).
——. *The Nicomachean Ethics*, ed. and trans. Roger Crisp (Cambridge, 2000).
Arnold, Matthew. 'Up to Easter', *Nineteenth Century*, 21 (1887), 629–43.
——. *The Study of Celtic Literature* (London, 1910).
——. *Culture and Anarchy and Other Writings*, ed. Stefan Collini (Cambridge, 1993).
Babbitt, Irving. *Rousseau and Romanticism* (Boston and New York, 1919).
——. *Democracy and Leadership* (Boston and New York, 1924).
Beaumont, Gustave de. *Ireland: Political, Social and Religious*, 2 vols., ed. W. C. Taylor,
        (London, 1839).
Bentham, Jeremy. *The Handbook of Political Fallacies* (New York, 1962).
——. *A Fragment on Government*, ed. J. H. Burns and H. L. A. Hart (Cambridge, 1988).
——. *The Principles of Morals and Legislation* (Amherst, 1988).
Besant, Walter. *The Pen and the Book* (London, 1899).
Bodkin, Matthias. *Recollections of an Irish Judge: Press, Bar and Parliament* (London, 1914).
Bolingbroke [Henry St. John]. *Political Writings*, ed. David Armitage (Cambridge, 1997).
Buckle, Henry Thomas. *History of Civilization in England*, 3 vols. (London, 1869).
Burke, Edmund. *The Works of the Right Honourable Edmund Burke*, vol. 6 (London, 1815).
——. *The Works of the Right Honourable Edmund Burke*, vol. 10 (London, 1818).
——. *The Correspondence of Edmund Burke. Volume 6: 1789–91*, ed. Alfred Cobban and
        Robert A. Smith (Cambridge and Chicago, 1967).
——. *The Correspondence of Edmund Burke. Volume 9: 1796–97*, ed. R. B. McDowell and
        John A. Woods (Chicago, 1970).
——. *The Writings and Speeches of Edmund Burke. Volume 2: Party, Parliament and the
        American Crisis, 1776–1774*, ed. Paul Langford, William B. Todd (Oxford, 1981).
——. *The Writings and Speeches of Edmund Burke. Volume 8: The French Revolution, 1790–
        1794*, ed. Paul Langford, L. G. Mitchell, William B. Todd (Oxford, 1989).
——. *The Writings and Speeches of Edmund Burke, Volume 6: India: The Launching of the
        Hastings Impeachment, 1786–1788*, ed. Paul Langford, P. J. Marshall, William B.
        Todd (Oxford, 1991).
——. *The Writings and Speeches of Edmund Burke. Volume 9. I: The Revolutionary War,
        1794–1797, II: Ireland*, ed. Paul Langford, R. B. McDowell, and William B. Todd
        (Oxford, 1991).
——. *The Writings and Speeches of Edmund Burke. Volume 3: Party, Parliament and the
        American War, 1774–1780*, ed. Paul Langford, Warren M. Elofson, John A.
        Woods, William B. Todd (Oxford, 1996).
Bryce, James. *Modern Democracies*, 2 vols. (London, 1921).

Campbell, George Douglas [Duke of Argyll]. *Irish Nationalism: An Appeal to History* (London, 1893).

Carlyle, Thomas. *Critical and Miscellaneous Essays*, 6 vols. (London, 1872).

——. *On Heroes and Hero-Worship* (London, 1872).

——. *The French Revolution*, 2 vols. ([1837] London, 1889).

Cicero. *Laelius, On Friendship and The Dream of Scipio*, trans. J. G. F. Powell (Warminster, 1990).

——. *On the Commonwealth and On the Laws*, ed. James E. G. Zetzel (Cambridge, 1999).

Comte, Auguste. *The Positive Philosophy of Auguste Comte*, 2 vols., trans. Harriet Martineau (London, 1853).

Connolly, James. *Collected Works*, 2 vols. (Dublin, 1988).

Constant, Benjamin. *Political Writings*, ed. and trans. Biancamaria Fontana (Cambridge, 1998).

Davis, Thomas. *The Poems of Thomas Davis*, ed. Thomas Wallis (Dublin, 1846).

——. *Essays Literary and Historical*, ed. D. J. O'Donoghue (Dundalk, 1914).

Dewey, John. *The Public and Its Problems* (Athens, 1927).

Dicey, A. V. *New Jacobinism and Old Morality* (London, n.d.).

——. *A Fool's Paradise* (London, 1913).

Disraeli, Benjamin. *Vindication of the English Constitution in a Letter to a Noble and Learned Lord* (London, 1835).

Donovan, Dick [pseud. for Joyce Emmerson Muddock]. *The Crime of the Century; Being the Life Story of Richard Pigott* (London, 1904).

Dowden, Edward. *New Studies in Literature* (London, 1895).

——. *Studies in Literature, 1789–1877* (London, 1906).

Drennan, William. *A Letter to Edmund Burke, Esq.; By Birth an Irishman, By Adoption an Englishman, Containing Some Reflections on Patriotism, Party-Spirit, and the Union of Free Nations. With Observations upon the Means on which Ireland Relies for Obtaining Political Independence* (Dublin, 1780).

——. *An Address to the Volunteers of Ireland, by the Author of a Letter to Edmund Burke, Esq., Containing Reflections on Patriotism, Party Spirit, and the Union of Free Nations* (Dublin, 1781).

——. *Letters of Orellana, An Irish Helot, to the Seven Northern Counties not Represented in the National Assembly of Delegates, Held at Dublin, October 1784, for Obtaining a More Equal Representation of the People in the Parliament of Ireland* (Dublin, 1785).

Duffy, Charles Gavan. *Ballad Poetry of Ireland*, 40th edn. (Dublin, 1869).

——. *Young Ireland: A Fragment of Irish History, 1840–1850* (London, 1880).

——. *Four Years of Irish History, 1845–1849*, 2 parts (London, 1883).

——. *Thomas Davis: The Memoirs of an Irish Patriot, 1840–1845* (London, 1890).

——. *My Life in Two Hemispheres*, 2 vols. (London, 1903).

Duffy, Charles Gavan, George Sigerson and Douglas Hyde. *The Revival of Irish Literature* (London, 1894).

Dunlop, Andrew. *Fifty Years of Irish Journalism* (Dublin, 1911).

Durkheim, Emile. *The Division of Labour in Society*, trans. H. D. Halls (Houndmills, Basingstoke and London, 1984).

Dutton, G. H. J. *A Delineation of the Character and Talents of the Late C. S. Parnell, M.P. and the Right Hon. W. H. Smith, M.P.* (Skegness, 1891).

Eckermann, Johann. *Goethe's Conversations with Eckermann*, rev. edn., trans. J. Oxenford (London, 1892).

Eglinton, John [pseud. for William Magee]. *Pebbles from a Brook* (Dublin, 1901).

——. *Bards and Saints* (Dublin, 1906).

——. *Irish Literary Portraits* (London, 1935).

Eliot, T. S. *Selected Prose of T. S. Eliot*, ed. Frank Kermode (London, 1975).

Ferguson, Adam. *An Essay on the History of Civil Society*, ed. Fania Oz-Salzberger (Cambridge, 1996).

Finneran, Richard J., George Mills Harper and William M. Murphy, eds. *Letters to W. B. Yeats*, 2 vols. (London and Basingstoke, 1977).

Flood, Henry. *A Letter to the People of Ireland on the Expediency and Necessity of the Present Associations in Ireland in Favour of Our Own Manufactures with Some Cursory Observations on the Effects of a Union* (Dublin, 1779).

Goethe, Johann Wolfgang Von. *The Autobiography of Goethe: Truth and Fiction Relating to My Own Life*, 2 vols., trans. John Oxenford (Honolulu, 2003).

Gogarty, Oliver St. John. *Going Native* (New York, 1940).

Gonne MacBride, Maud. *The Gonne–Yeats Letters, 1893–1938: Always Your Friend*, eds. Anna MacBride White and A. Norman Jeffares (London, 1992).

Grattan, Henry. *Speeches of the Rt. Hon. Henry Grattan*, 2nd edn. (Dublin, 1853).

Gregory, Augusta, ed. *Ideals in Ireland* (London, 1901).

——. *Our Irish Theatre* (Gerrards Cross, 1972).

——. *Poets and Dreamers: Studies and Translations from the Irish* (Gerrards Cross, 1974).

——. *Lady Gregory's Diaries, 1892–1902*, ed. James Pethica (Gerrards Cross, 1996).

Griffith, Arthur. 'Preface', in John Mitchel, *Jail Journal* (Dublin, 1913), ix–xvi.

——. 'Preface' in Thomas Davis, *Thomas Davis: The Thinker and Teacher*, ed. Arthur Griffith (Dublin, 1914), v–xiv.

Hazlitt, William. *The Life of Napoleon Buonaparte*, 2nd edn. (London, 1852).

Healy, T. M. *Letters and Leaders of My Day*, 2 vols. (London, 1928).

Hegel, G. W. F. *Philosophy of History*, trans. J. Sibree (New York, 1902).

——. *Phenomenology of Spirit*, trans. A. V. Miller (Oxford, 1977).

——. *Hegel's Aesthetics: Lectures on Fine Art*, 2 vols., trans. T. M. Knox (Oxford, 1975).

——. *Hegel and the Human Spirit: The Jena Lectures on the Philosophy of Spirit of 1805–6*, trans. Leo Rauch (Detroit, 1983).

——. *Elements of the Philosophy of Right*, ed. Allen W. Wood, trans. H. B. Nisbet (Cambridge, 1991).

Heidegger, Martin. *Nietzsche IV: Nihilism*, trans. Joan Stambaugh, David Farrell Krell and Frank A. Capuzzi (New York, 1982).

Heinrick, Hugh. *The Irish in England* (Liverpool, 1874).

Hobbes, Thomas. *Leviathan*, ed. Richard Tuck (Cambridge, 1996).

——. *On the Citizen*, ed. Richard Tuck and Michael Silverthorne (Cambridge, 1998).

Hobson, J. A. *The Psychology of Jingoism* (London, 1901).

Huggesson, Edward [Baron Brabourne]. *Facts and Fictions in Irish History: A Reply to Mr. Gladstone* (Edinburgh and London, 1886).

Hulme, T. E. *The Collected Writings of T. E. Hulme*, ed. Karen Csengeri (Oxford, 1994).

Humboldt, Wilhelm. *The Sphere and Duties of Government*, trans. Joseph Coulthard (London, 1854; repr. Bristol, 1996).

Hume, David. *Political Essays*, ed. Knud Haakonssen (Cambridge, 1994).

Hyde, Douglas. *Beside the Fire: A Collection of Irish Gaelic Folk Songs* (London, 1890).

——. *A Literary History of Ireland from the Earliest Times to the Present Day* (London, 1899).

Ingram, John K. *The Present Position & Prospects of Political Economy* (London, 1878).

James, Henry. *A London Life and The Reverberator* (Oxford, 1989).

——. 'The Papers', in *Complete Stories, 1898–1910*, ed. Denis Donoghue (New York, 1996), 542–638.

Jefferson, Thomas. *Political Writings*, ed. Joyce Appleby and Terence Ball (Cambridge, 1999).

Joyce, James. *Dubliners*, ed. Terence Brown (London, 1992).

——. *Ulysses*, ed. Jeri Johnson (Oxford, 1993).

——. *Occasional, Critical and Political Writing*, ed. Kevin Barry (Oxford, 2000).

Kant, Immanuel. *Lectures on Ethics*, trans. Louis Infield (London, 1930).

Keary, C. F. *The Journalist* (London, 1898).

Kennedy, Kevin [pseud. for William P. Ryan]. *Starlight through the Roof* (London, 1895).

Le Bon, Gustave. *The Crowd: A Study of the Popular Mind* (London, 1896).

Lecky, W. E. H. *History of European Morals from Augustus to Charlemagne*, 2 vols. (London, 1869).

——. *Democracy and Liberty*, 2 vols. (Indianapolis, 1981).

Lewis, Wyndham, ed. *Blast*, 1 (1914).

——. *The Art of Being Ruled* (London, 1926).

——. *Time and Western Man*, ed. Paul Edwards (Santa Rosa, 1993).

Lively, James, and John Rees, eds. *Utilitarian Logic and Politics: James Mill's 'Essay on Government', Macaulay's Critique and the Ensuing Debate* (London, 1990).

Longinus, 'On the Sublime', in *Aristotle/Horace/Longinus: Classical Literary Criticism*, trans. T. S. Dorsch (London, 1965), 97–158.

Lyneworth, Warde, and Percy Russell. *Fate's Grim Sport* (London, 1895).

McCarthy, Justin. 'Charles Stewart Parnell', *Contemporary Review*, 60 (1891), 625–36.

McCarthy, Michael J. F. *Mr. Balfour's Rule in Ireland* (Dublin, 1891).

——. *The Irish Revolution. Volume 1: The Murdering Time, from the Land League to the First Home Rule Bill* (Edinburgh and London, 1912).

MacDonagh, Michael. 'In the Bye-Ways of Rural Ireland', *Nineteenth Century*, 48 (July 1900), 75–88.

——. *William O'Brien* (London, 1928).

MacGill, Patrick. *Children of the Dead End: The Autobiography of a Navvy* (Ascot, 1980).

Machiavelli, Niccolò. *Discourses on Livy*, trans. Harvey C. Mansfield and Nathan Tarcov (Chicago and London, 1996).

McKenna, Stephen. *While I Remember* (London, 1921).

Maine, Henry Sumner. *Popular Government* (London, 1885).

Maistre, Joseph, de. *Considerations on France*, ed. and trans. Richard A. Lebrun (Cambridge, 1994).

Mandeville, Bernard. *The Fable of the Bees; or, Private Vices, Publick Benefits*, 2 vols., ed. F. B. Kaye (Indianapolis, 1988).

Marx, Karl. *Later Political Writings*, ed. and trans. Terrell Carver (Cambridge, 1996).

——. *Selected Writings*, 2nd edn., ed. David McLellan (Oxford, 2000).

Marx, Karl, and Friedrich Engels. *The German Ideology*, ed. and trans. S. Ryanskaya (Moscow, 1964).

Meagher, Thomas Francis. *Meagher of the Sword: Speeches of Thomas Francis Meagher in Ireland 1846–1848*, ed. Arthur Griffith (Dublin, 1916).

Meinecke, Friedrich. *Cosmopolitanism and the National State*, trans. Robert B. Kimber (Princeton, 1970).

——. *Historism: The Rise of a New Historical Outlook*, trans. J. E. Anderson (London, 1972).

Mill, John Stuart. *The Collected Works of John Stuart Mill. Volume 12: Earlier Letters, 1812–1848*, ed. Francis Mineka (Toronto and London, 1963).

——. *The Collected Works of John Stuart Mill. Volume 10: Essays on Ethics, Religion and Society*, ed. J. M. Robson and D. P. Dryer (Toronto and London, 1969).

——. *The Collected Works of John Stuart Mill. Volume 18: Essays on Politics and Society*, ed. J. M. Robson (Toronto and London, 1977).

——. *The Collected Works of John Stuart Mill. Volume 19: Essays on Politics and Society*, ed. J. M. Robson (Toronto and London, 1977).

——. *The Collected Works of John Stuart Mill, Volume 24: Newspaper Writings*, ed. A. and J. M. Robson (Toronto and London, 1986).

Mitchel, John. *Jail Journal; or, Five Years in British Prisons* (Glasgow, 1876).

Molesworth, Robert. *An Account of Denmark as It was in the Year 1692* (London, 1694).

Molyneux, William. *The Case of Ireland Stated by William Molyneux*, repr. from the 1st edn. of 1698 (Dublin, 1977).

Montague, C. E. *A Hind Let Loose* (London, 1910).

Montesquieu [Charles-Louis de Secondat]. *The Spirit of the Laws*, ed. and trans. Anne M. Cohler, Basia Carolyn Miller and Harold Samuel Stone (Cambridge, 1989).

Montgomery, H. de. F. *Correspondence with Mr. Gladstone and Notes on the Pamphlet* (Dublin, 1887).

Moody, T. W., and Richard Hawkins, ed. *Florence Arnold-Forster's Irish Journal* (Oxford, 1988).

Moore, George. *Confessions of a Young Man* (London, 1917).

——. *The Untilled Field* (Gerrards Cross, 1976).

——. *The Lake* (Gerrards Cross, 1980).

——. *Hail and Farewell: Ave, Vale, Salve*, ed. Richard Cave (Gerrards Cross, 1985).

Moore, Sturge. *W. B. Yeats and T. Sturge Moore: Their Correspondence, 1901–1937*, ed. Ursula Bridge (London, 1953).

Morley, John. *Edmund Burke: A Historical Study* (London, 1867).

——. *Recollections*, 2 vols. (New York, 1907).

Morris, William. *Collected Works. Volume 22: Hopes and Fears for Art, Lectures on Art and Industry* (London, 1914).

——. *Collected Works. Volume 23: Signs of Change, Lectures on Socialism* (London, 1915).

Morrow, John, ed. *Young England, The New Generation: A Selection of Primary Texts* (London, 1999).

Mussolini, Benito. *The Doctrine of Fascism*, trans. E. Cope (Florence, 1938).

Nietzsche, Friedrich. *The Works of Friedrich Nietzsche. Volume 3: The Case of Wagner. Nietzsche Contra Wagner. The Twilight of the Idols*, trans. Thomas Common (London, 1899).

——. *Thus Spoke Zarathustra*, trans. R. J. Hollingdale (London, 1961).

——. *The Will to Power*, ed. Walter Kaufmann, trans. Walter Kaufmann and R. J. Hollingdale (New York, 1968).

——. *The Gay Science*, trans. Walter Kaufmann (New York, 1974).

——. *Beyond Good and Evil*, trans. R. J. Hollingdale, intro. Michael Tanner (London, 1990).

——. *On the Genealogy of Morality*, ed. Keith Ansell-Pearson, trans. Carol Diethe (Cambridge, 1994).

——. *The Birth of Tragedy and Other Writings*, trans. Ronald Speirs (Cambridge, 1999).

——. *The Anti-Christ, Ecce Homo, Twilight of the Idols and Other Writings*, ed. Aaron Ridley and Judith Norman, trans. by Judith Norman (Cambridge, 2005).

O'Brien, William. *Recollections* (London, 1905).

——. *The Parnell of Real Life* (London, 1926).

O'Connor, Arthur. *The State of Ireland*, ed. James Livesey (Dublin, 1998).

O'Connor, Frank 'The Old Age of a Poet', *Bell*, 1, 5 (1941), 7–18.

O'Connor, James. *Recollections of Richard Pigott* (Dublin, 1889).

O'Connor, T. P. *The Parnell Movement* (London, 1886).

——. 'The New Journalism', *New Review*, 1 (1889), 423–34.

——. *Charles Stewart Parnell; A Memory* (London, New York, and Melbourne, 1891).

——. *Memoirs of an Old Parliamentarian*, 2 vols. (London, 1929).

O'Donnell, F. H. *A History of the Irish Parliamentary Party* (London, 1910).

O'Grady, Standish. *The Crisis in Ireland* (Dublin, 1882).

———. *Selected Essays and Passages* (Dublin, 1917).

O'Hara, M. M. *Chief and Tribune: Parnell and Davitt* (Dublin and London, 1919).

O'Shea, Katherine. *Charles Stewart Parnell: His Love Story and Political Life*, 2 vols. (London, 1914).

Oldcastle, John [pseud. for Wilfrid Meynell]. *Journals and Journalism: With a Guide for Literary Beginners* (London, 1880).

Orwell, George. *Essays* (London, 1968).

Ostrogorski, Moisei. *Democracy and the Organization of Political Parties*, 2 vols., trans. Frederick Clarke (London, 1902).

Owen-Madden, Daniel. *Ireland and Its Rulers since 1829*, 3 parts (London, 1843–44).

Paley, William. *The Works of William Paley with Additional Sermons Etc. Etc.*, 6 vols. (London, 1830).

Parnell, John Howard. *Charles Stewart Parnell: A Memoir* (London, 1916).

Paul-Dubois, L. *Contemporary Ireland* (Dublin, 1908).

Plato. *Gorgias*, trans. Robin Waterfield (Oxford, 1994).

———. *The Republic*, ed. G. R. F. Ferrari, trans. Tom Griffith (Cambridge, 2000).

Rousseau, Jean-Jacques. *The Discourses and Other Early Political Writings*, ed. and trans. Victor Gourevitch (Cambridge, 1997).

———. *The Social Contract and Other Later Political Writings*, ed. and trans. Victor Gourevitch (Cambridge, 1997).

Ryan, Frederick. *Criticism and Courage and Other Essays* (Dublin, 1906).

Ryan, William P. *The Plough and the Cross* (Point Loma, 1910).

———. *The Pope's Green Island* (London, 1912).

———. *Daisy Darley; or, The Fairy Gold of Fleet Street* (London and Toronto, 1913).

Savage, Mermion, *The Falcon Family, or Young Ireland* (London, 1844).

Schiller, Friedrich. *On the Aesthetic Education of Man in a Series of Letters*, ed. and trans. Elizabeth M. Wilkinson and L. A. Willoughby (Oxford, 1967).

———. *On the Naïve and Sentimental in Literature*, trans. Helen Watanabe O'Kelly (Manchester, 1981).

Schmitt, Carl. *Political Theology: Four Chapters on the Concept of Sovereignty*, trans. George Schwab (Chicago and London, 1985).

———. *Political Romanticism*, trans. Guy Oakes (Cambridge, 1986).

———. *The Concept of the Political*, trans. George Schwab (Chicago and London, 1996).

Smith, Adam. *An Inquiry into the Nature and Causes of the Wealth of Nations*, 2 vols., ed. R. H. Campbell, A. S. Kinner, and W. B. Todd, (Oxford, 1976).

———. *The Theory of Moral Sentiments*, ed. Knud Haakonssen (Cambridge, 2002).

Smith, R. J. *Ireland's Renaissance* (Dublin, 1903).

Spencer, Herbert. *Essays: Scientific, Political, and Speculative*, 2 vols. (London and Edinburgh, 1883).

——. *Political Writings*, ed. John Offer (Cambridge, 1994).

Staël, Anne Louise Germaine, de. *Considérations sur les Principaux Evénéments de la Révolution Françoise*, 3 vols. (London, 1818).

Sullivan, A. M. *New Ireland*, 2 vols. (London, 1877).

Swift, Jonathan. *The Drapier's Letters to the People of Ireland against Receiving Wood's Halfpence*, ed. Herbert Davis (Oxford, 1935).

——. *Complete Poems*, ed. Pat Rogers (London, 1983).

Synge, J. M. *Collected Works. Volume 2: Prose*, ed. Alan Price (London, 1966).

——. *Collected Works. Volume 4: Plays*, ed. Ann Saddlemyer (London, 1968).

Taine, Hippolyte. *Les Origines de la France Contemporaine: The Ancient Regime*, trans. John Durand (London, 1876).

——. *Les Origines de la France Contemporaine: The Revolution*, trans. John Durand, 3 vols. (London, 1878–1885).

Thierry, Augustin. *History of the Conquest of England by the Normans*, 2 vols. (London, 1847).

Tocqueville, Alexis, de. *The Old Regime and the French Revolution*, trans. Stuart Gilbert (New York, 1955).

——. *Democracy in America*, ed. Alan Ryan (London, 1994).

Toland, John. *Anglia Libera; or, The Limitation and Succession of the Crown of England Explain'd and Asserted* (London 1701).

Tone, Theobald Wolfe. *The Writings of Theobald Wolfe Tone, 1763–98. Volume 1: Tone's Career in Ireland to June 1795*, ed. T. W. Moody, R. B. McDowell and C. J. Woods (Oxford, 1998).

Tönnies, Ferdinand, de. *Community and Civil Society*, ed. Jose Harris, trans. Jose Harris and Margaret Hollis (Cambridge, 2001).

Webb, Thomas E. *The Irish Question: A Reply to Mr. Gladstone* (Dublin, 1886).

Weber, Max. *Economy and Society*, 2 vols., ed. Guenther Roth and Claus Wittich (Berkeley, 1978).

——. *From Max Weber: Essays in Sociology*, ed. H. H. Gerth and C. Wright Mills, new edn. (London, 1991).

Wilde, Oscar. *The Letters of Oscar Wilde*, ed. Rupert Hart-Davis (London, 1962).

——. *Collins Complete Works of Oscar Wilde* (Glasgow, 1999).

Yeats, J. B. *Letters to His Son W. B. Yeats and Others 1869–1922*, ed. with a Memoir by Joseph Hone (London, 1944).

Yeats, W. B. *The Celtic Twilight* (London and Stratford-upon-Avon, 1902).

——. *A Vision* (London, 1937).

——. *W. B. Yeats and T. Sturge Moore: Their Correspondence, 1901–1937*, ed. Ursula Bridge (London, 1953).

——. *The Letters of W. B. Yeats*, ed. Alan Wade (London, 1954).

——. *Autobiographies* (London, 1955).

——. *The Variorum Edition of the Poems of W. B. Yeats*, ed. Peter Allt and Russell K. Alspach (New York, 1957).

——. *The Senate Speeches of W. B. Yeats*, ed. Donald R. Pearce (London, 1960).

——. *Explorations* (London, 1962).

——. *The Variorum Edition of the Plays of W. B. Yeats*, ed. Russell K. Alspach, assisted by Catherine C. Alspach (London, Melbourne, Toronto, 1966).

——. *Essays and Introductions* (London, 1969).

——. *Uncollected Prose by W. B. Yeats. Volume 1*, ed. John P. Frayne (London, 1970).

——. *Memoirs*, ed. and transcribed by Denis Donoghue (London, 1972).

——. *Uncollected Prose by W. B. Yeats. Volume 2*, ed. John P. Frayne and Colton Johnson (London, 1975).

——. *Interviews and Recollections*, 2 vols., ed. E. H. Mikhail (London and Basingstoke, 1977).

——. *The Collected Letters of W. B. Yeats. Volume 1: 1865–1895*, ed. John Kelly and Erick Domville (Oxford, 1986).

——. *Prefaces and Introductions*, ed. William H. O'Donnell (Houndmills, Basingstoke, and London, 1988).

——. *Letters to the New Island* (Houndmills, Basingstoke, and London, 1989).

——. 'Four Lectures by W. B. Yeats', ed. Richard Londraville, in Warwick Gould, ed., *Yeats Annual No. 8* (Houndmills, Basingstoke, Hampshire and London, 1991), 78–122.

——. 'The Irish National Theatre', ed. David R. Clark, in Gould, ed., *Yeats Annual No. 8*, 144–54.

——. *The Collected Letters of W. B. Yeats. Volume 3: 1901–1904*, ed. John Kelly and Ronald Schuchard (Oxford, 1994).

——. *The Collected Works of W. B. Yeats. Volume 5: Later Essays*, ed. William H. O'Donnell (New York, 1994).

——. *The Collected Letters of W. B. Yeats. Volume 2: 1896–1901*, ed. Warwick Gould, John Kelly and Deirdre Toomey (Oxford, 1996).

——. *The Collected Letters of W. B. Yeats. Volume 4: 1905–1907*, ed. John Kelly and Ronald Schuchard (Oxford, 2005).

Secondary Works

Anderson, Benedict. *Imagined Communities*, rev. edn. (London, 1991).

Arendt, Hannah. *On Revolution* (London, 1990).

Aspinall, Arthur. *Politics and the Press 1780–1850* (Brighton, 1949).

Beckett, J. C. *The Making of Modern Ireland, 1603–1923* (London, 1966).

Bell, Quentin. *Virginia Woolf: A Biography* (New York, 1972).

Berlin, Isaiah. *Against the Current: Essays in the History of Ideas*, ed. Henry Hardy (London, 1979).

——. *Vico and Herder: Two Studies in the History of Ideas* (London, 1976).

——. *The Crooked Timber of Humanity*, ed. Henry Hardy (London, 2003).

Bew, Paul. *Ireland: The Politics of Enmity 1789–2006* (Oxford, 2007).

Billington, James H. *Fires in the Minds of Men: The Origins of the Revolutionary Faith* (New York, 1980).

Black, R. D. Collison. *Economic Thought and the Irish Question, 1817–1870* (Cambridge, 1960).

Bloom, Harold. *Yeats* (New York, 1970).

Bock, Gisela. 'Civil Discord in Machiavelli's *Istorie Fiorentine*', in Gisela Bock, Quentin Skinner and Maurizio Viroli, eds., *Machiavelli and Republicanism* (Cambridge, 1990), 181–201.

Bohlmann, Otto. *Yeats and Nietzsche: An Exploration of Major Nietzschean Echoes in the Writings of William Butler Yeats* (London, 1982).

Bourke, Richard. 'Sovereignty, Opinion and Revolution in Edmund Burke', *History of European Ideas*, 25, 3 (1999), 99–120.

——. 'Edmund Burke and the Politics of Conquest', *Modern Intellectual History*, 4, 3 (2007), 403–32.

Boyce, D. George. *Nineteenth-Century Ireland: The Search for Stability* (Dublin, 1990).

Boylan, Thomas, and Timothy P. Foley. *Political Economy and Colonial Ireland: The Propagation and Ideological Function of Economic Discourse in the Nineteenth Century* (London, 1992).

Brown, Malcolm. *The Politics of Irish Literature: From Thomas Davis to W. B. Yeats* (London, 1972).

Buckley, Mary. 'Thomas Davis: A Study in Nationalist Philosophy', Ph.D. thesis, University College Cork, 1980.

Burrow, J. W. *Whigs and Liberals: Continuity and Change in English Political Thought* (Oxford, 1998).

Butterfield, Herbert. *Man on His Past: The Study of the History of Historical Scholarship* (Cambridge, 1955).

Callanan, Frank. *The Parnell Split* (Cork, 1992).

——. *T. M. Healy* (Cork, 1996).

Canavan, Francis P. *The Political Reason of Edmund Burke* (Durham, 1960).

——. *Edmund Burke: Prescription and Providence* (Durham, 1987).

Castle, Gregory. *Modernism and the Celtic Revival* (Cambridge, 2001).

Chaudhry, Yug. *Yeats, the Irish Literary Revival and the Politics of Print* (Cork, 2001).

Chiron, Yves. 'The Influence of Burke's Writings in Post-Revolutionary France', in
    Ian Crowe, ed., *Edmund Burke: His Life and Legacy* (Dublin, 1997), 85–93.

Chisick, Harvey, ed. *The Press in the French Revolution* (Oxford, 1991).

Cobban, Alfred. *Edmund Burke and the Revolt against the Eighteenth Century: A Study of the
    Political and Social Thinking of Burke, Wordsworth, Coleridge and Southey*, 2nd edn.
    (London, 1960).

Conniff, James. 'Edmund Burke's Reflections on the Coming Revolution in Ireland',
    Journal of the History of Ideas, 47, 1 (1986), 37–59.

Connolly, S. J. 'Precedent and Principle: The Patriots and Their Critics', in S. J.
    Connolly, ed., *Political Ideas in Eighteenth-Century Ireland* (Dublin, 2000), 130–58.

——. *The Oxford Companion to Irish History*, 2nd edn. (Oxford, 2002).

Courtney, J. P. *Montesquieu and Burke* (Oxford, 1963).

Cullingford, Elizabeth. *Yeats, Ireland and Fascism* (London, 1981).

Curran, James, and Jean Seaton, eds. *Power without Responsibility: The Press and
    Broadcasting in Britain*, 5th edn. (London, 1997).

Curtin, Nancy. *The United Irishmen: Popular Politics in Ulster and Dublin, 1791–1798*
    (Oxford, 1994).

Dann, Otto, and John Dinwiddy, eds. *Nationalism in the Age of the French Revolution*
    (London, 1988).

Deane, Seamus. *Celtic Revivals: Essays in Modern Irish Literature, 1880–1980* (London,
    1985).

——. *Strange Country: Modernity and Nationhood in Irish Writing since 1790* (Oxford, 1997).

——. *Foreign Affections: Essays on Edmund Burke* (Cork, 2005).

Derrida, Jacques. *Of Grammatology*, trans. Gayatri Chakravorty Spivak (Baltimore and
    London, 1976).

——. *Margins of Philosophy*, trans. Alan Bass (Brighton, 1982).

Dinwiddy, J. R. *Radicalism and Reform in Britain, 1780–1850* (London, 1992).

Donlan, Seán Patrick. 'The "Genuine Voice of its Records and Monuments"?', in
    Seán Patrick Donlan, ed., *Edmund Burke's Irish Identities* (Dublin, 2007), 69–101.

Donoghue, Denis. *William Butler Yeats* (New York, 1971).

Donovan, Stephen. 'Literary Modernism and the Press, 1870–1922', doctoral
    dissertation, Göteburg University, 2001.

Dunn, John. *Western Political Theory in the Face of the Future* (Cambridge, 1993).

Eagleton, Terry. *Heathcliff and the Great Hunger: Studies in Irish Culture* (London and New
    York, 1995).

Elliott, Marianne. *Partners in Revolution: The United Irishmen and France* (New Haven and
    London, 1982).

Ellmann, Richard. *Yeats: The Man and the Masks* (London, 1979).

English, Richard. *Irish Freedom: The History of Nationalism in Ireland* (London, 2006).

Farrell, Brian, ed. *Communications and Community in Ireland* (Dublin and Cork, 1984).

Faulkner, Peter. *William Morris and W. B. Yeats* (Dublin, 1962).

Finley, M. I. *Democracy Ancient and Modern* (London, 1985).

Foley, Michael. 'Colonialism and Journalism in Ireland', *Journalism Studies*, 5, 3 (2004), 373–85.

Foster, R. F. *Paddy and Mr. Punch: Connections in Irish and English History* (London, 1995).

——. *W. B. Yeats: A Life. I: The Apprentice Mage, 1865–1914* (Oxford, 1997).

——. *W. B. Yeats: A Life. II: The Arch-Poet, 1915–1939* (Oxford, 2003).

Franco, Paul. *Hegel's Philosophy of Freedom* (New Haven and London, 1999).

Freyer, Grattan. *W. B. Yeats and the Anti-Democratic Tradition* (Dublin, 1981).

Fuchs, Michel. *Edmund Burke, Ireland, and the Fashioning of Self* (Oxford, 1996).

Furet, François. *Revolutionary France, 1770–1880*, trans. Antonia Nevill (Oxford, 1992).

Gadamer, Hans-Georg. *Truth and Method*, 2nd and rev. edn., trans. Joel Weinsheimer and Donald G. Marshall (London, 1989).

Garrigan, Sinéad. *Primitivism, Science, and the Irish Revival* (Oxford, 2004).

Gellner, Ernest. *Nations and Nationalism* (Oxford, 1983).

Gibbons, Luke. *Edmund Burke and Ireland* (Cambridge, 2003).

Glandon, Virginia. *Arthur Griffith and the Advanced Nationalist Press, Ireland: 1900–1922* (New York, 1985).

Gough, Hugh. *The Newspaper Press in the French Revolution* (London, 1988).

Greenfeld, Liah. *Nationalism: Five Roads to Modernity* (Cambridge, 1992).

Grene, Nicholas. 'Yeats and the Remaking of Synge', in Terence Brown and Nicholas Grene, eds., *Tradition and Influence in Anglo-Irish Poetry* (London and Basingstoke, 1989), 47–62.

Habermas, Jürgen. *The Structural Transformation of the Public Sphere*, trans. Thomas Burger, with the assistance of Frederick Lawrence (Cambridge, 1989).

Hampsher-Monk, Iain. *A History of Modern Political Thought: Major Political Thinkers from Hobbes to Marx* (Oxford, 1992).

Hampton, Mark. *Visions of the Press in Britain, 1850–1950* (Urbana and Chicago, 2004).

Harper, George Mills, ed. *Yeats and the Occult* (London and Basingstoke, 1975).

——. *The Making of Yeats's 'A Vision': A Study of the Automatic Script*, 2 vols. (Houndmills, Basingstoke, Hampshire and London, 1987).

Hayek, F. A. *The Road to Serfdom* (London, 1944).

Hearne, John M. 'Thomas Meagher: Reluctant Revolutionary', in John M. Hearne and Rory T. Cornish, eds., *Thomas Francis Meagher: The Making of an Irish American* (Dublin, 2006), 67–91.

Hill, Jacqueline. *From Patriots to Unionists: Dublin Civic Politics and Irish Protestant Patriotism 1660–1840* (Oxford, 1997).

Hirschman, Albert O. *The Passions and the Interests: Political Arguments for Capitalism before Its Triumph* (Princeton, 1977).

Hobsbawm, E. J. *Nations and Nationalism since 1780*, rev. edn. (Cambridge, 1990).

Hont, Istvan, and Michael Ignatieff. 'Needs and Justice in the *Wealth of Nations*', in Istvan Hont and Michael Ignatieff, eds., *Wealth and Virtue: The Shaping of Political Economy in the Scottish Enlightenment* (Cambridge, 1983), 1–44.

Hoppen, K. Theodore. *Elections, Politics and Society in Ireland, 1832–1885* (Oxford, 1994).

Howes, Marjorie. *Yeats's Nations: Gender, Class, and Irishness* (Cambridge, 1996).

Hume, J. L. *Bentham and Bureaucracy* (Cambridge, 1981).

Hutchinson, John. *The Dynamics of Cultural Nationalism* (London, 1987).

Inglis, Brian. *The Freedom of the Press in Ireland, 1784–1841* (London, 1954).

Insole, Christopher. *The Politics of Human Frailty: A Theological Defence of Political Liberalism* (London, 2004).

Inwood, Michael. *A Hegel Dictionary* (Oxford, 1992).

Jackson, Alvin. *Ireland 1798–1998* (Oxford, 1998).

Jones, Aled. *Powers of the Press: Newspapers, Power and the Public in Nineteenth-Century England* (Aldershot, 1996).

Jones, H. S. *Victorian Political Thought* (London and Basingstoke, 2000).

Keane, John. *The Media and Democracy* (Cambridge, 1991).

Keane, Patrick. *Yeats's Interactions with Tradition* (Columbia, 1987).

Kedourie, Elie. *Nationalism*, 4th edn. (Oxford and Cambridge, 1993).

Kelly, John. 'Parnell in Irish Literature', in D. George Boyce and Alan O'Day, eds., *Parnell in Perspective* (London, 1991), 242–83.

Kinzer, Bruce. *England's Disgrace?: J. S. Mill and the Irish Question* (Toronto, 2001).

Kohn, Hans. *The Idea of Nationalism, Its Meaning and History* (New York, 1964).

Koot, Gerard, M. *English Historical Economics, 1870–1926* (Cambridge, 1987).

Koss, Stephen. *The Rise and Fall of the Political Press in Britain* (London, 1990).

Lee, Joseph. *The Modernisation of Irish Society 1848–1918* (Dublin, 1973).

——. 'The Social and Economic Ideas of O'Connell', in Kevin B. Nowlan and Maurice R. O'Connell, eds., *Daniel O'Connell: Portrait of a Radical* (Belfast, 1984), 70–86.

Leerssen, Joep. *Remembrance and Imagination: Patterns in the Historical and Literary Representation of Ireland in the Nineteenth Century* (Cork, 1996).

Legg, Marie-Louise. *Newspapers and Nationalism: The Irish Provincial Press 1850–1892* (Dublin, 1999).

Lloyd, David. *Nationalism and Minor Literature: James Clarence Mangan and the Emergence of Irish Cultural Nationalism* (Berkeley, 1987).

Long, Douglas G. *Bentham on Liberty: Jermy Bentham's Idea of Liberty in Relation to his Utilitarianism* (Toronto and Buffalo, 1977).

Loughlin, James. 'Constructing the Political Spectacle: Parnell, the Press and National Leadership, 1879–86', in D. George Boyce and Alan O'Day, eds., *Parnell in Perspective* (London, 1991), 221–41.

Lyons, F. S. L. *Ireland since the Famine*, rev. edn. (London, 1973).

——. *Culture and Anarchy in Ireland, 1890–1939* (Oxford, 1979).

McBride, Ian. 'The School of Virtue: Francis Hutcheson, Irish Presbyterians and the Scottish Enlightenment', in George Boyce, Robert Eccleshall and Vincent Geoghen, eds., *Political Thought in Ireland since the Seventeenth Century* (London and New York, 1993), 73–99.

——. 'Nationalism and Republicanism in the 1790s', in S. J. Connolly, ed., *Political Ideas in Eighteenth-Century Ireland* (Dublin, 2000), 159–69.

McCartney, Donal. *W. E. H. Lecky: Historian and Politician, 1838–1903* (Dublin, 1994).

McCormack, W. J. *From Burke to Beckett* (Cork, 1994).

——. *Blood Kindred. W. B. Yeats: The Life, the Death, the Politics* (London, 2005).

——. 'Edmund Burke, Yeats and Leo Frobenius: "The State a Tree"?', in Seán Patrick Donlan, ed., *Edmund Burke's Irish Identities* (Dublin, 2007), 226–62.

MacDonagh, Oliver. *Ireland: The Union and Its Aftermath* (London, 1977).

——. *States of Mind: A Study of Anglo-Irish Conflict, 1780–1980* (London, 1983).

——. *O'Connell: The Life of Daniel O'Connell, 1775–1847* (London, 1991).

McDonald, Joan. *Rousseau and the French Revolution, 1762–1792* (London, 1965).

MacIntyre, Alistair. 'Poetry as Political Philosophy: Notes on Burke and Yeats', in *Ethics and Politics: Selected Essays, Volume 2* (Cambridge, 2006), 159–71.

MacNeice, Louis. *The Poetry of W. B. Yeats* (London, 1967).

Mahoney, Thomas. *Edmund Burke and Ireland* (Cambridge, 1960).

Marcus, Phillip L. *Yeats and the Beginning of the Irish Renaissance* (Ithaca and London, 1970).

Maume, Patrick. 'Young Ireland, Arthur Griffith and Republican Ideology: The Question of Continuity', *Éire-Ireland*, 34, 2 (1999), 155–74.

Miller, David. *On Nationality* (Oxford, 1995).

Molony, John N. *A Soul Came into Ireland: Thomas Davis 1814–45. A Biography* (Dublin, 1996).

Moore, Margaret. *The Ethics of Nationalism* (Oxford, 2001).

Morrissey, Thomas. *William Martin Murphy* (Dundalk, 1997).

Mulvey, Helen. *Thomas Davis and Ireland: A Biographical Study* (Washington, 2003).

Murphy, William Michael. *The Parnell Myth and Irish Politics, 1891–1956* (New York, 1986).

North, Michael. *The Political Aesthetic of Yeats, Eliot, and Pound* (Cambridge, 1990).

Oakeshott, Michael. *Rationalism in Politics and Other Essays*, new edn. (Indianapolis, 1991).

O'Brien, Conor Cruise. *Parnell and His Party* (Oxford, 1957).

——. 'Passion and Cunning: An Essay on the Politics of W. B. Yeats', in A. Norman Jeffares and K. G. W. Cross, eds., *Excited Reverie: A Centenary Tribute to William Butler Yeats 1865–1939* (London, 1965), 207–78.

——. *The Great Melody: A Thematic Biography of Edmund Burke* (London, 1992).

O'Brien, William. *Edmund Burke as an Irishman* (Dublin, 1926).

O'Cathaoir, Brendan. *John Blake Dillon, Young Irelander* (Dublin, 1990).

O'Day, Alan. 'Nationalism and Political Economy in Ireland: Isaac Butt's Analysis', in Roger Swift and Christine Kinealy, eds., *Politics and Power in Victorian Ireland* (Dublin, 2006), 109–18.

O'Ferrall, Fergus. *Catholic Emancipation and the Birth of Irish Democracy* (Dublin, 1985).

O'Flaherty, Eamon. 'Burke and the Irish Constitution', in Seán Patrick Donlan, ed., *Edmund Burke's Irish Identities* (Dublin, 2007), 102–16.

O'Hegarty, P. S. *A History of Ireland under the Union, 1801 to 1922* (London, 1952).

O'Neill, Patrick. *Ireland and Germany: A Study in Literary Relations* (New York, 1985).

Oommen, T. K. *Citizenship, Nationality and Ethnicity* (Cambridge, 1997).

Oram, Hugh. *The Newspaper Book: A History of Newspapers in Ireland, 1649–1983* (Dublin, 1983).

Pappin, Joseph. *The Metaphysics of Edmund Burke* (New York, 1993).

Pocock, J. G. A. 'Burke and the Ancient Constitution: A Problem in the History of Ideas', in *Politics, Language and Time: Essays on Political Thought and History* (New York, 1973), 202–32.

——. *The Machiavellian Moment, Florentine Political Thought and the Atlantic Republican Tradition* (Princeton, 1975).

——. 'The Political Economy of Burke's Analysis of the French Revolution', in *Virtue, Commerce, and History: Essays on Political Thought and History, Chiefly in the Eighteenth Century* (Cambridge, 1985), 193–212.

——. 'Introduction', in Edmund Burke, *Reflections on the Revolution of France*, ed. J. G. A. Pocock (Indianapolis, 1987).

——. 'Edmund Burke and the Redefinition of Enthusiasm: The Context as Counter-Revolution', in François Furet and Mona Ozouf, eds., *The French Revolution and the Creation of Modern Culture. Volume 3: The Transformation of Political Culture, 1739–1848* (Oxford, 1989), 19–43.

Popkin, Jeremy D., ed. *Media and Revolution, Comparative Perspectives* (Lexington, 1995).

——. *Revolutionary News: The Press in France, 1789–1799* (Durham and London, 1990).

Potter, Simon J., ed. *Newspapers and Empire in Ireland and Britain* (Dublin, 2004).

Quinn, James. 'John Mitchel and the Rejection of the Nineteenth Century', *Éire-Ireland*, 38, 3 and 4 (2003), 90–108.

Rawls, John. *Political Liberalism* (New York, 1993).

Robbins, Caroline. *The Eighteenth-Century Commonwealthman* (Cambridge, Mass., 1959).

Rose, Gillian. *Hegel Contra Sociology* (London, 1981).

Rosen, Frederick. *Jeremy Bentham and Representative Democracy: A Study of the Constitutional Code* (Oxford, 1983).

——. *Classical Utilitarianism from Hume to Mill* (London and New York, 2003).

Ryder, Sean. 'Young Ireland and the 1798 Rebellion', in M. Geary, ed., *Rebellion and Remembrance in Modern Ireland* (Dublin, 2001), 135–47.

Schama, Simon. *Citizens: A Chronicle of the French Revolution* (London, 1989).

Schuchard, Ronald. 'Eliot as an Extension Lecturer', *Review of English Studies*, 25, 98
    (1974), 165–66
——. 'Yeats, Arnold, and the Morbidity of Modernism', *Yeats: An Annual of Critical and
    Textual Studies*, 3 (1985), 88–106.
Schumpeter, Joseph A. *Capitalism, Socialism & Democracy* (London, 1943; repr. 2000).
Simes, Douglas. 'Ireland, 1760–1820', in Hannah Barker and Simon Burrows,
    eds., *Press, Politics and the Public Sphere in Europe and North America, 1760–1820*
    (Cambridge, 2002), 113–39.
Skinner, Quentin. *Liberty before Liberalism* (Cambridge, 1998).
Small, Stephen. *Political Thought in Ireland, 1776–1798: Republicanism, Patriotism and
    Radicalism* (Oxford, 2002).
Smith, Anthony D. *The Ethnic Origins of Nationalism* (Oxford, 1991).
——. *Nationalism: Theory, Ideology, History* (Cambridge, 2001).
Stallworthy, Jon. *Between the Lines: Yeats's Poetry in the Making* (Oxford, 1963).
Stanfield, Paul Scott. *Yeats and Politics in the 1930s* (London, 1988).
Stanlis, Peter, J. *Edmund Burke and the Natural Law* (Ann Arbor, 1965).
Steele, E. D. 'J. S. Mill and the Irish Question: Reform, and the Integrity of the
    Empire, 1865–1870', *Historical Journal*, 13 (1969), 419–50.
Steinman, Michael. *Yeats's Heroic Figures: Wilde, Parnell, Swift, Casement* (London, 1983).
Stöter, Eva. '"Grimmige Zeiten": The Influence of Lessing, Herder and the Grimm
    Brothers on the Nationalism of the Young Irelanders', in Glenn Hooper and
    Leon Litvack, eds., *Ireland in the Nineteenth Century: Regional Identity* (Dublin,
    2000), 173–80.
Strauss, Leo. *Natural Right and History* (Chicago, 1953).
Swift, Roger. 'Thomas Carlyle and Ireland', in D. George Boyce and Roger Swift,
    eds., *Problems and Perspectives in Irish History since 1800* (Dublin, 2004), 117–46.
Taylor, Charles. *Philosophy and the Human Sciences. Philosophical Papers 2* (Cambridge, 1985).
——. *The Ethics of Authenticity* (Cambridge and London, 1991).
Taylor, M. W. *Men versus the State: Herbert Spencer and Late Victorian Individualism* (Oxford,
    1992).
Thuente, Mary Helen. *The Harp Re-Strung: The United Irishmen and the Rise of Irish Literary
    Nationalism* (Syracuse, 1994).
Torchiana, Donald. *W. B. Yeats and Georgian Ireland*, 2nd edn. (Washington, 1992).
Trilling, Lionel. *Sincerity and Authenticity* (London, 1974).
Vincent, Andrew. *Nationalism and Particularity* (Cambridge, 2002).
Viroli, Maurizio. *For Love of Country: An Essay on Patriotism and Nationalism* (Oxford, 1995).
Watson, George. 'Yeats, Victorianism, and the 1890s', in Marjorie Howes and John
    Kelly, eds., *The Cambridge Companion to W. B. Yeats* (Cambridge, 2006), 36–58.
Whelan, Kevin. 'The United Irishmen, the Enlightenment and Popular Culture', in
    David Dickson, Dáire Keogh and Kevin Whelan, eds., *The United Irishmen:
    Republicanism, Radicalism and Rebellion* (Dublin, 1993), 269–96.

———. *The Tree of Liberty: Radicalism, Catholicism and the Construction of Irish Identity, 1760–1830* (Cork, 1996).

Wilkins, Burleigh. *The Problem of Burke's Political Philosophy* (Oxford, 1967).

Williams, Bernard. *Ethics and the Limits of Philosophy*, 3rd edn. (London, 1993).

———. *Truth and Truthfulness: An Essay in Genealogy* (Princeton and Oxford, 2002)

Wood, Allen. *Hegel's Ethical Thought* (Cambridge, 1990).

Worden, Blair. 'Marchamont Nedham and the Beginnings of English Republicanism, 1649–1656', in David Wooton, ed., *Republicanism, Liberty, and Commercial Society, 1649–1776* (Stanford, 1994), 45–81.

Yack, Bernard. 'The Myth of the Civic Nation', in Ronald Beiner, ed., *Theorizing Nationalism* (Albany, 1999), 103–18.

Zeldin, Theodore. *France 1848–1945: Taste and Corruption* (Oxford, 1980).

Index